POLICY
CHOICES

POLICY CHOICES

FREE TRADE AMONG NAFTA NATIONS

Edited by Karen Roberts and Mark I. Wilson

Michigan State University Press
Institute for Public Policy and Social Research
East Lansing

All Michigan State University Press books are produced on paper which meets
the requirements of American National Standard of Information Sciences—
Permanence of paper for printed materials ANSI Z39.48-1984.

Michigan State University Press
East Lansing, Michigan 48823-5202

Michigan State University Institute for Public Policy and Social Research
Public Policy Series

03 02 01 00 99 98 97 96 1 2 3 4 5 6 7 8 9

Library of Congress Cataloging-in-Publication Data

Policy choices : free trade among NAFTA nations / edited by Karen Roberts
and Mark I. Wilson
        p.   cm. — (Michigan State University Institue for Public Policy
   and Social Research public policy series)
     Includes bibliographical references and index.
     ISBN 0-87013-415-9
     1. Free Trade—North America. 2. North America—Economic integration.
   3. United States—Commercial policy. 4. Canada. Treaties, etc. 1992 Oct. 7.
   I. Roberts, Karen. II. Wilson, Mark I.
   HF1746.P64 1996
   382'.71'097—dc20   96-26073
                                                               CIP

Published with the support of the Institute for Public Policy and Social
Research, Michigan State University

Acknowledgements

This project received generous funding from the Canadian Embassy in Washington, D.C., which provided a grant to run the conference that formed the basis of this volume. We would also like to acknowledge the financial support of several units at Michigan State University: the Canadian Studies Centre; the Center for Latin American and Caribbean Studies; the Eli Broad College of Business and the Eli Broad Graduate School of Management; the International Business Center and Center for International Business Education and Research, International Studies and Programs; the School of Labor and Industrial Relations; and the Office of the Provost.

The editors would also like to thank the IPPSR program staff. AnnMarie Schneider, Sheila Triplett, and Chris Joslin organized and managed the conference. Frani Bickart both worked on the conference and edited the book. Andrew Padon and Wayne Hutchison also assisted with editing. The contributions of copy editor Elizabeth Johnston deserve special mention.

In addition, the editors would like to express appreciation to the following for their timely and insightful reviews of the papers in this book: Joel Cutcher-Gershenfeld, Peter Dorman, Steve Gold, James Granato, Phyllis Grummon, Harry Holzer, Daniel Kruger, Refugio Rochin, Alexander von Eye, and Carol Weissert.

Finally, we thank Jack Knott, director of the Institute for Public Policy and Social Research, for his continued support in bringing this volume in the Public Policy Series to fruition.

Contents

20 P7

APPENDICES

Foreword

The Institute for Public Policy and Social Research at Michigan State University is pleased to be able to offer the third volume in its Public Policy Series. The first two volumes covered a broad range of policy issues, many of which have been the subject of vigorous debate and new legislative activity. This volume differs from the first two in that it focuses on the effects of the North American Free Trade Agreement (NAFTA) on a variety of public policy issues of concern both in Michigan and in the nation. The goal of the series continues to be to present the range of information needed by policy makers to understand the scope of various policy decisions. Each volume is designed to articulate the questions that need to be both asked and answered in order to shape sound policy. Karen Roberts and Mark Wilson of the editorial board deserve special recognition for organizing the conference on which this book is based, as well as for their key roles in bringing this volume to publication. We hope that you continue to find these volumes useful.

Jack Knott
Director
Institute for Public Policy and Social Research

Introduction

Global economic integration is a fact of life for people in both the developed and developing worlds. One response to the structural changes imposed by an integrated economy is the development of large-scale trading blocs. For the populations of North America, the signing of the North American Free Trade Agreement (NAFTA) signaled the creation of a formal trading bloc and an important shift in the configuration of the political economy, production methods, work organization, trade relations, and cultural perceptions of the three member countries: Canada, Mexico, and the United States.

In this volume, the discussion of NAFTA focuses on issues of importance from a policy perspective. The objective is to serve as a resource for policy makers who must operate in an environment influenced by free trade. Chapters cover a range of policy-related topics and are designed to frame the issues confronting policy makers in order to enable them to make informed decisions.

This book is the third volume in the Public Policy Series issued by the Institute for Public Policy and Social Research (IPPSR) at Michigan State University. Unlike previous volumes in the series, this book was preceded by a conference in November 1994 at which most of the authors presented a preliminary version of their chapter. The conference also included presentations by speakers from the three member countries who framed the political, social, and economic context for NAFTA in their home countries, plus a panel discussion about NAFTA on the shop floor, all of which are included in this volume.

The book is divided into four parts. It begins with an overview of the political economy of NAFTA. This is followed by separate sections

1

focusing on three policy areas: agriculture, economic development, and workplace change. Three appendices complete the volume. The first is a transcript of a panel discussion held at the conference, "NAFTA on the Shop Floor." The second is a timeline of events leading up to the passage of NAFTA. The third is a data summary showing trade relations among the three countries.

The first section presents the political economy perspective of the three nations. The Canadian consul general in Detroit, Donald Wismer, traces the evolution of NAFTA from the Automotive Pact signed in the 1960s by Canada and the United States. While noting worries about protecting a way of life and social structure highly valued by Canadians, he discusses the need for continued evolution of free trade and the attendant agreements for the mutual enrichment of the participating countries.

A similar perspective from Mexico is described in the chapter by Manuel Chavez and Scott Whiteford. While recognizing the inevitability of free trade, particularly between Mexico and the United States, they note several Mexican concerns that were not resolved by NAFTA. In particular, they focus on the absence of strong protection for labor standards and social benefits, the lack of requirements on capital investment, and U.S. insistence on a wider hemispheric trade agreement as a possible vehicle for U.S. economic dominance of the region.

The U.S. context for NAFTA is presented by David Arsen, who emphasizes the diverse reactions to the agreement, ranging from calls for greater protectionism to demands for greater market freedom. He analyzes how these various responses to NAFTA indicate, within the United States, the varying incidence of NAFTA benefits across firms and workers and across different income groups.

The second section deals with agriculture, which accounts for a large share of trade between the United States and each of the other two countries. The United States annually exports approximately $3.6 billion in agricultural products to Canada and about $2.9 billion to Mexico. David Schweikhardt and Kandeh Yumkella provide an overview of agricultural trading patterns among the three nations. They then detail the provisions and timing of the removal of trade barriers under NAFTA and how these will affect trade. They note several concerns for the future, including the possibility that macroeconomic policy and a potential hemispheric trade agreement may affect the expected benefits to U.S. agriculture from NAFTA.

The chapter by James McDonald is an in-depth analysis of the difficulties facing the dairy industry in Mexico. McDonald analyzes the relative lack of competitiveness of Mexican dairy farmers and argues compellingly that they are likely to lose ground to U.S. producers with the implementation of NAFTA.

The chapters in the third section, on economic and public policy dimensions of NAFTA, discuss responses to some of the potential negative effects of the agreement. Corinne Krupp examines dumping as an unfair trade practice under NAFTA and provides a brief overview of antidumping laws, including their history, their current state, and the associated policy challenges. She chronicles the ongoing reform of existing laws, details recent proposals, and discusses their likely enactment and the implementation of various scenarios for policy makers.

David Arsen, Mark Wilson, and Jonas Zoninsein analyze manufacturing activity as trade barriers fall. They use a shift-share model to examine past trends and discuss the implications for the future. They clearly reject the conventional wisdom that the United States will lose manufacturing jobs to its trading partners, and find instead that Canada will lose jobs to Mexico. They show that in Michigan, however, the transportation equipment industry is vulnerable to competition from both countries.

The chapter by Richard Hill and Kuniko Fujita provides a prescriptive analysis for localities to respond to potential job loss in the face of free trade. They argue that economic planning at the local level, supported by coordination across all levels of government, is a promising route for protecting and advancing economic competitiveness. Their discussion is based on the Japanese "Flying Geese" model of promoting relatively even economic development, and a detailed case study of economic planning in the prefecture of Osaka is used to illustrate their point.

The final chapter in this section, by Lynn Duggan, addresses some of the social welfare implications of NAFTA. Duggan uses an economic framework to ask what sorts of government intervention may be needed to mediate the negative effects of free trade. She focuses on how women divide their time between paid and unpaid work and how NAFTA will pressure them to spend more time in the labor market and less time performing unpaid work at home. She then discusses the current state of publicly provided support to supplement unpaid work at home.

The final section addresses workplace and workforce changes likely to result from NAFTA. One expectation has been that NAFTA will reduce the flow of illegal immigration from Mexico to the United States. The chapter by Robert Aponte closely examines the issue and concludes that this is an unlikely outcome in the near future. He then analyzes migratory patterns to determine where Mexican immigrants are likely to settle, and suggests that Michigan is not a probable destination.

Richard Block's chapter begins with the premise that economic integration with Mexico poses comparable challenges to the U.S. and Canadian labor markets. He then examines the industrial relations factors that will lead to different responses. He presents two models: the negotiated outcome, whereby responses are negotiated through collective bargaining, and the unilateral outcome, whereby management designs the response. Block suggests that Canadian responses are likely to be negotiated, whereas U.S. responses are more likely to be unilateral.

The chapter by Karen Roberts, Doug Hyatt, and Peter Dorman examines possible changes in the employment structure resulting from competition among the three countries under free trade. The chapter describes the gradual shift in both the United States and Canada toward contingent work arrangements and the relationship between these structural changes and competition due to free trade. The structure of the Mexican labor market and differences between the formal and informal sectors are examined. The authors discuss possible changes in all three countries' structures in response to free trade.

Joseph Ofori-Dankwa addresses the microissue of tolerance for diversity in the workplace. His premise is that global integration has heightened attention to diversity at the expense of commonalities across workers and cultures. The concept of diversimilarity is developed, and its workplace implications are examined.

I.
The Political Economy
of NAFTA:
Three Perspectives

Perspectives from Canada

Donald T. Wismer

It is difficult to provide "perspectives" from Canada in only a few pages, since NAFTA with its annexes is a couple of feet thick. I decided to avoid a detailed sectoral analysis of the agreement's effect on Canada and to focus instead on where Canada stands with respect to freer and fairer trade more generally. In my view, any Canadian perspectives on free trade must make reference to the Canada-U.S. Free Trade Agreement, to NAFTA, the General Agreement on Tariffs and Trade (GATT) Uruguay Round, and to where we hope to go in the future.

Let me start with a bit of history. Canada's first real experience with free trade with the United States goes back to the 1960s, when we signed the Automotive Pact as well as a Defense Sharing Agreement. Both of these accords worked very well from Canada's point of view. Manufacturers in the automotive and defense industries in each country received duty-free access to and national treatment by the other party, subject to agreed upon guidelines on content, volume, and quality standards. Trade and investment increased substantially in both directions. Notwithstanding the success in these two areas and a strong multilateral commitment to liberal trade going back to the founding of the GATT in 1947, Canadian governments have shied away from broadening free trade with the United States out of fear of cultural domination and loss of sovereignty. By the mid-1980s, however, the Canadian economy was in such bad shape that the Mulroney government decided a "leap of faith" was required, and our 1988 election was passionately fought over free trade with the United States. Sentiment was high. Here are a few quotations from those days:

Best friends or not, the U.S. sometimes acts like the bully on the block. Canadians derive many benefits from their proximity to the U.S., but they have to pay a price for it, too. How high a price remains negotiable, but economic, cultural and political sovereignty must be protected constantly or else be lost. The Loyalists knew that, the Fathers of Confederation knew it, and so, one hopes, do Canadians and their governments in the late 20th century.[1]

In public debates in Canada, the key words, those that determine the winner of the debate are "equity" and "fairness"; in the U.S., the comparable determining words are "freedom" and "efficiency."[2]

When I sought the leadership of my party five years ago I said that Canada and the United States were one another's best friend and greatest ally. Nothing in my experience in government—and we have known tensions and serious disagreement—has led me to revise my views about the profound value of an exemplary relationship between two of the world's greatest democracies.[3]

George Bush wants a kinder, gentler country: it's called Canada.[4]

In the end, the Conservatives carried the day, and we negotiated the Free Trade Agreement (FTA) to put pressure on our economy, to increase our productivity, and to establish a dispute settlement mechanism that would not leave us open to bullying from U.S. trade remedies. The FTA definitely led to higher productivity in Canada and benefited both the United States and Canada, but because the FTA did not specifically define what constitutes a subsidy or dumping, we have continued to be frustrated by U.S. actions with respect to a number of trade disputes, particularly those having to do with wheat, steel, and softwood lumber.

When the United States and Mexico announced that they were going to negotiate a free trade deal soon after the FTA, we did not really feel ready for it, but we could not afford to be left out. There was a danger for us that if the United States arranged a number of separate bilateral agreements it would become a hub for new investment and we would be a disadvantaged spoke. We also wanted to encourage democratic economic development in Mexico, recognizing its wonderful market potential with a population of 85 million, and acknowledge that it could act as a beacon to other Latin American countries. We participated in NAFTA, and so far it has been very good for us. If we look at trade statistics for 1993 compared with those of 1990, Canadian exports to the United States increased from $112 billion to $151 billion. Imports from the United States rose from $88 billion to $114 billion. Looking at Mexico over that period, our exports rose from $656 million to $825 million, which is not bad, but Mexico's exports to Canada increased from $1.7 billion to $3.7 billion. During the first six months of 1994, our trade boomed in both directions with each country. In trade with the United States, both our exports and imports are up 18 percent over 1993, and in trade with Mexico our exports are up 24 percent and our imports 36 percent. Canada has not suffered any major dislocations, and the automotive industry has especially benefited.

An essential element of our decision to proceed with NAFTA was the creation of working groups on subsidies and dumping that will address long-standing Canadian concerns about disputes arising from countervailing and antidumping duties. These groups are to complete their search for solutions that reduce the possibility of disputes from the operation of trade remedy laws by the end of December 1995.

What NAFTA reflects—and reinforces—is the emergence of a more truly integrated North American economy, one that goes beyond more intensive trade linkages to encompass converging infrastructures, common distribution networks, and an increasingly intricate web of cross-border production.

The movement toward closer economic integration is not limited to the northern half of the hemisphere. In addition to NAFTA, Mexico has also entered into a free trade arrangement with Venezuela and Colombia. A revived Andean pact will link the economies of Peru, Bolivia, Colombia, Ecuador, and Venezuela through freer trade. Argentina, Brazil, Paraguay, and Uruguay have signaled their intention to move the MERCOSUR (those countries' free trade bloc) farther toward a full common market. Nowhere in the world has the drive for economic liberalization and reform been more vigorous and more far-reaching than in this hemisphere, in both North and South America.

Despite these rapid advances in recent years, there are signs that this revolution of market liberalization may be faltering. After playing a leading role in securing the successful conclusion of both NAFTA and the Uruguay Round, by 1994 the United States seemed in danger of losing its momentum for freer trade. This danger is already evident in the context of current Canada/U.S. bilateral relations. Although we enjoy the world's largest trade relationship, one in which the vast majority of our two-way trade flows without impediment, we have encountered a number of corrosive disputes that reflect, for the most part, the triumph of narrow, protectionist interests over a broader trade vision.

Largely in reaction to perceived U.S. uncertainty, other countries in Latin America have begun to reevaluate their own options. Not surprisingly, separate bilateral deals, or even an exclusive South American free trade area, have begun to look increasingly attractive to some as the prospects for full hemispheric integration appear to grow dimmer.

The dangers of losing direction at this critical juncture cannot be overstated. Trade agreements are not static institutions. They are living, dynamic arrangements. Like bicycles, they thrive on momentum. NAFTA has no choice but to move forward at this time, deepening its rules as well as broadening its membership, or else risk slipping backward. For Canada, this would mean living with an agreement that is essentially unfinished and, by extension, living with a growing number of imperfect solutions to the frictions associated with closer economic integration. Any loss of momentum could also mean missing a historic opportunity to build bridges to the newly emerging economies of Latin America in a way that is both comprehensive and nondiscriminatory. Perhaps most important, a loss of momentum could risk a fundamental change in the orientation of NAFTA itself from an open, dynamic arrangement to a more closed, inward-looking bloc.

Certainly, it is no secret that the increasingly cautious approach of the United States toward NAFTA expansion is fueled largely by protectionist forces, which were just barely kept at bay during the difficult passage of NAFTA legislation through the U.S. Congress in late 1993. Unless we can ensure that the NAFTA door is kept open to Chile, Argentina, and other would-be partners, there is a very real risk that it will remain permanently closed.

What we need at this point is an overarching trade and investment policy for the Americas—a larger, bolder vision that could serve to overshadow and ultimately overwhelm more parochial and divisive concerns. In short, we need a policy that reflects the openness, energy, and dynamism of our economies; that recognizes the creative synergy that can emerge from the marriage of developing and developed economies; and that reaches out to all countries willing to commit to more intensive, more comprehensive rules-based trade.

NAFTA can provide the foundation for such a policy. With the political will, it could be the nucleus for a wider free trade association that could, in time, include countries throughout the Western Hemisphere and beyond. With the right commitment, it could emerge as a new kind of economic association, one defined not by geography but by a collective commitment to deeper levels of free trade: the nucleus of a new global GATT-plus.

The underlying idea would not be to replace the existing multilateral system, still less to set up a discriminatory regional bloc, but instead would be to establish a coalition of countries willing to move farther and more quickly toward the goal of trade and investment liberalization. A wider free trade association could also be one engine to drive the more cumbersome, but centrally important, multilateral negotiating process that we all must encourage in the World Trade Organization.

The original justification for the Canada-U.S. Free Trade Agreement and for the subsequent trilateral agreement with Mexico was really just that: to push forward in areas where our degree of economic integration called for a deeper and more comprehensive regime of rules than GATT itself could provide. In areas such as dispute settlement, investment, trade in services, and procurement, NAFTA has already moved well beyond the kind of consensus that has been achieved in the larger and more slow-moving multilateral context. In other critical areas such as trade remedy law, Canada is working hard to deepen the agreement.

Both Canada and Mexico have also signaled their desire to move quickly on NAFTA expansion in the Western Hemisphere. Although it is critical to obtain Chilean accession, there is no reason that, in time, all countries agreeing to abide by NAFTA rules should not be welcome, nor is there any reason to limit this expansion to the Western Hemisphere.

As for the three existing NAFTA partners, broadening the agreement offers more than access to growing markets. It offers new partnerships and new alliances to tackle the hard trade issues of the future and provides a more balanced negotiating framework in which to achieve these goals. It also offers us a powerful tool in our dealings with the rest of the world by demonstrating that those countries unwilling to move toward greater liberalization risk being left behind in the wake of dynamic regionalism.

As such, NAFTA has the potential to set in motion an external, competitive dynamic to reduce tariff and nontariff barriers worldwide; that is, it has the potential to kick-start a new round of global trade liberalization. Ultimately, it is to the multilateral trading system in general—and to the newly created World Trade Organization in particular—that we must look for the long-term future of free trade, but the process must start now. Canada, the United States, and Mexico have laid the foundations for a new kind of economic order. We have eschewed the constraints of a customs union or a common market in favor of a much more open economic area, one whose inherent dynamic is to reduce barriers and to expand to others.

Changes of this magnitude require vision and political will. NAFTA has certain mechanisms to help make this happen; roughly 25 NAFTA commissions, committees, and working groups will deal with the nuts-and-bolts questions of enhancing our free trade area. Public interest has understandably focused on the labor and environmental commissions, but other groups will also meet regularly to address the more prosaic stuff of trade, such as rules of origin, standards for agriculture, telecommunications standards, labeling of textile and apparel goods, and temporary entry for business people.

By far the most important and most far-reaching of these working groups are the two established recently, at Canadian prompting, to address the continued absence of common rules governing the application of trade remedy laws, which really have no economic rationale in a free trade area. We know that it will not be an easy task to agree on these issues; we also know that our success in this endeavor will signal whether North America's common economic interests can transcend narrow domestic concerns.

Another area in which NAFTA—or a NAFTA-plus—can move forward is investment. Increasingly, servicing a foreign market means achieving a presence there, whether through joint ventures, strategic partnership, or direct capital investment. Already we have seen a spectacular growth in cross-border investment within North America itself and within the Western Hemisphere as a whole. In a world in which trade is not only about what you make but also about how and where you make it, an advanced investment code should be one of the central rationales of NAFTA.

Here, as elsewhere, Canada can take a leading role, even in the face of apparent U.S. uncertainty. We have a unique opportunity to push the hemispheric agenda forward and a unique opportunity to help chart the trade policy map of the next several years or even decades. After all, the defining characteristic of Canada's foreign policy has been the commitment to international rule-making and consensus-building.

Canada's security and prosperity have always been inextricably linked to the health of international systems. Our enduring strategy for working toward shared goals and interests has consistently been to build a shared architecture of international rights and obligations. When the countries of the Western Hemisphere gather at the Summit of the Americas in Miami in December 1994, Canada at least will have a clear message to deliver.

NOTES

1. J. L. Granatstein, historian, "Canada and the United States," *The Canadian Encyclopedia*, 2d ed. (Edmonton: Hurtig Publishers, 1988).
2. Richard Gwyn, correspondent, "Cultural Sovereignty: Myth or Reality?" in James Chacko, ed., *Proceedings of the 28th Annual Seminar on Canadian American Relations* (Windsor: Centre for Canadian-American Studies, University of Windsor, 1987).
3. Brian Mulroney, Prime Minister, addressing a joint sitting of the U.S. Congress, 27 April 1988, quoted in the *Toronto Star* the following day.
4. Message on signs at a Liberal rally in St. John's Fld., referring to U.S. President George Bush and the Free Trade Agreement, 15 November 1988, quoted by David Vienneau in the *Toronto Star* the following day.

Beyond the Market: Political and Socioeconomic Dimensions of NAFTA for Mexico

Manuel Chavez and Scott Whiteford

To most observers NAFTA represents 2,000 pages of detailed and complicated trade regulations and tariffs, but little that resembles a public policy instrument. Yet, upon looking at the historical relationships between the United States and Mexico and the United States and Canada in particular, and at the pre-NAFTA processes in these countries, it is clear that NAFTA is not only a trade instrument but also a policy mechanism that regulates and cements the sociopolitical and economic integration well underway before the signing. We argue that NAFTA formalized trade and economic processes already linking the three nations, that Michigan companies were some of the leaders in this process, and that the formalization provided by NAFTA enhanced the efficiency of the process.[1]

When the indigenous corn growers rebelled in Chiapas, taking the name of Zapatistas, they chose the anniversary of the NAFTA signing as the day to launch their offensive. The choice symbolizes their perception of the Mexican government's priorities (in domestic as well as international policy) and their vulnerability in the post-NAFTA era. While the plight of the Zapatistas resulted from endogenous as well as exogenous factors, it captured the imagination of many Mexicans because it jarred them into reconsidering the philosophy and potential effects of many of President Salinas's domestic reforms as he prepared Mexico for NAFTA. These included educational reform, constitutional changes in the agrarian reform laws, massive

15

privatization of state-owned companies, restructuring of the banking system, and the creation of new social support programs. Thus, the very potential of NAFTA led to profound domestic and policy changes in Mexico.

Because of the nature of the NAFTA negotiations, side agreements evolved as an attempt to change interdependent labor and environmental regulations in the three countries that had contradictory content and intentions. In the process, NAFTA not only led to the creation of new institutions in all three countries, but also in some cases profoundly influenced how domestic laws were regulated.

NAFTA emerged during a period, following the fall of the Soviet Union, when free trade and privatization were seen as keys to economic growth for people everywhere. The reduction of government regulations and tariff barriers are included in this formula. In many ways the enactment of this philosophy enhances the position of the industrial nations, which have often been blocked by trade regulation and import substitution policies.

In examination of the Mexico-United States relationship, we focus on the different perspectives of NAFTA and attempt to answer two questions. First, is the creation of NAFTA an entirely new initiative, or does it regularize trade and social policies that have been building over the last twenty years?[2] Second, how does NAFTA influence domestic programs and the way in which these become international issues, particularly when they deal with immigration and the environment?

To answer these questions, we begin with a review of the nature and context of the interdependency between Mexico and the United States, including the growth in Michigan exports to Mexico. This section is followed by a discussion of NAFTA's effect on domestic policies, with a special focus on Mexico. Finally, we analyze how domestic policies or programs become international issues, focusing in particular on environmental problems and immigration.

At the domestic level, NAFTA represents very different challenges for Mexico and the United States. President Salinas saw the agreement as a means to modernize his country by integrating the Mexican economy with that of the United States, thus creating greater access to new technology, capital, and markets. For both the Republican and Democratic administrations that negotiated NAFTA on the U.S. side, the agreement gave U.S. companies greater opportunities to invest in Mexico, greater access to inexpensive labor, and access to a growing market.

As we will show, President Salinas initiated a series of domestic reforms to prepare Mexico for NAFTA. While the United States did not develop any specific programs in anticipation of NAFTA, new binational programs were created to help resolve environmental and social problems between the two countries. The Border Environmental Cooperation Commission (BECC), the North American Developmental Bank (NADBANK), and the North American Commission for Environmental Cooperation were created to define border problems, develop solutions, and generate funding to implement them. *look these up*

INTERDEPENDENCE AND INDUSTRIALIZATION ON THE NEW FRONTIER

Three of the most obvious symptoms of interdependence between Mexico and the United States are *maquiladora* production, crossings along the border, and population settlements in border states and municipalities. *Maquiladoras* (in-bond plants) were created by an agreement between the United States and Mexico in 1965. In part, they were intended to solve a problem resulting from cessation of the Bracero Program, which had dealt with agricultural guest workers for 20 years. At the end of that program many migrants who had repatriated to Mexico did not return home, but chose to remain in the border towns, waiting for an opportunity to cross back to the United States and obtain either the same or a better job. They wanted employment in the United States but legally were prohibited, and these half-million workers put pressure on the already precarious infrastructure of the border towns. In response the Mexican government created the National Border Program to stimulate development in the region,[3] assisted on the U.S. side by a new initiative, the Border Industrialization Program (BIP).

Under BIP, U.S. companies that wanted to locate plants on the Mexican side of the border would receive preferential tax treatment on the goods they produced there. Sections 806.30, 807, and 808 of the U.S. Tariff Schedule Code were revised so that only the value added during manufacturing was taxed. Most of these plants were in accord with provisions clearly stipulating "articles assembled abroad."[4] Three years after BIP began, only a few companies were participating—by 1968 ten companies had located operations in Tijuana—and by 1970, there were only 55 such plants in all of Mexico, employing about 20,000 workers (see table 1).

Table 1.
Maquila Industry in Mexico and Selected Cities, 1970-90.

	1970	1975	1980	1985	1987	1989	1990
MEXICO							
Plants	—	454	620	760	1,259	1,795	2,014
Personnel	20,327	67,214	119,546	211,968	322,743	437,064	468,392
TIJUANA							
Plants	25	99	123	192	317	478	531
% of Mex. total	—	21.81	19.84	25.26	25.18	26.63	26.37
Personnel	—	7,844	12,343	25,913	40,000	58,590	65,893
% of Mex. total	—	11.67	10.32	12.22	12.39	13.41	14.07
JUAREZ							
Plants	30	86	121	168	233	261	292
% of Mex. total	—	18.94	19.52	22.11	18.51	14.54	14.50
Personnel	—	19,775	39,402	77,592	100,446	122,452	129,156
% of Mex. total	—	29.42	32.96	36.61	31.12	28.02	27.57
MATAMOROS							
Plants	—	40	50	35	68	94	93
% of Mex. total	—	8.81	8.06	4.61	5.40	5.24	4.62
Personnel	—	9,778	15,231	20,686	28,730	38,268	38,305
% of Mex. total	—	14.55	12.74	9.76	8.90	8.76	8.18

Source: "Estadistica de la Industria Maquiladora de Exportacion 1975-1986," INEGI.SPP, 1987; "Avance de Informacion Economia," Industria Maquiladora de Exportacion, INEGI, February 1991.

By 1980, the number of "production-sharing" firms had significantly increased, to 620 plants employing almost 120,000 workers. From 1975 to 1985, the share of Mexican employment in the *maquiladoras* more than doubled, rising from 1.84 percent to 4 percent.[5] Two cities, Tijuana and Juarez, had emerged as the most important for *maquiladora* production.

Federal officials in Mexico paid close attention to the effects, problems, costs, benefits, and potential for expansion of the *maquiladoras*. By 1987, it was evident to public officials in both countries that the program was suceeding. In that year more than 1,200 plants accounted for almost 323,000 jobs, a doubling in two years in both sites and employment. By 1990, 2,014 *maquiladoras* employed almost half a million people. Tijuana, south of San Diego, has more of these plants than any other city in northern Mexico. During the Mexican economic crisis and peso devaluation of 1995, the *maquiladoras* have been the most stable economic sector and the leaders in Mexican exports and growth.

The media have popularized the notion that most of the border crossings between Mexico and the United States are illegal, but U.S. Immigration and Naturalization Service reports indicate otherwise. For example, in 1989 more than 60 million people legally crossed at just one point of entry, between Tijuana and San Diego, or more than twice the total population of Canada. In 1988, a number almost equal to the U.S. population crossed the Mexican border legally; of these 226 million, 60 percent were not U.S. citizens.[6] The magnitude of legal crossings is evidence of the high degree of interaction and interdependence along the border of the two countries.

These crossings also reflect the rapid population growth on both sides of the border, shown in table 2. In 1970 almost 42 million people lived in the northern Mexican states and the U.S. Southwest. By 1980 the number had risen to more than 57 million, a net increase of 36 percent, and by 1990 the area had almost 63 million people, a net increase of 10 percent. Roughly one-fifth of the two countries' total populations live in these border states. This puts pressure on services, the environment, natural resources, infrastructure, employment, and political systems and adds to the development problems being addressed regionally by the two countries. Thus, NAFTA is only part of the binational processes already underway.

Table 2.
Population of U.S.-Mexico Border States, 1970 to 1990, in
Millions.

	1970	1980	1990
MEXICO			
Baja Calif.	870	1,227	2,000
Sonora	1,099	1,498	2,003
Chihuahua	1,613	1,935	2,336
Coahuila	1,115	1,561	2,030
N. Leon	1,695	2,464	3,476
Tamaulipas	1,457	1,925	2,448
Border	7,849	10,610	14,293
Mexico	48,225	69,393	87,400
% Border	16.28	15.29	16.35
US			
California	19,971	25,623	26,710
Arizona	1,775	3,053	3,449
New Mexico	1,011	1,424	1,520
Texas	11,199	15,986	16,479
Border	33,956	46,086	48,158
USA	203,306	226,505	248,249
% Border	16.70	20.35	19.40
Total			
Border			
US-Mex	41,805	56,696	62,451
% Change		35.62	10.15

Sources: U.S. Bureau of the Census, *U.S. Census of Population*, 1970,
1980, and 1990; INEGI, Secretaria be Programacion y Presupuesto,
Censos de Poblacion, 1970, 1980, and 1990.

INTEGRATION OR REGULARIZATION?

As suggested in the previous section, the changing nature of the interdependence between Mexico and the United States has meant that policies intended solely for the border region have been extended beyond that region, linking industry, development, private-sector growth, and labor markets in both countries. In turn, these policies have induced other social and economic interactions that have become more complex and intertwined over time. The original policies did not anticipate the dozens of new ramifications that emerged between 1965 and 1985.

Border economic development occurred without government intervention. NAFTA, as a political process, followed the economic transition. Sinclair states that government intervention has a crucial influence on the structure of markets and the patterns of international trade,[7] but for Mexico and the United States, intergovernmental agreements have emerged to control trends that developed with no direct state intervention. In the Mexican case, this has contributed to a total shift of national growth and developmental policy, namely, the abandonment after 40 years of the import substitution model (ISM). Beginning in the 1940s, ISM led to the creation, strict implementation, and maintenance of high tariffs and inward protectionist policies in Mexico. In the early 1970s Mexican officials started to recognize the resulting inefficiencies, but resisted change mainly for ideological and political reasons. Two major problems were associated with ISM and the economic development of Mexico: the very inefficient and unproductive industrial base and the emergence of noncompetitive commercial markets.

In addition, the state realized that there were inefficiencies in its own functioning.[8] Centralization and concentration in the Mexican political-economic system became impediments to boosting the economy. Decisions made mostly in Mexico City and a cumbersome bureaucracy meant that state and local officials were virtually excluded from policy making. Moreover, there was no significant participation of Mexican corporations and entrepreneurial organizations in formulating economic policy. At times, relations between the state and the private sector were confrontational, as during the administrations of Luis Echeverría (1970-76) and José Lopez Portillo (1976-82).

At the same time, there was a growing recognition in Mexico of the potential significance of its proximity to the United States, which, instead of being viewed as a threat to economic development poised to overwhelm Mexican business, could be viewed as a source of growth and a model of private-sector investment. The increasing activity along the border prompted the Mexican authorities, despite the history of U.S. invasions and border disputes, to reexamine the logic of continued resistance to creating new alliances. The political discourse of the official party (PRI) remained dry and cold when referring to their northern neighbor, reflecting doubt and suspicion, but in the early 1980s many factors interacted to challenge this approach. An unproductive industrial sector, a stagnant economy, the collapse of international oil prices, and increasing monetary and inflationary problems stimulated changes in economic development policies and national policies toward the United States.

Two initiatives were designed for this transition. One was formulated to guide domestic economic development and the other sought to link domestic change with a foreign policy of North American cooperation. This represented total renunciation of the political philosophy that had dominated since the Mexican Revolution. Throughout the 1980s, more and more Mexican leaders proposed policy shifts, calling for a closer relationship with the United States and a more outward-oriented economic strategy.[9] The policy adopted combined opening the country to foreign investment with what is referred to as managed interdependence—that is, explicit government intervention in the economic and trade relationships evolving between Mexico and the United States.[10]

In Mexico, economic integration and free trade among the three NAFTA countries was not understood as the whole solution to Mexican underdevelopment, but this was conceived of as the best strategy to promote growth and stability.[11] The realities of failed policies, the recognition of new international trends, and interdependent economic activities forced Mexico to rethink and reformulate domestic policies. Economic reform was not simply a novelty of policy formulation but, as stated by Delal, "was born of necessity."[12]

Meanwhile, in the United States little policy attention was directed toward strengthening the relationship with Mexico. In the private sector, corporate strategy was international and global, but looked to Europe and Asia. Mexico was avoided because of its cumbersome bureaucracy and obscure laws. In 1965, the Johnson administration initiated a change by agreeing to the *maquiladora* program, which was seen essentially as a benefit to U.S. corporations and not as a precursor to free trade with Mexico.

Nevertheless, several large corporations were actively engaged in expansion activities in Mexico. General Motors and Ford were among those with a long tradition there. The automobile industry had moved into Mexico during the 1940s, mainly to assemble cars for consumption in that country,[13] and most of the plants were located in Mexico City. No major changes occurred until the 1980s, when Chrysler started to use Mexico as a platform for export to Latin America. By the 1990s there were automotive factories all over the country, with high-technology plants close to the border in order to facilitate transportation and supervision. Many of the border operations produced auto parts destined for U.S. plants and clearly fit the international "production-sharing" model begun by BIP.[14] Before NAFTA was passed, the auto sector was already taking advantage of proximity, labor markets, and productivity. Moreover, they have been able to expand even in periods of recession in Mexico. Indeed, Chrysler was expanding and upgrading its plants in Toluca and Juarez at the beginning of 1995.

In the 1990s, following what the Michigan companies had done 50 years before, more companies learned to work in another culture and to adapt for flexible production operations. General Electric (appliances), Motorola, IBM, Hewlett Packard, and Rexnord are among those that expanded south of the border, and many other companies have relocated part of their overseas manufacturing to Mexico. Currently, Apple Computer, Pepsi, Compaq, and many middle-sized auto suppliers in Michigan are studying their options in this regard.

In view of the economic, social, educational, and political forces at work, a perplexed Washington wanted to regulate, normalize, and control events at an early stage rather than wait for them to become more complex and require a more complicated formula.[15] In official circles there was also a recognition of the need for integration with neighbors in order to aggregate economies in the face of such challenges as the European Economic Union. NAFTA also presented a way to facilitate corporate penetration of Latin American tariffs and trade barriers in the name of economic development. Thus, the integration at the continental level begun by the Canada-United States Free Trade Agreement in 1988 was expanded to Mexico in 1993, and other countries in the hemisphere, such as Chile, were offered promises of affiliation. Negotiations are well underway in 1995, and NAFTA offers the possibility of testing open markets and expanding them throughout the region.

The assessment and evaluation of NAFTA's effects is keeping observers and policy makers busy. In Mexico, the government is looking to see whether economic stabilization results. In the United States also, companies and policy makers are following events closely, especially along the border. Clearly, Texas and California are the closest trading partners with Mexico, ranking first and second, respectively, in 1990, with trade valued at $13.3 billion and $4.7 billion. Yet, Michigan was third among the exporters to Mexico, with a considerable $1.4 billion in trade.

Michigan exports have followed a peculiar pattern in recent years. As seen in table 3, from an increase of almost 13 percent in 1991, they declined by 13.8 percent in 1992 and by 8 percent in 1993, mainly due to the political discourse generated in Michigan against the agreement. In figure 1, the dotted line represents more than $5 billion in estimated trade when components produced in Michigan but not directly exported from the state are taken into account.[16] Preliminary figures from the Michigan International Trade Authority indicate that in 1994, when NAFTA started, exports to Mexico increased to $1.5 billion, or a net rise of 17.5 percent. Manufacturing is the sector of the state economy with the largest share of these exports. Analysts expect that exports to Mexico will decline in 1995 as a consequence of its inflationary and monetary problems.

Table 3.
Michigan Exports to Mexico, 1987-93 in thousands of dollars.

Sector	1987	1988	1989	1990	1991	1992	1993
Agriculture	2,463	2,721	1,915	6,910	3,289	6,586	5,370
Mining	2,324	1,209	289	4,379	3,120	3,845	8,286
Manufact.	1,071,690	1,311,025	1,523,886	1,396,142	1,545,755	1,246,366	1,021,378
Other	1,392	2,441	194,468	30,628	79,245	163,834	282,483
Total	1,077,870	1,317,396	1,720,558	1,438,058	1,625,000	1,420,640	1,295,192

Source: Michigan International Trade Authority; Adjusted data from the U.S. Bureau of the Census, Foreign Trade Division, and reports from the Michigan Deptartment of Commerce.

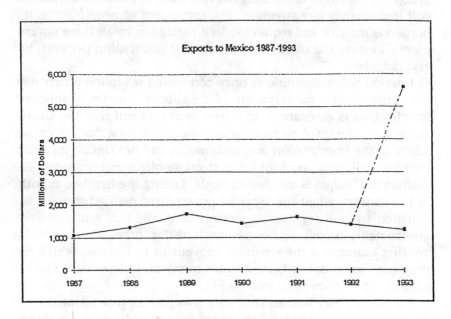

Figure 1.
Michigan Exports to Mexico.

BEYOND THE MARKET: NAFTA'S EFFECT ON DOMESTIC AFFAIRS

To understand NAFTA as an instrument of public policy, it is important to recognize the regional political economy of North America. A combination of political and economic factors flow back and forth over national borders every day. For instance, no two countries in the world are more sensitive to the fluctuation of the U.S. dollar than Canada and Mexico.[17] A decision on domestic interest rates by the U.S. Federal Reserve Board has immediate repercussions in the neighboring economies. While political integration is not on the horizon, political involvement among the three partners is certainly expected to grow. Now more than ever, each country is aware that in formulating policies it needs to calculate effects on and reactions from its partners.[18]

When there are tensions or conflicts that affect trade or binational logistics along the borders, parties in the dispute need only block the bridges or highways connecting the two countries and the authorities will immediately pay attention. The movement of people across the borders is massive and requires federal regulation by all three governments. In sum, the three countries are not just trading partners, but also neighbors.

Internal political problems once considered sovereign affairs may now involve the participation of neighbors, usually unsolicited. Immigration is an example of a persistent problem that the United States has attempted to solve with domestic policy, but, as proponents of the Immigration and Reform Control Act (IRCA) have discovered, unilateral decisions for bilateral problems will not work. The conflict in Chiapas is another example. During the first two months of the conflict, when the Mexican government decided to solve the situation by military means, pressure from the U.S. and Canadian governments forced authorities to look for other avenues.[19] Yet another example is the separatist movement in Quebec, which has prompted some in the United States to say an independent Quebec should not be allowed to join NAFTA.[20]

Democracy and human rights are two themes that are at the top of the binational agendas. The presence of outside observers during recent elections in Mexico indicates that not only independent groups, but also members of the U.S. Congress will be active in overseeing political events there. In the area of human rights, Mexico does not have an impeccable record. Since some archaic Mexican functionaries, particularly in law enforcement agencies, still practice their own law, a more direct intervention will probably occur.[21] Though uncomfortable with the interference, many Mexicans see NAFTA as a means to change some of the old deficiencies and vices of their political system. [22]

Other issues that may create conflict include how the United States will manage its foreign policy toward Latin America and Mexico's reaction if invasions and occupations are involved.[23] In this regard, Canada and Mexico present a common front against intervention that sooner or later will collide with the historical U.S. policy of interventionism, including the embargo of Cuba.

WHEN DOMESTIC POLICY BECOMES INTERNATIONAL IN THE NAFTA ERA: ENVIRONMENT AND MIGRATION

Several key problems appear to be domestic issues, but have emerged as binational problems. Environmental quality along the U.S.-Mexican border is one of the most crucial considerations for people living there, and pollution recognizes no national boundaries. For example, pollution of the Colorado River affects the water shared with Mexico, particularly in the area of Mexicali, where it is used for both human consumption and irrigation.[24] Another example is Tijuana, whose sewage discharges into the ocean soil San Diego beaches and cause health and ecological problems in Southern California generally.

Air quality has also emerged as a pressing issue, particularly in the Juarez-El Paso region. During the 1980s the problem was tackled by El Paso authorities, who enforced EPA standards for U.S. urban areas in the erroneous belief that the remedy lay on their side of the border. But air has no citizenship and it was discovered that part of the problem was lower standards for auto emissions in Juarez, although the main source of pollution was the emissions of vehicles waiting (often almost an hour) to pass through local U.S. border stations. Furthermore, *maquiladoras* in northern Mexico also contributed to contamination of the region. Most of the garbage and chemicals from these factories were dumped into the waterways feeding the Rio Grande River, which has caused serious health problems for communities on both sides of the border.

Although the United States did not develop any specific initiatives in anticipation of NAFTA, several new binational programs were created to help resolve environmental and social problems along the border with Mexico. Examples are the Border Environmental Cooperation Commission (BECC), the North American Development Bank (NADBANK), and the North American Commission for Environmental Cooperation.

In addition to the environment, shifts in labor migration patterns have created issues requiring binational attention. Labor markets in both countries respond rapidly to changes in their structural conditions, and this affects migration.[25] Recruiting for the service, construction, and landscaping sectors in Southern California works nicely at noon in the main plazas of Tijuana. Houston employers do their hiring during weekends in such Mexican border cities as Matamoros, Reynosa, and Rio Bravo.[26] There are cases in which Midwestern companies from 2,000 miles away have hired agricultural labor on the streets of Nuevo Laredo.[27]

Labor market interdependency has been spurred by growth in the U.S. demand for domestic help and child care over the last 15 years, particularly for those with a basic knowledge of English. Recruiting is done through advertisements in local newspapers and magazines in northern Mexico. Recently, demand has increased for health aides and elderly care workers with good English and professional skills. Local papers in Houston, Los Angeles, and San Diego frequently have advertisements seeking caretakers and live-in companions, answered by people from as far away as Guadalajara and San Luis Potosi, located in central Mexico. It is clear that a binational network links buyers and sellers of labor, and this is likely to grow in view of the constant increases in U.S. labor costs in these sectors.

In the analysis of migration patterns, it is necessary to study the sources of both expulsion, or push, factors, and attraction, or pull, factors. The latter have been outlined in the previous discussions; now we will discuss some of the conditions that determine push variants. Liberalization and privatization of Mexican agriculture and reconversion of the industrial base are occurring almost simultaneously. Both are intended to open new avenues of investment and to revitalize production, but these reforms were made with the understanding that they would cause major population dislocation.

Since 1992, the Mexican government has implemented a series of profound changes in agriculture. Possibly the most important was the modification of Article 27 of the Mexican Constitution to allow—although not force—the privatization of previously inalienably controlled land, the *ejido*. Other changes included reduced price supports for agricultural commodities, less subsidization of irrigation water and fertilizer, and cutbacks in state credits for small producers. All of these were meant to stimulate private investment in agriculture and make the Mexican agricultural sector more competitive with agricultural imports.[28] In the process, the historical social contract between the state and the peasantry was negated. Policy makers knew that one of the major effects would be massive migration from the countryside. Unpublished but official projections estimate that 4 million people will leave agriculture and move to the major cities by 2010.

These changes were put into place before NAFTA was signed, but were designed to prepare Mexico for the competition of the NAFTA era. While some argued that the country needed to make these changes, with or without NAFTA, the impending agreement certainly forced the pace.

In the process, Mexican domestic policies have played an important role in moving the nation toward the economic and social "joining" of NAFTA. They have served to increase foreign investment in Mexican agriculture, and they have promoted migration to the United States. Cities in Mexico, already crowded, are receiving even more rural newcomers, and the competition for good jobs is fierce. The government has instituted a new program of emergency employment in infrastructure construction, creating jobs that are temporary but relatively well paid. The most desirable employment, however, is in the new industries, including the expanding assembly plant sector. Despite these opportunities in some urban-industrial areas and in the border cities, legal and illegal Mexican migration is expanding. There are several reasons for this, led by the wage differential for comparable work (about seven times higher in the United States), especially with the peso devaluation of 1995.

These push and pull factors, despite attempts to curb them, remain dynamic and attest to the high degree of interdependency in this unique binational labor market, where the demand for inexpensive, relatively educated, loyal, and productive workers will continue to affect labor migration well into the future. Remedies for these problems have been attempted unilaterally by federal, state, and local authorities, but these solutions have not lasted. It has become clear to policy makers that these problems are bilateral and that solving them requires the participation of all the jurisdictions involved.

Interlocking job markets and migration also have created social networks that are binational in character. Ties based on kinship, community of origin, ethnicity, and class link such diverse regions as Oaxaca, located in southern Mexico, to towns in Oregon and Michigan. Like migration itself, the networks are not limited to low-income populations but also include professionals and business people. The presence of migrants may generate a political reaction, such as the passage of Proposition 187 in California. Although the Michigan population of Mexican origin continues to grow, its size is still small compared to that of California.

When the managers, technicians, and supervisors of U.S. corporations move to Mexico, the process is seldom called migration nor the
people migrants, even though many retire there. U.S. workers in
Mexico participate in many different sectors of the economy, from
agriculture to industry, and the country is also attracting a growing
number of North American retirees, who settle in such communities
as Jalisco and Oaxaca. Many of these people resist learning Spanish
and interacting with Mexicans, and along with a growing Mexican
frustration with Americanization (promoted by the expansion of
such chains as McDonalds, Pizza Hut, Kentucky Fried Chicken,
Walmart, and the Price Club), this may lead to the reemergence of
anti-Americanism.

THE POLITICAL AND ECONOMIC CONTEXTS OF THE DISAGREEMENTS

Several issues, not only economic but also political, were not
resolved with the formalization of NAFTA. One is the protection of
labor standards. Rather than enhance workers' rights, the labor side
agreement is expected to maintain the status quo established by each
country's legislation. In addition, no labor mobility is contemplated
by the agreement, except professionals and/or intrafirm reloca-
tions.[29] No mention is made of government responsibilities to facilitate education and training for workers who may require these as a
consequence of NAFTA adjustments. Also, there are no policies and
guidelines for planning for future labor needs. Social benefits such as
health care, work insurance, pensions and retirement plans, profit
sharing, and child care provision are not included in the present text
of NAFTA.[30] The North American Commission for Labor
Cooperation, created with the signing of the agreement, will eventually need to address how the rights and benefits of workers will be
provided.

Another unresolved issue is that transnational corporations
(TNCs) are expected to benefit the most from NAFTA, but it is unclear
to what extent they will help minimize the negative social effects
resulting from industrial and capital mobility. In addition, TNCs
seem to enjoy preferential tax treatment as long as they follow the
percentage limits of the rules of origin. No provisions are contem-

Reeducation

plated to regulate the mobility of capital, such as the minimum period capital must be committed to a particular investment. Although it was agreed that the three countries will exchange fiscal information, no specific regulations were established.

A third issue that is implicit in NAFTA is an inducement toward regionalism. It is clear that other countries in the world will see NAFTA as an example of how to aggregate their economic capacities. The strategy is evident: competition is better managed if a few blocs are competing among themselves than if hundreds of countries are competing with one another. The recent formation of MERCOSUR by Brazil, Argentina, Paraguay, and Uruguay is an example of this trend to regionalization. Fourth, NAFTA has critical implications for Latin American foreign policy in the next century. The Enterprise of the Americas Initiative (EAI), suggested by President Bush, contemplates intercontinental trade for the Americas,[31] to promote market reforms in the respective countries. During the December 1994 Summit of the Americas in Miami, President Clinton announced that by the year 2005 there will be a free trade region from the Yukon to Tierra del Fuego.[32] It seems clear that Washington favors a policy of integration, regardless of the party in the White House. Such an approach would mean not only economic gains for corporations, but also greater U.S. political control over the region.[33] While most of the Latin American presidents at the Miami summit supported the idea, they raised other concerns, including democratization, monetary and fiscal policies, and the war on drugs.[34] Nevertheless, the U.S. delegation insisted on hemispheric trade as the central theme. There is no question about which country will exercise the most control in the hemisphere when the Western Hemisphere Free Trade Agreement (WHAFTA) becomes a reality. The asymmetry of power and wealth clearly indicates that the United States will have regional hegemony through economics, commerce, and trade specifically.

In sum, many of the models that assess the economic effects of NAFTA fail to include all of the social issues mentioned above.[35] Two critics, Grinspun and Cameron,[36] have noted the lack of socially oriented variables and mention that most of the general equilibrium models tell a shortsighted story because they do not examine intrafirm trade, income distribution, macroeconomic imbalances, differentials in human capital, and environmental costs. Grinspun adds that many of these components are key to the successful integration of economies, and their absence undermines the modeling of NAFTA's effects.[37] Most models fail to assess two major areas affected by economic integration: the human and the environmental contexts.

CONCLUSION

We have argued that a process was underway to create a new set of relationships between Mexico and the United States before NAFTA was negotiated and signed. Yet the ties of capital, labor, markets, and culture connecting the two countries received a major stimulus from the simple prospect of NAFTA being forged. In Mexico, significant reforms were implemented in preparation. The signing of NAFTA has led many U.S. firms and agricultural producers to readjust their long-term planning, but neither the State of Michigan nor the federal government has made any major shifts in domestic policy because of NAFTA.

When President Zedillo took office, Mexico faced a new set of crises, in part endogenous and in part due to Mexico's links with the international financial market. As one political analyst put it, "Mexico is at the point that old structures are ready to die, and new ones are not ready to be born."[38]

Mexican immigration, stimulated by internal and external pressures, has generated a strong reaction in the United States. NAFTA was promoted in the United States as a way to stimulate economic growth in Mexico and thus generate the jobs to limit migration. Like all policy shifts, however, it will be years before the total social and economic effects can be evaluated.

At the same time, it is possible that privatization, coupled with NAFTA, is contributing to a growing inequality of income in Mexico. Many rural Mexicans faced with growing inflation are tempted to seek work in the United States. Whole communities are becoming dependent on remittances sent home by migrant workers. NAFTA was never designed to address social problems, yet the agreement has immense social implications, both domestic and international.

NAFTA could well become just a footnote in history as tariffs fall with GATT and as other nations of the Americas join, as many predict, what is now the North American trade bloc. This is certainly the goal of U.S. policy. Yet the concerns of many who opposed NAFTA—

such as the reduction of local control and the concentration of power that can result from the new trade blocs—linger. The seeds of social unrest that erupted in Chiapas may find fertile soil elsewhere in the hemisphere. Unless Mexico and other Latin American countries can either generate new jobs or create social programs that enhance living conditions, NAFTA's promise of a higher standard of living will be replaced by discontent and resistance in all three countries. Social movements do not wait for the last evaluation before they emerge.

NOTES

1. Sidney Weintraub, ed., "Free Trade in the Western Hemisphere," *Annals of the American Academy of Political and Social Science* 526 (Newbury Park: Sage Periodical Press, 1993); Robert A. Pastor, *Integration with Mexico: Options for U.S. Policy* (New York: Twentieth Century Fund, 1993).
2. By regularization, we mean the creation of formal norms, rules, and policies that control and frame operations and activities in economic and social contexts.
3. Manuel Chavez, "The State, Elites, and Urban Development: The Political Economy of the U.S. Mexico Border Region" (Ph.D. diss., University of Wisconsin - Milwaukee, 1993).
4. Bernardo A. Gonzalez and Rocio Barajas, *Las Maquiladoras. Ajuste Estructural y Desarollo Regional* (Tijuana: El Colegio de La Frontera Norte, 1989); Leslie Sklair, *Assembling for Development: The Maquila Industry in Mexico and the United States* (San Diego: Center for U.S. Mexico Studies, University of California - San Diego, 1993).
5. Gonzalez and Barajas, *Las Maquiladoras.*
6. U.S. Department of Justice, Immigration and Naturalization Service *Yearbook*, various years.
7. Scott Sinclair, "NAFTA and U.S. Trade Policy: Implications for Canada and Mexico," in *The Political Economy of the North American Free Trade* (New York: St. Martin's Press, 1993), 228.
8. Maria de Los Angeles Pozas, *Industrial Restructuring in Mexico: Corporate Adaptation, Technological Innovation, and Changing Patterns of Industrial Relations in Mexico* (San Diego: University of California - San Diego, 1993).
9. Banco Nacional de Mexico, Department of Economic Research, "Reflections on Mexican Development," *Review of the Economic Situation of Mexico* 70, no. 822 (1994): 223-29.
10. Sidney Weintraub, *A Marriage of Convenience: Relations between Mexico and the United States* (New York: Twentieth Century Fund, 1990); Jorge Bustamante, Clark W. Reynolds, and Raúl Hinojosa, *U.S.-Mexico Relations: Labor Markets Interdependence* (Stanford: Stanford University Press, 1992).

11. M. Delal Baer, "North American Free Trade," *Foreign Affairs* 70, no. 4 (fall 1991): 130-49.
12. Ibid.
13. Rafael Fernandez de Castro, Monica C. Verea, and Sidney Weintraub, eds., *Sectoral Labor Effects of North American Free Trade* (Austin: U.S. Mexican Policy Studies Program, University of Texas at Austin, CISAN-UNAM, ITAM, 1993).
14. Sergio Sánchez, "El Sector Automotriz ante el Tratado de Libre Comercio," in *Sectoral Labor Effects of North American Free Trade* (Austin: U.S. Mexican Policy Studies Program, University of Texas at Austin, CISAN-UNAM, ITAM, 1993).
15. Weintraub, *Marriage of Convenience* and "Free Trade," 204-9.
16. The data need to be examined with care, because the Michigan Department of Commerce switched database assumptions for 1993, including all goods that had "significant origin" in Michigan but were finally assembled outside the state.
17. Gary C. Hufbauer and Jeffery J. Schott, *North American Free Trade: Issues and Recommendations* (Washington, D.C.: Institute for International Economics, 1992).
18. Adolfo Aguilar, "La Dimension Politica," in *El Tratado de Libre Comercio: Entre el Viejo y el Nuevo Orden* (D.F. Mexico: UNAM-CISAN, Ciudad Universitaria, 1992); Bustamante, Reynolds, and Hinojosa, *U.S.-Mexico Relations*; Ricardo Grinspun and Maxwell A. Cameron, eds., *The Political Economy of the North American Free Trade Agreement* (New York: St. Martin's Press, 1993); Pastor, *Integration*; Weintraub, *Marriage of Convenience*.
19. "La Influencia Externa en el Conflicto de Chiapas" *El Financiero*, 18 March 1994, p. 5.
20. "An Independent Quebec?" *Wall Street Journal*, 3 March 1994, p. A7.
21. One issue that seems to be a serious contender for political harmonization is control of drugs and reduction of the increasing power of narcotics traffickers. Since this matter also affects the national security of the United States, pressure will probably grow to persuade Mexico and Canada to join a trinational law enforcement effort to tackle contraband and drug smugglers.
22. Jorge Castarsuade Mexico and Canada to join *Foreign Affairs* 72 (September/October 1993): 66-80; Aguilar, "La Dimension Politica," 120-35.
23. Remedios Gomez Arnau, "El Tratado de Libre Comercio y su Impacto en la Relacion Diplomatica Bilateral Mexico-Estados Unidos," in *El Tratado de Libre Comercio: Entre el Viejo y el Nuevo Orden* (D.F. Mexico: UNAM-CISAN, Ciudad Universitaria, 1992).
24. Scott Whiteford, "Troubled Waters: The Regional Impacts of Foreign Investment and State Capital in the Mexicali Valley," in *Regional Impacts of U.S.-Mexico Relations* (San Diego: U.S. Mexican Studies Center, University of California - San Diego, 1986).

25. Bustamante, Reynolds, and Hinojosa, *U.S.-Mexico Relations*.
26. Alenjandra Salas, "Libre Comercio y Políticas Econf Califor*El Cotidiano* 5, no. 1 (1991): 3.
27. Manuel Chavez, "Migration Forces in the Midwest: The Pull Factor" in *Immigration and Ethnic Communities: A Latino Focus*, ed. Refugio Rochin (East Lansing: JSRI - Michigan State University, 1996).
28. Scott Whiteford and Francisco Bernal, "Campesinos, Water, and the State," in *The Reform of the Mexican Agrarian Reform* (New York: Columbia University Press, 1995).
29. *North American Agreement on Labor Cooperation*, (Washington, D.C.: U.S. Government Printing Office, 1993), 28-34.
30. "North American Labor Laws, How They Stack up to Each Other," *El Financiero*, 15 May 1993, 14-15.
31. "The Enterprise of the Americas," *New York Times*, 20 August 1990.
32. "On Eve of Miami Summit Talks, U.S. Comes Under Fire," *New York Times*, 9 December 1994, pp. 1, 4.
33. Jonathan Hartlyn, Lars Schoultz, and Augusto Varas, eds., *The United States and Latin America in the 1990s: Beyond the Cold War* (Chapel Hill: University of North Carolina Press, 1992).
34. "What the Summit of the Americas Promises," *Washington Post*, 11 December 1994, p. A1.
35. Clark W. Reynolds, Leonard Waverman, and Gerardo Bueno, eds., *The Dynamics of North American Trade and Investment: Canada, Mexico, and the United States* (Stanford: Stanford University Press, 1991).
36. Grinspun and Cameron, *Political Economy*, 7-10.
37. Ibid., 110-19.
38. Casta, 110-19.

The NAFTA Debate in Retrospect: U.S. Perspectives

David D. Arsen

It is understandable that the North American Free Trade Agreement commands such widespread interest, even with the passage of time since its implementation. NAFTA addresses global forces that are widely perceived as relentlessly affecting the character and trajectory of contemporary economic and social life. NAFTA did not create these forces. Rather, the agreement was an attempt to mold them, to promote some developments and to undermine others. The range of effects is remarkably broad, including patterns of employment and income growth; transnational corporate strategy; environmental, business, and social regulation; sovereignty; and governance.

NAFTA eliminated trade barriers between Canada, Mexico, and the United States, some immediately and others more gradually over a period of up to 15 years. On this count it accelerated and locked in place an established progression toward expanded and liberalized trade in the region. The Canada-U.S. Free Trade Agreement was already in place. Prior to NAFTA, Mexico had substantially reduced trade-weighted tariffs from an average of 23 percent in 1985 to only 6.5 percent by 1990, and they were reduced further still before NAFTA's implementation.[1] U.S. tariffs against Mexican goods were even lower. These are small barriers, constituting virtually free trade even before NAFTA went into effect.

More significant than the provisions regarding trade are those pertaining to investment. Indeed, a far larger share of the two thousand pages in the agreement pertain to investment than to trade. NAFTA is appropriately seen as an economic constitution, the rules for the establishment of long-term economic relations in an integrated market comprising more than 360 million people. The desire to set out such rules is entirely sensible. Differences of opinion, however, naturally will arise regarding just what those rules ought to be.

NAFTA offers an intriguing study of the political role of expert opinion in public policy making. Economists are not generally the life of the party. But in the arena of authoritative, expert predictions of NAFTA's effects, economists held a virtual monopoly. They relied heavily on arguments from economic theory that have been polished for more than a century and a half relating to the mutual benefits of international specialization and trade. Buttressed by the predictions of sophisticated economic models, NAFTA proponents achieved an early and influential jump on the debate. Critics, mostly noneconomists, could offer nothing on the same level of methodological sophistication and typically came off as misguided alarmists.

U.S. public opinion on NAFTA split sharply along class lines. Polls revealed wide support among high-income and college-educated Americans, while production and nonmanagerial workers opposed the accord by equally wide margins. Large corporations and business associations lobbied hard for the treaty's passage. Unions were steadfast in their opposition.

The pattern of public opinion posed a little-noticed conundrum for economic science. Economists have a doctrinal commitment to the proposition that individuals make decisions and act in a rational, self-interested manner. Average citizens are regularly assumed to make all sorts of esoteric calculations in order to anticipate correctly the course of future events (for example, one's future lifetime tax burden associated with contemporary government budget deficits, or the future inflationary consequences of present-day monetary policy). NAFTA presented economists with an awkward choice between preserving the rationality hypothesis, which would imply that roughly half the population, mostly concentrated in the bottom half of the income distribution, correctly anticipated adverse consequences from NAFTA, or abandoning the rationality hypothesis to assume widespread irrational preferences. With few exceptions, economists abandoned their standard behavioral postulate and embraced the latter interpretation.

The NAFTA debate did not end with the treaty's passage. Indeed, the dramatic financial crisis that erupted in Mexico barely one year after NAFTA's implementation has served to reopen the debate and redirect public attention to U.S.-Mexican relations. One rarely observes a case in which social science's predicted effects of public policy are so clearly and publicly stated and also open to (presumed) ready assessment by average citizens after the fact. NAFTA's pitched political battle failed to produce an open and reflective dialogue among interested parties holding opposing views. Supporters tended to offer forceful claims of economic benefits, while brushing aside the distributional and broader political economic concerns of opponents. Many opponents, meanwhile, perceiving adverse consequences from a deal they did not help to shape, offered hasty reactions, often too shrill and lacking sufficient development. This chapter seeks to further a more constructive dialogue on a range of NAFTA issues of enduring significance.

TWO FACES OF NAFTA

In the debates, NAFTA proponents successfully presented themselves as optimistic, open to change, forward-looking, and cosmopolitan. Their opponents, by comparison, were effectively cast as shortsighted, misguided, supporters of special interests, and nationalistic. All this is an apt characterization of some NAFTA opponents—those who might be called nationalist opponents—led notably in the United States by Ross Perot and Patrick Buchanan.

The objections of others in the United States, as well as in Mexico and Canada, turn on different concerns, however. I will call this group cosmopolitan opponents. They do not oppose free trade or wider economic integration. Rather, their concerns center on the rules under which that integration takes place. Although they have received less attention, the cosmopolitan opponents raise the more pertinent and interesting objections. Between them, the NAFTA proponents and cosmopolitan opponents offer two sharply different visions of the accord.

For NAFTA proponents, orthodox trade theory provides the essential justification for the agreement: When each country specializes in producing whatever it produces relatively efficiently, the economic pie grows and consumers reap the benefits of greater productivity as competition forces prices down. Living standards increase due to a more efficient international division of labor, as each country exports the surplus of goods it produces relatively efficiently in exchange for relatively low-cost imports. This view acknowledges that trade liberalization may generate losers (for example, displaced workers and capital owners in industries lacking comparative advantage), but the gains to winners in free trade are sufficient to compensate the losers fully and still come out ahead. So, in principle, winners could compensate losers through an appropriate government transfer mechanism.

According to proponents, Mexico stood to gain a disproportionate share of NAFTA's economic benefits. This is because U.S.-Mexico trade represents a large share of Mexico's total trade, but only a small portion of the U.S. total. Also, NAFTA's trade and investment liberalization represented a greater shift in Mexican than in U.S. or Canadian policy. By replacing the Mexican government's traditional interventionist economic role with an increased role for private domestic and foreign firms, proponents predicted that NAFTA would trigger robust Mexican growth. This, it turn, would benefit the United States and Canada through growing export markets in a more prosperous Mexico.

Predictions of NAFTA-induced Mexican growth carried important implications for a number of contentious nontrade issues. Proponents argued that Mexican growth would eventually slow or reverse the economic incentives underlying Mexican immigration to the United States. Rising incomes would also lead Mexicans to demand improved environmental conditions. In addition, more vigorous private-sector competition and an expanding middle class would establish the economic prerequisites for moving Mexico toward a more open and democratic political structure.

NAFTA's cosmopolitan opponents do not share the proponents' abiding faith in the social benefits attained from private businesses acting in response to profit incentives. They view NAFTA as an elite-driven political strategy that shifts power to transnational corporations (TNCs), and away from workers and government. From this perspective, NAFTA represents a "continental bill of rights" for TNCs. It makes significant advances in protecting investors' rights, which will encourage TNCs to shift production from the United States and Canada to Mexico. Yet, in promoting a continental market, NAFTA secures very little for labor and environmental rights and, indeed, seriously restricts citizens' capacity through their national and subnational governments, to raise or maintain standards in these areas.

Opponents focus on what they regard as NAFTA's perverse distributional consequences in all three countries. By locating operations in Mexico, TNCs can lower production costs while maintaining barrier-free access to the North American market. Simultaneously, the threat of capital mobility to Mexico will undercut both wage demands and business regulations in the United States and Canada. Critics maintain that NAFTA's provisions fail to assure Mexican wage growth, so Mexico's labor surplus, weak unions, and macroeconomic austerity will prevent wages from rising even as foreign investment increases. Rather than reducing product prices for consumers, critics see these cost reductions flowing primarily to higher profits for large corporations. In short, by this view, NAFTA's benefits will flow disproportionately to the top of the income distribution, while its costs will be borne by lower-income households.

THE STRATEGIC CONTEXT

A key promise of trade liberalization is always that the establishment of stable and clear rules will take politics out of trade. In reality, conflicting interests and the exercise of power heavily influence an agreement's specific content and implementation. Countries generally seek to maximize the gains from opening foreign markets to their exports while minimizing the losses to import-sensitive domestic industries. Yet differing circumstances in the three NAFTA countries were associated with distinctive objectives and bargaining strength in the NAFTA negotiations.

For the United States, NAFTA represented a strategic response to economic challenges from Europe and Japan and an opportunity to reinforce its power base in the Western Hemisphere. For a quarter century following World War II, the U.S. lead in productivity generated international competitiveness and supported a dominant U.S. role in international institutions. As economic advances in Europe and Japan narrowed the productivity gap, U.S. producers encountered sustained and serious competitive challenges in markets at home and abroad. In response, over the last two decades U.S. businesses have moved aggressively on several fronts to enhance their competitiveness through improving productivity and reducing costs.

One strategy for improving price competitiveness, particularly relevant to U.S. manufacturers, is the establishment of production facilities in low-wage countries to serve the U.S. market. Among low-wage countries, Mexico offers the significant advantage of proximity. Yet the potential cost savings of direct investment in poor countries must always be weighed against the risk that investors' rights are less secure and the chronic tendency of governments in developing countries (including Mexico) to seek control over the pattern of domestic development through regulations on foreign direct investment. Accordingly, in the NAFTA negotiations, the United States sought to establish rules that both protected the rights of foreign investors and eliminated regulations imposed by Mexico on foreign investment. The United States also sought to open for foreign investment certain Mexican industries, such as energy and financial services, that were extensively regulated or dominated by government-owned enterprises. NAFTA promised to bolster U.S. investors' confidence in Mexico by improving market access and offering important commitments on future government activities.

NAFTA's benefits for U.S. manufacturers in competition with producers in other advanced countries turn on a number of features. On the one hand, Japan is not part of a formal regional free trade area. On the other hand, the European Union (EU) does not include any country with wage levels nearly as low as Mexico's. The EU also commits member countries to a range of costly harmonization in the area of social policy. Unlike the EU, NAFTA is not a customs union, so the United States maintains a high degree of autonomy in its economic relations with countries outside the free trade area. Finally, the United States secured rules-of-origin provisions that restrict barrier-free access to goods with specified percentages of their value produced in North America. These protective measures were designed to limit the market access of firms from other advanced countries that rely on established networks for sourcing production from sites outside North America.

Given its heavy dependence on exports to the United States, a central Canadian objective in both the Free Trade Agreement (FTA) and NAFTA negotiations was to ensure against U.S. protectionism. Tariff barriers were relatively minor, and far less important to Canada than avoiding nontariff barriers resulting from existing and future applications of U.S. trade remedy laws, particularly countervailing and antidumping duties and 301 and "super 301" actions.[2] The United States has increasingly resorted to these defensive trade measures against some countries. The actions taken against Canada focused on agricultural, fish, forestry, and natural resource products. The FTA's liberalization of nontariff barriers disappointed many Canadians, and there was hope that the NAFTA negotiations could provide greater assurances on this front.

The primary Mexican rationale for NAFTA was the country's pressing need for external capital inflows and foreign exchange. Mexico's 1982 foreign debt crisis was the catalyst for its subsequent liberalization. Saddled with heavy debt servicing and forced austerity in domestic macroeconomic policy, the Mexican economy was stagnant through most of the 1980s. Through NAFTA, Mexico sought to stimulate the inflow of foreign investment and to generate foreign exchange by establishing the country as an export platform in manufactured goods. Apart from the need for foreign exchange, Mexican officials came to embrace foreign investment as an essential part of a strategy to expand domestic employment and modernize technologically backward industries. These reforms were largely consistent with U.S. objectives and followed considerable and sustained pressure from multilateral agencies (e.g., IMF, Inter-American Development Bank, World Bank), which followed Washington's policies by conditioning credit flows on Mexico's implementation of the right policies.

Several forces worked to strengthen the bargaining position of the United States in the NAFTA negotiations relative to the other two countries. First, Mexico's acute need for foreign investment weakened its hand. Indeed, the desire to secure more accommodating relations with the international financial community accounted for Mexico's extensive unilateral trade liberalization in the years prior to the NAFTA accord.

Second, internal political institutions worked to strengthen the U.S. bargaining position.[3] Whereas U.S. trade negotiators are sensitive to the views of Congress and powerful interest groups, the Canadian Parliament is less permeable to special interests and had little influence during the negotiating process. So long as the prime minister could control the House of Commons, the trade accord could be passed in Canada through traditional party discipline. In

Mexico, the 70-year dominance of the ruling Institutional Revolutionary Party (PRI) meant that Congress was malleable, so the Mexican negotiators were relatively free from domestic political constraints, but this was a weakness, not a strength. The Mexican representatives could not credibly claim domestic political constraints to extract concessions from the United States and Canada. These differences in internal politics account for both the importance of fast-track authorization to Canada and Mexico and the torrent of Canadian and Mexican concessions secured by the Clinton administration on the eve of the U.S. House vote on NAFTA.[4]

Third, as the largest of the three economies, the United States was in a position to demand concessions. Trade theory predicts that when a small country opens to trade with a large country, it experiences a disproportionate share of the benefits.[5] In addition, the importance of a strong multilateral system of nondiscriminatory rules is greater for smaller, weaker countries than it is for strong countries, since the strong will enjoy greater success in securing their interests in a lawless environment. It follows, therefore, that the United States, needing some incentive to support a system that would potentially bestow disproportionate benefits on the smaller economies, was in a position to demand side payments in the form of disproportionate influence in the establishment and management of the rules of this system.

The side payments demanded essentially took three forms: (1) The establishment of special provisions to protect certain import-sensitive industries (such as fruits, vegetables, sugar, and other agricultural goods) and rules of origin for a number of manufactures (including textiles, fabrics, steel products, cars, and auto parts). (2) National treatment for U.S.-based TNCs operating in Mexico and Canada so that U.S. firms would reap a satisfactory portion of the benefits of future growth there. Key features included the elimination of maximum proportions for foreign equity, local sourcing and exporting requirements, review procedures for external investors, and increased protection for firms' intellectual property rights. (3) Sufficient ambiguity in the definition of subsidies and unfair trade practices to permit the dispute settlement mechanism to provide discretion for U.S. application of trade remedies against Canada and Mexico.

While NAFTA's benefits will be felt in all three countries, the strength of the U.S. bargaining position clearly increased the likely flow of returns to U.S. firms. These firms attained national treatment across the continent and enhanced access to Canada and Mexico's banking systems and energy resources. The United States also sought to use the negotiated elements of NAFTA to spur GATT (now known as the World Trade Organization) to adopt its positions regarding investment rules, financial services, intellectual property rights, agriculture, and government subsidies.

EFFECTS ON EMPLOYMENT AND EARNINGS

Certainly NAFTA's most hotly debated consequences were its effects on employment and earnings. Economists are right to stress the potential efficiency gains from NAFTA's trade and investment liberalization. Yet they tend to offer mechanistic, if not dogmatic, descriptions of how these efficiency gains will be distributed. A key issue concerns the implications of joining high- and low-wage countries within a single free trade area. Economists' predictions that countries with very different endowments will mutually benefit from free trade are deduced from very abstract models. Most employment predictions were based on computable general equilibrium (CGE) models, which embody textbook assumptions of perfect markets.[6] These models contain a huge number of equations that entail many hidden assumptions about unknown parameters and that fail to incorporate a wide range of specifically negotiated treaty features. Alternatively, the most widely publicized employment predictions were made by Gary Hufbauer and Jeffrey Schott, who adopted a different methodology, which they designated as a "historical" model.[7]

Abstraction is an unavoidable and essential feature of economic modeling, but one embedded assumption is particularly significant for the CGE models' employment predictions. These models employ the standard trade theory assumption of full employment both before and after trade liberalization. Consequently, employment effects are necessarily limited to shifting the workers displaced in one industry to instant reemployment in another. Since productivity growth is anticipated with specialization and trade, the assumption of full employment can only result in higher real incomes in aggregate. Such models, however, are not designed to predict overall employment creation or destruction, which accounts for the fact that they forecast either little or no change in the number of U.S. jobs.

The second significant assumption of the CGE models in the NAFTA context is that productive investment will not be diverted from the United States and Canada to Mexico. This is a striking assumption, given the robust growth of investment by TNCs in Mexico to serve the U.S. market and the clear objective of both Mexico and the United States to promote such investment through NAFTA. The standard modeling assumptions, however, go beyond ignoring possible shifts in the allocation of investment within the region to assume that NAFTA will create new investment in North America. New foreign direct investment (FDI) in Mexico is assumed to come from countries outside North America and from U.S. firms which divert their FDI to Mexico from the other low-wage countries where it otherwise would have been placed. Both of these effects are plausible, even if their magnitude cannot be confidently projected, but less plausible is the additional assumption that none of the induced FDI in Mexico from non-NAFTA countries would have been placed in the United States. Indeed, a large and rising share of this FDI has come from Japanese and European firms which are establishing Mexican production facilities to serve the entire North American market. Finally, the standard models ignore the possibility that jobs associated with foreign investment in Mexico may simply displace existing employment in less efficient firms or transform these firms into subsidiaries of TNCs, rather than create net increases in employment. Despite rapid growth in FDI, Mexico's total manufacturing employment has *declined* every month since September 1990.[8] In short, forecasts of employment benefits in all three NAFTA countries are hardly surprising: the economic models have systematically ignored those effects that could produce employment losses.

Alternatively, Hufbauer and Schott predicted that by 1995 NAFTA would generate net employment gains of 130,000 in the United States and more than 600,000 in Mexico. The U.S. gains were premised on a U.S. trade surplus with Mexico, implicitly requiring capital flows to that country. Mexican imports of U.S. capital goods, in turn, would facilitate the expansion of Mexican employment, which was assumed to be constrained by the shortage of capital equipment. Obviously, Mexico's financial crisis soon conspired to render Hufbauer and Schott's projections hopelessly optimistic. For the foreseeable future, Mexico will be forced to implement contractionary macroeconomic policies, depressing domestic employment and import demand, and consequently U.S. employment as well. In retrospect, Hufbauer and Schott's key error was to underestimate the enduring constraint of Mexico's foreign debt burden and its vulnerability to dramatic losses of portfolio investment.

While critics can readily identify tenuous assumptions regarding future patterns of foreign investment, it is quite another matter to offer superior predictions. Since the determinants of FDI are not well understood, those critics who tried to estimate its diversion from the United States to Mexico due to NAFTA were themselves forced to employ highly speculative and tenuous assumptions. There simply are no suitable precedents on which to base such predictions.

On balance, despite model biases and the uncertain course of future events, the aggregate employment projections of NAFTA proponents, in all likelihood, were a good deal closer to the mark than Ross Perot's alarmist prediction of vast U.S. job losses.[9] The net effect of NAFTA on the number of jobs in each country is likely to be rather small. Many people will lose jobs, but many others will gain them. Clearly, in the short run, the peso crisis and Mexico's current deep recession have produced unanticipated trade-related net job losses in the United States. Over the long run, however, the availability of work in each country will depend much more on macroeconomic policies than on trade policies.

This leaves open the question of the precise nature of employment specialization induced by trade liberalization. Which jobs will be gained and lost in each country? U.S. manufacturing workers find little solace in the economy's impressive capacity over the last decade, whatever its genesis, to generate the low-wage service sector employment that has offset job losses in manufacturing. What will be the pattern of employment shifts across occupations (skilled and unskilled), industries, and subnational regions? These are key questions, and the answers are far from clear.

NAFTA proponents envision an induced pattern of specialization in which U.S. and Canadian employment in capital-intensive and high-tech operations will expand, while Mexico will gain jobs in more labor-intensive and low- or standardized-technology industries. Consequently, a key predicted benefit of NAFTA for U.S. workers is a shift in the composition of domestic employment toward more good jobs, those with relatively high skills and high wages, including specifically jobs in U.S. capital goods industries and advanced services.

Empirical support for this hopeful scenario is mixed.[10] The prediction is certainly consistent with the labor-intensive manufacturing employment attracted to Mexico in the first-generation *maquiladora* plants, but more recent FDI in Mexico has represented increasingly capital-intensive and technologically advanced production. Harley Shaiken reports on a number of high-tech ventures in Mexico with the ability to produce complex products at quality and productivity levels comparable with U.S. levels and rivaling those in Japan.[11] Given further development of Mexican skills, infrastructure, and internal supplier networks, it is not unreasonable to acknowledge that a range of high-wage production jobs in the United States and Canada are at risk. The precise nature of these adjustments will largely depend on corporate sourcing strategies and patterns of intrafirm trade.

Apart from effects on the number and type of jobs available, there remains the issue of how trade liberalization will affect wages and income distribution—in other words, how the gains from trade will be distributed. Orthodox economic theory is wedded to the notion that market forces lead to a distribution of earnings across individuals that corresponds to individual productivity. As productivity increases, earnings rise in lockstep. This idea was used to deflect claims that firms would move production to Mexico seeking low-wage labor, the reason being that if lower Mexican wages were matched by lower labor productivity, then unit labor costs would not be reduced by shifting production to Mexico. The productivity gap would also protect U.S. and Canadian wages from being battered down by competition from Mexican wages. But few observers dispute the vast potential for TNCs to narrow the productivity gap by attaining First World standards of technical efficiency and quality in Mexican operations. By orthodox view, this will be accompanied by equivalent rises in Mexican wages, which in turn will expand Mexican consumer demand for U.S. exports.

These theoretical conventions should not be mistaken for a description of empirical reality. Powerful forces constrain Mexican wage growth even as productivity rises. Even after reversing the heavy job losses associated with its current recession, Mexico has a chronic labor surplus of roughly 30 million. Job growth could proceed for a very long time before exerting generalized upward pressure on wages. By then, this pressure could be offset by the inclusion of several additional low-wage countries in a hemisphere-wide trade bloc. Mexico's history of government co-option of official unions and repression of independent labor movements has left workers without strong organizations to secure higher real wages.

Recurring and large peso devaluations also can instantly throw the wage-productivity balance out of whack. The 60 percent peso devaluation since NAFTA's implementation has not changed Mexican productivity, but has suddenly made Mexican wages dramatically cheaper in dollar terms. The associated drop in unit labor costs has created strong additional incentives for foreign firms to shift production to Mexico, which will simultaneously undercut production wages in the United States and Canada.

Those skeptical of the wage-productivity relationship need not focus on Mexico, for the presumed linkage has been broken in U.S. manufacturing as well. From 1950 to 1973, the growth of real wages closely tracked the growth of labor productivity in U.S. manufacturing, but between 1979 and 1994, real wages for U.S. manufacturing workers declined at an annual rate of 0.8 percent (an 11.8 percent reduction), despite an annual growth rate of 3.4 percent in labor productivity.[12] In these two periods, productivity growth in U.S. manufacturing was virtually identical, but in the latter period, production workers as a group did not gain any portion of that growth in rising incomes. Instead, their real incomes fell.

Research to explain the drop in real wages and the increase in overall income inequality has been the focus of much attention among economists lately. Many factors seem to be at work (such as declines in unionization and the real minimum wage, deindustrialization, and demographic factors), but a growing number of studies are pointing to international trade as a possible contributing force.[13] In the real world, the distribution of firm earnings among wages, salaries, and profits is conditioned by bargaining strength. NAFTA not only facilitates firms' cost savings and profitability via international capital mobility and intrafirm trade, but also strengthens their bargaining position with workers. Over the last 15 years or so, income inequality has increased in all three NAFTA countries. This does not verify that the simultaneous growth in international trade is the cause, but it is consistent with the concern raised by the treaty's critics.

MEXICAN DEVELOPMENT AND THE PESO CRISIS

Mexico's economic restructuring represents a dramatic departure from its previous strategy of import-substitution industrialization (ISI), that is, the use of public policy to increase domestic production of formerly imported items for the home market.[14] From the 1940s through the 1970s, the Mexican government promoted industrial growth through high tariffs and import license requirements, as well as through subsidies to fledgling industries through tax and credit policies. The ISI regime supported rapid expansion and extensive capitalization of Mexican factories, and real GDP grew at a remarkable average annual rate of 6.5 percent between 1965 and 1980. Still, ISI produced important weaknesses, including an inefficient industrial oligarchy that failed to produce competitive exports or ease the country's dependence on imported capital goods and technology (with serious consequences for the balance of payments and industrial sector when peso depreciations occurred), as well as an income distribution so highly concentrated that it restricted the growth of internal markets. In the 1970s the Mexican government was always the driving force in the economy. The government had plenty of money from oil exports. When that was not enough to sustain the massive expenditures necessary to support the ISI regime, the government borrowed on world capital markets. A series of external shocks eventually put an end to that strategy, and in August 1982 Mexico announced that it could no longer service its huge external debt.

In the wake of this crisis, the Mexican government undertook a variety of austerity and liberalization measures at the insistence of the international financial community. Drastic cuts in government spending transformed the budget deficit into a surplus by the late 1980s. State enterprises were privatized and government regulations were relaxed. International creditors rolled over Mexico's existing debt (usually converting interest to principal, thus increasing the long-term burden) and eventually offered some modest relief under the U.S.-sponsored Brady Plan of 1989.

These structural adjustments were designed to facilitate Mexico's ability to service its debts (by cutting import demand and attracting capital inflows), but they caused severe cuts in the standard of living for ordinary Mexicans and a massive transfer of capital out of the country. From 1980 to 1986 Mexico's annual growth rate of real GDP fell to only 0.4 percent, while the population increased at a rate of 2.2 percent. The associated decline in average living standards reversed years of previous development. Real wages fell by 30-50 percent, depending on the measure used, while unemployment and poverty increased.

Mexican policy in the late 1980s shifted toward securing foreign exchange to meet debt obligations by promoting the country as an export platform for manufactured items produced by FDI. Reduced restrictions on industrial product imports and FDI were accompanied by an accelerated flow of investment to Mexico. Mexican GDP growth recovered to an average annual rate of 2.9 percent between 1987 and 1992. While an improvement, this pace was still well below that of the ISI period, and it was insufficient to restore real wages and average living standards to the levels attained before the debt crisis.

Mexican economic performance lagged in the late 1980s because the austerity and liberalization policies that stimulated FDI simultaneously depressed domestic production. High interest rates, weak domestic demand, and intensified import competition wiped out many Mexican firms. Despite rapid employment growth in TNC subsidiaries, total manufacturing jobs in Mexico declined by 5 percent between 1985 and 1992.[15]

In this context, the Mexican government embraced NAFTA to deliver, through further increases in FDI, the growth stimulus that stabilization, structural adjustment, and liberalization in the 1980s had failed to achieve, a stimulus missing since the demise of ISI. Given its massive adjustments, Mexico's economy seemed poised for take off, if only there were sufficient investment to fuel it. This prospect raised widespread (and unrealistic) anticipation in Mexico of the imminent transformation to advanced country living standards and set the stage for crushing disappointment when the financial crisis unfolded barely one year after NAFTA took effect.

The financial crisis that erupted in December 1994 inevitably raises questions about the coherence and sustainability of Mexico's growth strategy. Mexico's gross domestic product is down more than 6 percent in 1995, and domestic politics are more volatile than ever. By comparison, the United States has not experienced an economic contraction of this magnitude since the Great Depression. According to the Clinton administration and many economists, there is nothing fundamentally wrong with Mexico's liberalization program or

NAFTA. Mexico is simply the temporary victim of official mismanagement, primarily the misguided decision to defend the peso in
1994 rather than let it depreciate sooner and more gradually. But
while it may be granted that official mismanagement and political
turmoil played a role, it does not necessarily follow that Mexico's
NAFTA strategy represents a viable program for broadly based
national growth.

Mexico faces a chronic balance-of-payments constraint on growth,
which was only temporarily eased in the early 1990s by a massive
inflow of speculative portfolio investment. The liberalization
between 1987 and 1994 produced growing trade and current account
deficits. During this period Mexican exports increased by 61 percent,
but imports rose by 361 percent, contributing to a current account
deficit of $28 billion (8 percent of GDP) by 1994. However, between
1990 and 1993 this growing deficit was exceeded by rising net capital inflows, leading to a balance-of-payments surplus, which forced a
brief appreciation of the peso and enabled Mexico to increase its foreign exchange reserves.

Yet it is essential to recognize that FDI represented only about one-
quarter of the 1990-93 capital inflow. Most of the inflow was portfolio investment (purchases of stocks, bonds, and other financial
assets), propelled by expectations of NAFTA-induced Mexican
growth. In 1993, FDI in Mexico climbed to $4.9 billion, but net port-
folio investment inflows, so-called hot money, amounted to $27.9
billion. These inflows produced booming financial markets in
Mexico but very little increase in real output, and GDP growth fell to
0.4 percent in 1993.

In 1994, while FDI and Mexico's trade and current account deficits
continued to increase, portfolio investment (although still a positive
net inflow) took a nosedive. Consequently, portfolio capital inflows
were no longer sufficient to cover Mexico's yawning current account
deficit. This left a huge overall gap in the balance of payments, which
by the end of the year fully depleted the country's foreign exchange
reserves. Mexico was forced to depreciate the peso, which in turn
posed a serious threat to the value of Mexican financial assets in
terms of foreign currencies. This burst the speculative bubble, and the
desperate rush by investors to dump peso-denominated assets caused
a huge and devastating outflow of portfolio investment, which
forced a rapid 40 percent depreciation of the peso against the U.S.

dollar in the winter of 1995. By autumn 1995, the exchange rate was hovering at about 7.5 pesos to the dollar as compared with approximately 3 pesos in the last year before the crisis—roughly a 60 percent devaluation. Mexico once again faces, with a vengeance, a balance-of-payments constraint to growth.

The peso devaluation eases this constraint by making exports more competitive, decreasing imports, and encouraging FDI all at once. But devaluation does not eliminate the need for draconian macroeconomic austerity (e.g., interest rates above 50 percent and growing government budget surpluses) because of the sharp inflationary pressures it triggers. Failure to control domestic inflation offsets devaluation's favorable influence on trade and FDI because real devaluation turns out to be a good deal less than the nominal devaluation. Moreover, control of inflation is critical for persuading foreign and Mexican portfolio investment to return. Thus far, just as in the early 1980s, Mexican policy has been geared to reassuring Wall Street and foreign investors by maintaining tight money, high interest rates, and harsh fiscal tightening that not only limits inflation and peso depreciation, but also represses domestic growth.

Mexico faces an unhappy contradiction that NAFTA supporters failed to anticipate. It cannot grow unless it attracts foreign investment and increases exports, but it cannot attract foreign investment unless it adopts sufficiently contractionary domestic policies to offset the real growth that results from export success. Squeezed by high interest rates and weak domestic demand, Mexican banks, businesses, and households are all teetering on the verge of bankruptcy. Given its current economic circumstances, it will be difficult to avoid further political instability, which would only translate into further wariness among foreign investors. Moreover, in committing to NAFTA's provisions, Mexico has foresworn use of policies (such as capital controls, targeted credit and export subsidies, tariffs, and import licensing) that might provide transitional relief from this bind and that have been used so effectively in the Korean model of industrialization.[16] More than ever, Mexico must now assume a passive stance. Its economic fate rests squarely on the future decisions of foreign investors.

NONTRADE ISSUES

The NAFTA debate generated an unusual coalition of opposing groups concerned about the treaty's effects on a range of nontrade issues, including the environment, labor standards, human rights, and democracy. Indeed, one outcome of the negotiations was closer contact among organizations interested in these issues across the three countries. A common concern is that NAFTA, by limiting business regulations and facilitating capital mobility, will promote forces that erode existing social and environmental programs and make the implementation of new ones more difficult. The result envisioned by critics is a downward harmonization of social and environmental standards through a process designated as social dumping, whereby jurisdictions threatened with import competition and the exit of local firms seek to enhance their competitiveness by reducing standards and hence business costs. Specifically, critics fear that the United States and Canada will gradually converge toward Mexican standards.[17]

It should be noted that in an era of heightened economic globalization such pressures may be present even in the absence of NAFTA, so the relevant question is whether the agreement went far enough in addressing these issues. But the answer must be mindful of two important counterarguments. The first is the legitimate risk that social and environmental regulations can be used as protective barriers, if free entry of imports is restricted to countries that observe stipulated standards. The second is the concern that national sovereignty in the determination of social and environmental standards may be compromised if free trade is made contingent upon them.

NAFTA supporters offer a twofold response to the social dumping charge. One line of argument defends the integrity of the treaty's environmental and social standard provisions, including the labor and environmental side agreements and the associated dispute settlement mechanisms. NAFTA, for example, is said to be the "greenest" trade accord ever negotiated. The establishment of tighter standards could be protective and could interfere with national sovereignty. The second type of argument maintains that social and environmental standards are a positive function of a country's level of economic development. As nations become richer, their populations naturally demand that these standards be higher. Advanced country standards are not yet appropriate for Mexico, but as free trade stimulates income growth, Mexicans will demand higher standards through their political system.

In response to the criticisms of labor and environmental groups, the Clinton administration negotiated side agreements to the original treaty formulated during the Bush presidency. The relevant question is whether these provisions have any "teeth." Rather than set standards, the side agreements seek to promote voluntary compliance with existing national law, but they take only the smallest step toward creating supranational institutions to assure enforcement or upward harmonization.

Under NAFTA, complaints concerning violations of labor or environmental standards can only be lodged with the established international commissions by one of the national governments. The grievances of labor unions and environmental or other organizations cannot be heard unless a national government can be persuaded to voice them. Thus far, most complaints have been raised by U.S. groups regarding violations of Mexican laws, but the U.S. government has consistently refused to take up the cases. Even if a government were to pursue an alleged violation through the elaborate multistage dispute resolution mechanisms, the potential penalties (usually fines paid by the national government of the country in which the violations occur) would scarcely constitute a daunting prospect for offending private businesses. As NAFTA supporters such as Hufbauer and Schott recognized, the environmental and labor side agreements fall short in many respects, which is why they recommended that these agreements be revisited once NAFTA took effect.[18]

The entire class of nontrade issues falls under the more fundamental problem concerning the assignment of social decision making between the economic and political spheres. The treaty does not tie economic integration to a deepening of participatory democracy. Indeed, it does the opposite by deliberately seeking to shift a wide range of decisions from the political sphere to the private sector. For most economists, accustomed to detailing the real and unfortunate mischief politics plays with otherwise superior market outcomes, this is a desirable shift. But that assessment is less clear-cut if the political processes by which the rules are established and enforced are disproportionately responsive to powerful economic interests at the expense of other parties.

NAFTA is not just about free trade; it is also antigovernment. Its rules are designed to remove from electoral pressures the basic features of the liberalization framework. NAFTA extends the space within which large corporations can move unfettered by government restrictions. The flip side is that the treaty inhibits the ability of the citizenry to collectivety determine its welfare through government activity. Limits on the freedom of democratic action will restrict not only inappropriate efforts to protect otherwise unviable domestic production, but also government policies aimed at assuring worker rights and safety, protecting the environment, and regulating use of nonrenewable natural resources, since any of these can be challenged under NAFTA as barriers to trade or investment.

Finally, in restricting the power of national and subnational governments, NAFTA has not substituted representative supranational institutions for the loss of voter sovereignty. Instead, there is a shift in decision making to unelected, unrepresentative corporate and technical bureaucracies set up to handle dispute resolution. The European Union, by contrast, seems to have gone further to assure that its commission, parliament, and court are representative.

CONCLUSION

Basic components of contemporary economic life—investment, finance, technology, communications, production, and distribution—are relentlessly transnational. This internationalism has the capacity to generate sweeping economic change and development. Yet it also inhibits the ability of the nation-state to stabilize its economy and fulfill its traditional responsibilities, to redress income imbalance, to regulate business, and to provide social services. This is a fundamental tension of our time. NAFTA commands attention because it helps shape the trajectory of economic internationalism in North America. Its long-run consequences for a range of important issues are still uncertain, but the effects will surely be experienced, often indirectly, by households, firms, and communities across the continent in countless private decisions regarding where and how goods and services are produced and sold. The fallout from Mexico's financial crisis will surely continue to generate employment trends sharply at odds with NAFTA proponents' projections. It is difficult to see how this can be reversed, unless Mexico receives significant relief from its current foreign debt burden. Beyond the macroeconomic constraints, NAFTA should produce important improvements in economic efficiency. Yet it would be a mistake to restrict the analysis to these potential benefits. My hunch is that among NAFTA's most important impacts will be changes in income distribution and the responsiveness of government to citizen preferences, which most citizens in all three countries will regard as undesirable. It is important, therefore, to appreciate that NAFTA's implementation does not foreclose further refinement of domestic policies and the rules of economic internationalism to foster favorable developments in these latter areas, if the political will is present.

NOTES

1. Gary Hufbauer and Jeffrey Schott, *North American Free Trade: Issues and Recommendations* (Washington, D.C.: Institute for International Economics, 1992), 23.
2. Antidumping laws provide relief to domestic production through punitive duties on imports judged to be priced below the "normal" price charged in the exporter's home market. Countervailing duties are assessed against imports judged to be subsidized by foreign government programs. Section 301 is a provision of the U.S. Trade Act of 1974 that creates wide powers to retaliate against any foreign government practice that is "unreasonable, or discriminatory and burdens or restricts United States commerce." Super 301 refers to provisions of the 1988 U.S. Omnibus Trade and Competitiveness Act, which broadens the scope of Section 301 (for example, mandating trade sanctions for violations of U.S. intellectual property rights and for countries having a chronic trade surplus with the United States).
3. Ricardo Grinspun and Maxwell Cameron, "The Political Economy of North American Integration: Diverse Perspectives, Converging Criticisms," in *The Political Economy of North American Free Trade*, Grinspun and Cameron, eds. (New York: St. Martin's Press, 1993), 3-25.
4. Accounts of the Clinton administration's "bazaar" method of dealing for votes are given in *The New York Times*, 11 November 1993, p. A11, and *The Nation*, 20 December 1993, p. 752.
5. This is because the large economy will dominate in the determination of prices after liberalization, generating less change in prices and resource allocation in the large country than in the small. The small country also stands to reap greater benefits from newly available economies of scale. For

a discussion linking these predictions to side payments in trade negotiations, see Gerald K. Helleiner, "Considering U.S.-Mexico Free Trade," in *The
Political Economy of North American Free Trade*, Grinspun and Cameron,
eds., (New York: St. Martin's Press, 1993), 45-60.

6. CGE models are summarized in Congressional Budget Office, *Estimating the
Effects of NAFTA: An Assessment of the Economic Models and Other Empirical
Studies* (Washington, D.C.: CBO), June 1993.

7. Hufbauer and Schott, *North American Free Trade*, chap. 3.

8. *New York Times*, 10 October 1995, p. A1.

9. Ross Perot and Pat Choate, *Save Your Job, Save Your Country: Why NAFTA
Must Be Stopped—Now* (New York: United We Stand, Inc., 1993).

10. See David Arsen, Mark Wilson, and Jonas Zoninsein, "Trends in
Manufacturing Employment in the NAFTA Region: Evidence of a Giant
Sucking Sound?" in this volume.

11. Harley Shaiken, "Advanced Manufacturing and Mexico: A New
International Division of Labor?" *Latin American Research Review* 29, no. 2
(1994): 39-71.

12. These calculations are based on data in the *Economic Report of the President*
(Washington, D.C.: U.S. Government Printing Office, February 1995), 324,
326, 330, 341.

13. Gary Burtless, "International Trade and the Rise in Income Inequality,"
Journal of Economic Literature 33, no. 2 (1995): 800-16.

14. This section draws extensively on the analysis in Robert Blecker, "NAFTA,
the Peso, and the Contradictions of the Mexican Economic Growth
Strategy," a paper delivered at the Eastern Economic Association meetings,
New York, March 1995. Unless otherwise noted, all data cited here are from
this source.

15. International Labour Office, *Year Book of Labour Statistics* (Geneva: ILO,
1993).

16. See Alice Amsden, *Asia's Next Giant: South Korea and Late Industrialization*
(New York: Oxford University Press, 1989).

17. Some observers cast the claim of social dumping more broadly, noting that
NAFTA does not set standards for universal social policies, such as unemployment insurance, social welfare, job training, or health programs.

18. Gary Hufbauer, Jeffrey Schott, and Philip Martin, *NAFTA Briefing Book*
(Washington, D.C.: Institute for International Economics, October 1993),
24.

II.
Agriculture After NAFTA

Economic Integration in North America: Consequences, Opportunities, and Challenges for the Michigan Food System

David B. Schweikhardt and Kandeh K. Yumkella

The global trend toward greater economic integration will present both expanded market opportunities and new competitive pressures for food and agribusiness firms in Michigan. In a state with one of the nation's most diverse agricultural sectors (ranging from grains to horticultural products, sugar beets, and livestock products), nearly every part of Michigan's food industry will be affected by the implementation of NAFTA. This chapter examines the agreement's effects, including the competitive relationships among the three NAFTA partners and the potential consequences of integration for Michigan producers.

Economic integration presents some unique challenges for the food industry. The harmonization of regulations (such as food safety), coordination of agricultural policies, and role of macroeconomic policies will all influence future trade relations among the partners. The effect of expanding NAFTA to other Latin American countries will also be examined.

U.S. AGRICULTURAL TRADE WITH MEXICO AND CANADA

Canada is the largest overall U.S. trade partner and Mexico is the third largest (Japan is second). During the past five years, U.S. exports to Canada have averaged $81 billion annually and U.S. imports from

Canada have averaged $92 billion (see figure 1). U.S. exports to Canada have grown by 9 percent each year since 1984, compared to an annual increase of 6 percent in U.S. imports from that country.

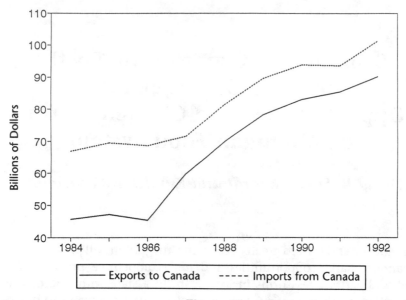

Figure 1.
U.S. Trade with Canada, 1984-1992.

The United States exported an average of $29 billion in products annually to Mexico during the same period, compared to annual imports averaging $30 billion. This represents a yearly increase of 17 percent in U.S. exports to Mexico since 1984. The United States recorded trade surpluses with its southern neighbor in 1991 and 1992 for the first time in the past decade (see figure 2). Mexico's exports to the United States have increased by 9 percent annually since 1984, and its imports of U.S. products accelerated after trade barriers were reduced in 1986.

Canada is the second largest buyer of U.S. agricultural exports, which have averaged $3.6 billion annually during the past five years, while U.S. imports of Canada's agricultural products have averaged $3.2 billion a year (see figure 3). Vegetables ($1.1 billion), live animals and meats ($890 million), and grains ($770 million) accounted for most of these U.S. exports in 1992. Live animals and meats ($1.8

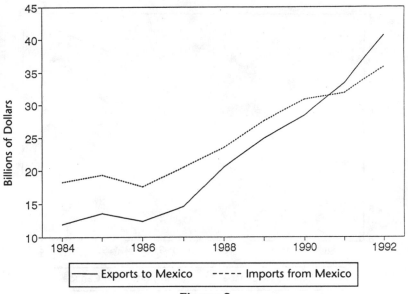

Figure 2.
U.S. Trade with Mexico, 1984-1992.

billion), grains ($778 million), and oilseeds ($320 million) led Canadian exports to the United States in that year. Since implementation of the U.S.-Canadian Free Trade Agreement in 1989, U.S. agricultural exports to Canada have increased, primarily vegetables, fruits, and poultry products. U.S. imports of live animals and grains from Canada have also grown.

U.S. agricultural exports to Mexico averaged $2.9 billion annually between 1988 and 1993, compared to $2.3 billion in imports. (See figure 4.) Live animals and meats ($1.3 billion), grains ($1 billion), and oilseeds ($715 million) were the main U.S. exports to Mexico in 1992. In that year Mexico exported nearly $400 million in noncompetitive agricultural products (bananas and coffee) to the United States, although vegetables ($809 million), live animals ($372 million), and fruits ($321 million) led the list of competitive products. Mexican trade barriers are higher than U.S. tariffs for many agricultural products, but Mexico has increased U.S. imports in this category by 14 percent annually since 1988. Excluding bananas and coffee, the U.S. agricultural trade surplus with Mexico rose from $780 million in 1988 to $1.8 billion in 1992.

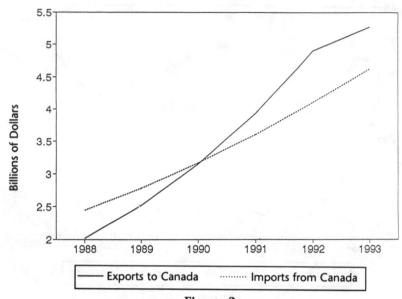

Figure 3.
U.S. Agricultural Trade with Canada, 1988-1993.

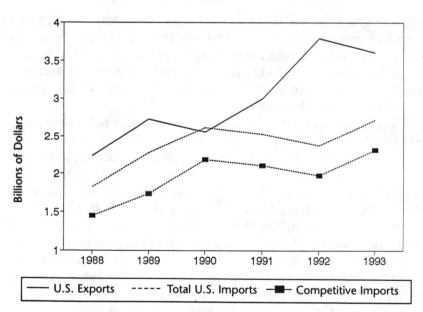

Figure 4.
U.S. Agricultural Trade with Mexico, 1988-1993.

The volume of trade between Canada and Mexico is much smaller than that of the United States with either of these countries. Measured in U.S. dollars, Canada's exports to Mexico have averaged $480 million annually since 1988, and the comparable import figure was $1.6 billion. In 1991 Canada exported $54 million in agricultural products to Mexico and imported $128 million from there. Canada sent primarily grains ($23 million), live animals and meat ($17 million), and dairy products ($12 million) during 1991 and received mainly fruits ($50 million), vegetables ($42 million), and tropical products (coffee, tea, and spices, $15 million).

NAFTA PROVISIONS AFFECTING AGRICULTURAL TRADE

Prior to 1985, Mexico used tariffs and import licenses to impose tight controls that protected its domestic markets. By restricting licenses, the government limited imports and maintained domestic prices above the world level. In 1985 more than 90 percent of Mexico's agricultural imports (covering 320 products) were controlled in this way. Mexico's average tariff was 23.5 percent, and some were as high as 100 percent, although the government began to reverse this policy after joining GATT in 1986. After this time, the maximum tariff was reduced to 50 percent, and the average dropped to 12.5 percent. Import licenses were eliminated in many industries but continued to be used for energy and agricultural products. U.S. duties on all products imported from Mexico are much lower (averaging 3 percent in 1991) than Mexican barriers to U.S. exports (10 percent).[1]

Mexican tariffs on agricultural imports were higher than U.S. barriers at the time NAFTA was enacted. The average U.S. tariff on these imports was 8 percent in 1991, and nearly one-quarter of U.S. agricultural exports to Mexico faced import licensing restrictions. The United States and Canada began removing most agricultural tariffs under the U.S.-Canadian Free Trade Agreement of 1989, and when the process is complete in 1998, only dairy and poultry products will still have barriers.

REMOVAL OF TARIFFS

NAFTA phases out tariffs, quotas, and import licenses between the United States and Mexico over fifteen years. Under the tariff structure prior to NAFTA, nearly 29 percent of U.S. agricultural imports from Mexico entered duty-free (zero tariff), and 15 percent of U.S. agricultural exports to Mexico were admitted duty free (see table 1).

Table 1.
Removal of U.S. and Mexican Agricultural Tariffs under NAFTA.

	U.S. imports from Mexico[a]	U.S. exports to Mexico[b]
Duty-free prior to NAFTA	29%	15%
Tariff removed in first year	35%	37%
Tariff phased out in 5 years	7%	3%
Tariff phased out in 10 years	25%	38%
Tariff phased out in 15 years	4%	7%

Source: U.S. International Trade Commission.
[a]Percentage of total value of U.S. agricultural imports from Mexico.
[b]Percentage of total value of U.S. agricultural exports to Mexico.

U.S. tariffs on another 35 percent of these imports were eliminated in 1994, at which time Mexico eliminated duties on an additional 37 percent of such products. Most of the commodities involved had low tariffs or were not traded in large volumes between the two countries.

The United States will phase out tariffs on an additional 7 percent of Mexican agricultural imports over five years, followed by 25 percent more over ten years. Mexico will do the same for 3 percent and then 38 percent of its U.S. agricultural imports. Finally, another 4 percent in the U.S. case and 7 percent in the Mexican case will have tariffs phased out over fifteen years.

REMOVAL OF IMPORT QUOTAS AND LICENSES

NAFTA requires the United States and Mexico to use a tariff rate quota (TRQ) system to eliminate import quotas and licensing requirements. The TRQ permits NAFTA partners to export a specified "in-quota" quantity to the other partners at a tariff rate lower than the pre-NAFTA amount (or zero in many cases). All additional exports above the in-quota volume will be assessed a higher "over-quota" tariff (equal to the pre-NAFTA figure). The in-quota volume will increase by 3 percent annually, and the over-quota tariff will be phased out by the end of the transition period. The TRQ mechanism allows trade to adjust gradually as import quotas and licenses are removed.

The United States will replace its Section 22 import quotas on sugar, dairy products, cotton, and peanuts with TRQs. Mexico will do the same for its import licenses on corn, dry beans, nonfat dry milk, cheese, poultry products, and potatoes. TRQs will also provide additional transition protection for some fruits and vegetables by permitting a specified in-quota quantity to be imported at a reduced tariff (but not duty-free) and assessing the full tariff on all over-quota imports. The in-quota volume also will increase by 3 percent annually, the in-quota tariff will be phased out, and the over-quota tariff eventually will be eliminated for these products. The United States will have TRQs for onions, fresh tomatoes, eggplants, chili peppers, squash, and watermelons imported from Mexico, which, in turn, will have TRQs for pork products and apples imported from the United States.

RULES OF ORIGIN

Rules of origin specify content requirements for products traded under the terms of NAFTA. Such rules are necessary to assure that goods are not shipped into the area from nonmember countries.[2] It is critical that only the goods produced by the partners are eligible for free trade status. Three general rules will apply to all agricultural and food products, and specific rules will apply to some products.

First, bulk commodities such as corn must be produced in a partner country to be traded under the terms of the agreement. Second, agricultural commodities imported from outside the region can be traded under the terms of NAFTA only if they have undergone a "significant transformation" in processing (defined as a change that causes their reclassification in the U.S. tariff schedule). Third, products cannot be traded under the terms of NAFTA if the value of inputs from outside the region exceeds 7 percent of the total value of the final product.

The specific rules of origin for certain agricultural products include the following:

- Raw sugar from nations outside NAFTA cannot be used to produce refined sugar or molasses for shipment to partner countries. Confectionery containing sugar imported from outside the region can be shipped to other NAFTA members.
- Milk from outside the region cannot be used to produce dry milk, cream, yogurt, cheese, ice cream, or other milk-based drinks that are shipped to NAFTA partners.
- Peanut butter shipped from Mexico to the United States must be produced from Mexican peanuts. Peanuts from non-NAFTA countries may be used to produce peanut butter in Canada for shipment to the United States. The latter rule is a continuation of one established by the U.S.-Canadian Free Trade Agreement.
- Citrus fruit from outside the region cannot be used to produce citrus juices for shipment to other NAFTA countries.
- Cotton from outside the region cannot be used to produce yarn or fabric for shipment to other NAFTA countries.
- Commodities from outside the region cannot be refined to produce vegetable oils for shipment to other NAFTA countries. Imported vegetable oils also cannot be used to produce margarine for shipment to other partners.
- Cigars and cigarettes cannot be traded under the terms of NAFTA if the value of tobacco from outside the region exceeds 9 percent of the total value of the final product.

To enforce these provisions, U.S. companies will be permitted to request a U.S. Customs Service audit of the origin of products imported from Canada and Mexico. The products of foreign companies refusing such an audit or found in violation of the rules will be denied access to the United States under the terms of NAFTA.

OTHER PROVISIONS

NAFTA contains several other provisions affecting agricultural trade. Among these are the following:

- Members of NAFTA can retain domestic commodity programs (including all existing U.S. farm programs).
- The partners can match export subsidies offered by countries outside NAFTA. For example, if the European Union (EU) uses export subsidies to ship agricultural products to Mexico, the United States is permitted to match these with its own export subsidies on shipments to Mexico.
- Members of NAFTA will be permitted to retain quality grades and standards for agricultural products. Such standards must be applied to both domestic and imported products.
- The partners can retain sanitary and phytosanitary regulations that protect human, animal, or plant health. Such regulations may exceed international standards if they are based on scientific evidence and are applied to both domestic and imported products. Any country challenging these regulations must prove that the standard is a violation of NAFTA.
- Partners can retain existing inspection policies at national borders.

THE POTENTIAL EFFECT OF NAFTA ON AGRICULTURAL TRADE

Agricultural trade between the United States and Mexico is expected to increase under NAFTA. Excluding trade in bananas and coffee, the United States has had a trade surplus with Mexico in competitive agricultural products since 1988, and this surplus is expected to continue.

Two factors will determine the influence of NAFTA on agricultural trade. First, Mexico's import licensing restrictions and tariffs create barriers that are much higher than U.S. duties on most agricultural products. U.S. agricultural exports to Mexico are expected to increase as these barriers are removed. Second, combined with NAFTA, internal reforms in Mexico are likely to raise incomes, which will increase the demand for food and, more importantly, lead to changes in the diet of Mexican consumers that will further expand U.S. exports. Several studies suggest that food consumption patterns begin to change significantly when income surpasses $3,000 per capita. At that level of economic development, consumers eat less grain and more meat, resulting in a demand for feed grains and protein supplements for livestock. Consumption of fruits and vegetables also increases with income growth.[3]

With a per capita income of $3,500 in 1991, Mexico is poised for such a dietary transformation. Incomes began to grow following domestic reforms and reductions in trade barriers in the late 1980s. This growth is expected to continue over the short and long term.[4] Studies suggest that NAFTA will increase Mexican GDP by as much as 11 percent by the end of the agreement,[5] which will contribute to higher demand for food in the short run and will accelerate the transformation of consumption patterns in the long run. Both factors will translate into more U.S. agricultural exports.

Most studies indicate that U.S. exports of corn, dry beans, soybeans, meat, nonfat dry milk, potatoes, and apples will increase under NAFTA. U.S. imports of some agricultural products are also expected to rise, especially of those products with the highest tariffs, such as fresh asparagus, cucumbers, peppers, tomatoes, broccoli, melons, and citrus fruit.[6] Mexico is not expected to increase its sugar exports to the United States during the early years of the agreement, but U.S. imports of sugar could grow during the final five years of the agreement if Mexico converts to corn sweeteners in its soft drink industry, which would require additional U.S. exports of corn or corn sweetener.[7]

The 1989 U.S.-Canadian Free Trade Agreement began a ten-year process to remove most tariffs on agricultural products, and this will continue under NAFTA. Canadian imports of U.S. fruits, vegetables, and poultry products have grown since the first agreement went into effect, as have U.S. imports of Canadian wheat and some livestock products. These trends are expected to continue.

CONTINUING ISSUES IN NORTH AMERICAN AGRICULTURAL TRADE

Trade agreements provide a framework of rules within which commercial exchange takes place and disputes can be resolved. Such agreements cannot anticipate every dispute that will arise, nor can they address every policy that affects trade. Issues will continue to emerge as the integration of North American agricultural trade proceeds, and these will have a significant effect on the future of that trade.

MACROECONOMIC POLICY AND EXCHANGE RATES

Due to its influence on exchange rates, macroeconomic policy is a major determinant of trade. NAFTA has no provisions to coordinate macroeconomic policies among the partners, leaving each nation to pursue its own course. While there is little prospect for any formal policy coordination by the members of NAFTA, macroeconomic policy and fluctuations in exchange rates are likely to be a major issue in the future. This factor is often overlooked but is a likely source of friction in trade relations. For example, while several causal factors were cited in the 1994 U.S.-Canadian wheat dispute, in which the United States accused Canada of dumping wheat in U.S. markets, the depreciation of the Canadian dollar (from 1.16 per U.S. dollar in 1990 to 1.38 in 1994) was rarely mentioned. Yet, this change reduced the price of Canadian wheat by 15 percent between 1990 and 1994 and contributed to increased U.S. imports. Similarly, the devaluation of the Mexican peso in late 1994 is likely to decrease U.S. exports of agricultural products to Mexico and increase U.S. imports of such products from Mexico in the short run. Exchange rates will assume more importance as the final trade barriers are removed under NAFTA.

NONTARIFF BARRIERS

As tariffs, quotas, and import licenses are eliminated under NAFTA, nontariff barriers are likely to cause an increasing number of trade disputes. These regulations, ranging from labeling and packaging laws to food safety requirements and inspection policies, will grow in importance as tariffs and quantitative barriers impose fewer limits on trade. Moreover, producers facing import competition may increase pressure for protection through nontariff barriers. Because these are usually less transparent than tariffs or quantitative barriers and often must be dealt with on a case-by-case basis, specific disputes will have to be resolved one at a time rather than negotiated through trade agreements. The definition of legitimate policies and the elimination of nontariff barriers that are simply protectionist measures will require continued attention.

THE EXPANSION OF NAFTA

The inclusion of other Latin American countries in NAFTA is likely to be a major issue in the future. With other trade blocs forming throughout the hemisphere, the United States must determine whether it prefers to negotiate with individual countries or to pursue mergers with these blocs. The Clinton administration has proposed admitting Chile to NAFTA, setting the stage for others to join in later years. An expanded NAFTA would create both opportunities for export and potential for increased import competition, depending on the tariff structures of the new members and their competitive relationship with U.S. producers.

CONCLUSION

The integration of agricultural trade through NAFTA creates both opportunities and competition for Michigan food producers. The agreement reduces many barriers to trade, but new issues are certain to arise. The continued evolution of trade policy will determine the extent to which Michigan farmers and food firms benefit from further economic integration in our hemisphere.

NOTES

1. U.S. International Trade Commission (USITC), *The Potential Impact on the U.S. Economy and Selected Industries of the North American Free Trade Agreement*, Publication No. 2596 (Washington, D.C.: USITC, 1993).
2. Ivan E. Kingston, "The Economics of Rules of Origin," in *Rules of Origin in International Trade: A Comparative Study*, Edwin Vermulst, Paul Waer, and Jacques Bourgeois, eds. (Ann Arbor: University of Michigan Press, 1994), 7-25.
3. Suzanne Marie Marks and Mervin J. Yetley, *Global Food Demand Patterns over Changing Levels of Economic Development*, Staff Report No. AGES 870910 (Washington, D.C.: Economic Research Service, U.S. Department of Agriculture, 1987); Roberta L. Cook, Carlos Benito, James Matson, David

Runston, Kenneth Shwedel, and Timothy Taylor, "Fruit and Vegetable Issues," in *The North American Free Trade Agreement: Effects on Agriculture*, Mechel Paggi, ed., vol. 4 (Park Ridge, Ill: American Farm Bureau Research Foundation, 1991).

4. U.S. Congressional Budget Office, *A Budgetary and Economic Analysis of the North American Free Trade Agreement* (Washington, D.C.: CBO, 1993); Gary C. Hufbauer and Jeffrey J. Schott, *NAFTA: An Assessment* (Washington, D.C.: Institute for International Economics, 1993).

5. USITC, *Potential Impact*.

6. Cook et al., "Fruit and Vegetable Issues"; Thomas Grennes, Julie Hernandez Estrada, Barry Krissoff, Jaime Matus Gardea, Jerry Sharples, and Constanza Valdez, *An Analysis of a United States-Canada- Mexico Free Trade Agreement*, Commissioned Paper no. 10 (International Trade Research Consortium, 1991); E. Wesley F. Peterson, "The Implications of a Free Trade Agreement with Mexico for U.S. Grain and Oilseed Exports," in *The North American Free Trade Agreement: Effects on Agriculture*, Mechel Paggi, ed., vol 3 (Park Ridge, Ill.: American Farm Bureau Research Foundation, 1991); U.S. Department of Agriculture, *Agriculture in the North American Free Trade Agreement: Analysis of Liberalizing Trade between the United States and Mexico*, Foreign Agricultural and Economic Report 246 (Washington, D.C.: Economic Research Service, 1992); USDA, *Effects of the North American Free Trade Agreement on U.S. Agricultural Commodities* (Washington, D.C.: Economic Research Service, Economic Staff Analysis, 1993); U.S. Department of Commerce, *North American Free Trade Agreement: Opportunities for U.S. Industries* (Washington, D.C.: International Trade Administration, 1993); USITC, *Potential Impact*; Congressional Budget Office, *Budgetary and Economic Analysis*; and U.S. General Accounting Office, *North American Free Trade Agreement: Assessment of Major Issues*, Report GAO/GGD-93-137B (Washington, D.C.: General Accounting Office, 1993).

7. Fred Kessel, Peter Bussanell, and Ron Lord, *Mexico's Sugar Industry: Current and Future Situation* (Washington, D.C.: USDA, 1993).

The Milk War: The Effects of NAFTA on Dairy Farmers in the United States and Mexico

James H. McDonald

With the passage of NAFTA on 1 January 1994, the economies of the United States, Mexico, and Canada were inextricably integrated. As the quotations below suggest, this integration has been fraught with problems, conflicts, and uncertainties.

> This is what we expected under the flawed rules of NAFTA. Mexico is clearly not the dairy export bonanza that NAFTA apologists claimed it would be. Mexican bureaucrats are throwing up roadblocks right and left, and we continue to be locked out of the Canadian market with no relief in sight. Meanwhile, we are bracing for a huge increase in cheap imports under GATT minimum access rules.[1]

> In El Paso and across the Mexican border in Juárez they call it the milk war. As soon as NAFTA took effect January 1, American milk, freed from Mexican licensing requirements, flooded across the Rio Grande.[2]

> Aside from the 12,000 liters of milk that [Mexican] dairy farmers gave away [to poor families in Celaya, Guanajuato], they also dumped another 1,000 liters as a measure to get the attention of the authorities and the store owners who sell milk. Only they can bring an immediate solution to the problem of low prices to the farmer.[3]

This chapter examines the effects of NAFTA on U.S. and Mexican dairy farmers as they struggle to survive in a globalizing economy. The primary focus is on how the new and complex transnational relationship created by NAFTA is likely to affect Michigan dairy farmers. While most researchers acknowledge the two-way flows of goods between NAFTA partners, agricultural research tends to emphasize the movement of capital and commodities from north to south. This process, many scholars feel, is controlled and dominated by transnational financial organizations, such as the World Bank or International Monetary Fund (IMF), who are increasingly setting policies that were formerly the function of national governments.[4] It will be argued that the globalization of agriculture and the subsequent restructuring of "national agricultures" (that is, agricultural economies built around national regulation and control[5]) not only affect the economic topography of Mexico, but also have indirectly contributed to the ongoing restructuring of the U.S. dairy industry, a restructuring whose historical roots date back 50 years.

A second objective of this chapter is to examine and explain the effects of NAFTA on nonpeasant, commercial, small-scale capitalist dairy farming in Mexico, with special emphasis on the State of Guanajuato in central Mexico. The radical transformation of the Mexican agricultural sector can be traced to the presidency of Miguel de la Madrid (1982-88) and was vigorously pursued by the administration of Carlos Salinas de Gortari (1988-94). Under pressure from the IMF and the World Bank, policies encouraging privatization and free trade have been steadily implemented over the past 12 years. This activity has intensified markedly in the agrarian sector since 1991, when subsidies and other forms of support were removed from most crops. One of the most striking changes occurred in 1992, when the revision of Article 27 of the 1917 Mexican Constitution created the legal structure for privatization of the *ejido* and allowed these agrarian communities to enter into economic partnerships with outside developers.[6] The hope was that foreign capital would fill the void left by the reversal of the historical policy of agrarian populism, which provided government support for the peasantry and private family farms. These major changes, culminating with the passage of NAFTA, have had a significant effect on numerous regions and sectors of Mexican agriculture. Most examinations of this restructuring, however, concentrate solely on the peasant sector and on the polarized discussion between the political Right, which extols the virtues of an idealized capitalist family farm while denouncing the inefficient socialist *ejido*, and the political Left, which has spent equal amounts of energy defending the *ejido*.[7] What is missing is any consideration of NAFTA's effects on middle-level family farmers whose enterprises are capitalist but small in scale. Free trade links the fates of the dairy sectors in Mexico and the United States more closely than in the past, so a clear understanding of the dairy industry in Mexico is imperative if we are to understand how NAFTA will affect that industry in Michigan.

It is useful to begin with an overview of Mexican food policy, followed by a discussion of the Mexican dairy industry's current attempts to adapt to a rapidly transforming political economy. Particular attention will be paid to how farmers are coping with NAFTA under conditions of rapid change. Against this backdrop, an analysis of NAFTA and Michigan's dairy industry will be presented. The chapter will conclude by considering the changes in the Mexican dairy industry and their implications for Michigan.

HISTORY OF MEXICAN FOOD POLICY

Article 27 of the 1917 Mexican Constitution provided for agrarian reform, a concession made to the peasant and indigenous sectors of the population after the 1910 revolution. Rural groups could petition for the return of land that had been, in various ways, usurped by large landowners living on haciendas. The new agrarian communities were known as *ejidos*. Agrarian reform was first seriously undertaken during the regime of Lázaro Cárdenas (1934-40), when 45 million acres were redistributed, as compared to 19 million acres under his predecessors.[8] In support of the newly established *ejidos*, Cárdenas initiated the National Ejidal Credit Bank to provide low-interest loans as well as technical and administrative assistance, and a number of agricultural colleges were also opened to provide both research on rain-fed agriculture and extension services to those communities. At the same time, haciendas subject to the reforms were allowed to keep 150 acres (usually their best land), which often included the main buildings, irrigation systems, roads, and the like.[9]

After 1940, government spending was redirected toward commercial agriculture and away from basic food production for the market and for subsistence. This is most evident in the massive investment in dams and large-scale irrigation systems.[10] A number of scholars note that *ejidos* and *minifundios* (private farms of less than ten acres) saw access to credit and extension services considerably reduced as funding and technical support went to large-scale producers of cash crops, such as wheat and cotton. Commercial export-oriented farmers became the vanguard of the Mexican green revolution, with its intensive technological inputs of machinery, agrochemicals, and irrigation.[11] Even so, by the late 1950s, Mexico was self-sufficient in the production of corn and beans.

In the mid-1960s there was a marked shift in crop production from staples to forage and export crops. By the mid-1970s, Mexico was no longer self-sufficient in corn or beans. The investment in major irrigation projects, originally defended as ensuring food self-sufficiency, now was justified as generating export crops for foreign exchange to fund Mexican industrialization.[12] Thus, from the mid-1960s to the present, the Mexican government policy has been to provide cheap basic foods for an underpaid urban and rural population primarily through importation.

Since the Cárdenas regime 60 years ago, there have been three attempts by the government to assist the basic food production sector. The first occurred in the late 1970s under President José López Portillo (1976-82) in the form of the Program for Public Investment for Rural Development (PIDER), funded by the World Bank. PIDER established a number of pilot projects designed to increase peasants' rain-fed agricultural yields (through technological inputs, extension services, and new sources of inexpensive credit) and to help develop new methods for marketing their harvests. These projects had serious problems, and the result was that midsized farmers were able to get inexpensive credit and produce on a scale that allowed them to sell directly to the government, while the poorest peasants were forced off the land.[13]

Given the dubious results of PIDER, President López Portillo made a second attempt with the Mexican Food System, known as SAM. It's goal was to assist market-oriented peasant agriculture through price supports, credit availability, and subsidized technological inputs. Production, processing, and consumption were subsidized by the government, but the result was similar to that of PIDER. Commercial farmers, middlemen, and midsized farmers benefited while poorer peasants were driven off the land,[14] and the program was terminated in 1983.

The third attempt, a program of subsidies called PROCAMPO (Program of Direct Rural Aid), was launched by President Carlos Salinas in 1993-94.[15] After ten years without aid and faced with escalating costs of production and intense global competition, Mexican farmers vigorously protested that they could not compete in international markets against First World agribusiness and farmers who received various forms of subsidies and price supports. When we consider that corn is the primary crop for almost half of all Mexican farmers and that they produce it at about twice the cost of their counterparts to the north, it becomes clear that the policies embarked upon by President de la Madrid and vigorously carried out by President Salinas had brought basic food producers to the brink of collapse.[16]

PROCAMPO was a response to this crisis. Enacted in October 1993, it provided growers of corn, wheat, sorghum, soybeans, rice, and/or cotton with a subsidy of $330 new pesos per hectare (about U.S. $100) for the 1993-94 agricultural cycle, increasing to $350 new pesos per hectare in 1994-95. As one Mexican researcher observed, "The peasant who farms [PROCAMPO crops] will have $1.83 pesos per day that will serve him well to buy a soft drink or [perhaps] buy a sandwich, though I doubt it will cost so little."[17] Others see PRO-CAMPO as a blatantly political move on the part of the Institutional Revolutionary Party (PRI) to recapture some of the rural vote lost over the last two presidencies. Many seem to agree that the program provides few long- or even short-term benefits to farmers,[18] prompting some to refer to it as "PRICAMPO." Yet others note that this was the only effort during Salinas's six-year term to support agriculture and counterbalance the PRI's shift away from agrarian populism. Many researchers have argued that taken together these policies are having and will continue to have very negative effects on both domestic and export crop production.[19]

Taking corn as an example, PROCAMPO will have the following effect on domestic crop prices. In 1993-94, the price of corn was $750 new pesos per ton (U.S. $250), but in the next cycle, that will begin to drop toward international levels, with a guaranteed price of $600 new pesos per ton (U.S. $200). At the same time, assume an annual inflation rate of 10 percent. Rather than drop, the guaranteed price of corn should rise to around $825 new pesos per ton (U.S.$275) in order for farmers to secure a profit. Furthermore, even with this drop in price, Mexican corn is not competitive, as the average price of corn in Michigan is currently U.S. $2.60 per bushel, or U.S. $102.15 per metric ton.

THE MEXICAN DAIRY INDUSTRY

GENERAL TRENDS

The Mexican dairy industry historically has been a small sector of the agricultural economy, and milk has never been a staple in the Mexican diet. Beginning in the 1970s, as part of the effort to fight malnutrition, especially in rural areas, milk was recognized by the Mexican government as an important component of a well-rounded diet. According to Barkin, 90 percent of all rural Mexicans experience both caloric and protein deficiency, and half that group is severely malnourished.[20] In the campaign to abolish malnutrition, subsidized basic foods were made available to the rural population through the National Company for Popular Subsistence (CONASUPO), the government's rural food distribution system. Although the Mexican dairy industry has expanded, especially since the 1970s, the government has augmented production shortfalls by importing large amounts of cheap powdered milk from the United States and Europe, selling it directly to consumers through CONASUPO outlets or to dairies, where it is processed into other products. In the 1980s and 1990s these imports rose markedly, while the domestic dairy industry has increased production despite a decrease in the number of farms. The trend, then, has been toward greater centralization of the Mexican dairy industry.

Historical data on Mexican dairy farming are virtually nonexistent, although some statistics are available from diverse sources. Reasonably accurate historical summaries were first released by major statistical agencies in Mexico only in the 1980s, and there are comparability problems. For example, producer price indices may take 1970 as the base for the 1970-80 period and then switch to 1980 as the base for 1980-90. Nevertheless, the information illustrates overall trends in the Mexican economy that have affected small-scale capitalist farming.[21]

Most researchers agree that the Mexican economy was relatively stable during the 1960s and 1970s. Inflation, for example, was a minor problem prior to 1976.[22] During the administration of

Table 1.
Macro- and Micro-Price Indices for Mexico, 1960-90.

Year	Macro Price Index[a]	Annual Increase (%)	Micro Price Index[b]	Annual Increase (%)
1960	23.6	-	24.8	-
1961	23.9	1.3	26.0	4.8
1962	24.3	1.7	25.9	-0.4
1963	24.4	0.4	26.5	2.3
1964	25.5	4.5	27.0	1.9
1965	25.9	1.6	28.0	3.7
1966	26.3	1.5	28.3	1.1
1967	27.0	2.7	29.2	3.2
1968	27.6	2.2	29.6	2.4
1969	28.3	2.5	30.2	2.0
1970	30.0	2.5	31.8	5.3
1971	31.1	3.7	33.4	5.0
1972	31.9	2.6	34.8	4.2
1973	37.0	16.0	37.1	6.6
1974	45.3	22.4	46.0	24.0
1975	50.0	10.4	54.2	17.8
1976	61.2	22.4	60.8	12.2
1977	86.4	41.2	78.2	28.6
1978	100.0	15.7	93.5	19.6
1979	118.3	18.3	110.1	17.8
1980	147.2	24.4	133.8	21.5
1981	183.3	24.5	171.0	27.8
1982	286.1	56.1	223.7	30.8
1983	593.2	107.3	469.9	110.1
1984	1,010.4	70.3	814.8	73.4
1985	1,551.6	53.6	1,309.8	60.8
1986	2,923.0	88.4	2,173.3	66.0
1987	4,440.9	104.3	-	-
1988	12,293.5	176.8	-	-
1989	16,542.6	34.6	-	-
1990	20,260.7	22.5	-	-

[a] Source: Banco de México, *Indicadores Economicos* (Mexico City: Banmex, 1990), III-H-25 to III-H-32(c); base year, 1978.

[b] Source: Consejos de las Cámaras Nacionales de Comercio, *Reportes*, 28 February 1990. Indexed figures are for January of each year; base year, 1978.

Table 2.
Mexican Consumer Price Indices by Commodity, 1960-90.

Year	General Index[a]	Increase (%)	Agriculture, Livestock, Fish[b]	Increase (%)	Gas, Oil, Other	Increase (%)	Electricity	Increase (%)
1960	24.79	-	-	-	-	-	-	-
1961	26.02	5.0	-	-	-	-	-	-
1962	25.85	-0.7	-	-	-	-	-	-
1963	26.49	2.5	-	-	-	-	-	-
1964	26.96	1.8	-	-	-	-	-	-
1965	27.98	3.7	-	-	-	-	-	-
1966	28.26	1.0	-	-	-	-	-	-
1967	29.20	3.3	-	-	-	-	-	-
1968	29.56	1.2	-	-	-	-	-	-
1969	30.21	2.2	-	-	-	-	-	-
1970	31.78	5.2	34.7	29.2	64.2	-	-	-
1971	33.35	4.9	33.8	-2.6	29.4	0.7	64.4	0.3
1972	34.81	4.4	36.1	6.8	30.0	2.0	65.2	1.2
1973	37.12	3.1	42.4	17.5	32.0	6.7	68.5	5.1
1974	46.00	24.0	55.7	31.4	55.4	73.1	79.9	9.9
1975	54.24	17.9	64.3	15.4	72.0	30.0	82.0	2.6
1976	60.76	12.0	70.8	10.1	76.7	6.5	86.0	4.9
1977	78.23	28.8	85.7	21.0	98.7	28.7	98.0	14.0
1978	93.52	19.5	100.0	16.7	100.0	1.3	100.0	2.0
1979	110.05	17.7	118.0	18.0	101.0	1.0	118.0	18.0
1980	133.78	21.6	151.7	28.6	105.0	4.0	144.4	22.4
1981	170.96	27.8	196.4	29.5	116.7	11.1	170.2	17.9
1982	223.73	30.9	264.8	34.8	274.9	135.6	242.0	42.2
1983	469.92	110.0	494.6	86.8	757.7	175.6	531.9	119.8
1984	814.82	73.4	812.1	64.2	1,175.3	55.1	938.8	76.5
1985	1,309.83	60.8	1,276.1	57.1	1,812.5	54.2	1,311.7	39.7
1986	2,173.25	65.9	2,386.9	87.0	3,740.9	106.4	2,761.3	110.5
1987	4,440.90	104.2	5,314.5	122.7	8,400.5	124.6	4,970.0	80.0
1988	12,293.50	176.8	11,289.7	112.4	18,047.3	114.8	10,209.3	105.4
1989	16,542.60	34.6	15,404.1	36.4	18,364.5	1.8	11,312.6	10.8
1990	20,260.70	22.5	19,976.5	29.7	22,514.0	22.6	27,523.6	143.3

[a] Source: Consejos de las Cámaras Nacionales de Comercio, *Reportes*, 28 February 1990. The indexed figure is for January of each year; base year, 1978.
[b] Source: Banco de México, *Indicadores Economicos* (Mexico City: Bannex, 1990), 6. The indexed figures are averages for each year; 1990 is estimated; base year, 1978 (100).

President Luis Echeverría (1970-76), the strict policy of pegging the peso to the dollar was loosened, a relaxation that continued under Echeverría's successor, José Lopez Portillo. In addition, the latter massively increased Mexico's foreign debt in order to develop oil reserves. Although inflation rose, it appeared to be offset by a bright future for the Mexican economy due to oil revenues. Economic growth continued until the drop in oil prices in 1982, at which point Mexico was left with a massive foreign debt. Since then the economy has been characterized by massive inflation (only recently controlled by the Salinas administration in 1988-94) and restructuring.

The rate of inflation in Mexico is best seen in macro- (wholesale) and micro- (consumer) price indices.[23] Table 1 shows that from 1960 to 1986 the macro index rose from 23 percent to 20,260 percent, and the micro index from 24 percent to 2,173 percent. The very minimal rise from 1960 to 1972 was followed by annual hikes between 1973 and 1983 averaging 25 percent (macro-index) and 20 percent (micro-index). After 1982, however, inflation was enormous, especially in 1983, 1987, and 1988.

From a consumer perspective, the cost of agricultural and livestock products rose slightly less than the general index from 1960 to 1990—20,260 percent versus 19,976 percent (see table 2). The main input costs for dairy farmers, petroleum products and electricity, increased considerably more than the selling price for agricultural and livestock products (table 2). Mechanized farms thus pay more for their inputs than they receive for their products. Gasoline and diesel prices were stable through the 1960s, but in the 1970s these rose, although diesel (the more important of the two for farming purposes) had a relatively minor cost increase. From 1980 to 1988, however, gasoline prices rose 17,507 percent and diesel prices rose 44,400 percent.

Dairy farmers may be even more seriously affected by these economic trends than other basic foods producers.[24] Milk trailed significantly behind even the traditionally heavily controlled retail price of corn, tortillas, and bread in its percentage increase in cost between 1960 and 1979 (see table 3). Wholesale data also reflect the gap between milk and the general index for the mid-1980s (see table 4). Furthermore, federally designated wholesale prices decreased in December 1990, from $820 pesos/liter to $780 pesos/liter. Although the wholesale price of milk increased 9,604 percent between 1978 and 1988, it was outstripped by the 10,237 percent rise in input costs

Table 3.
General Index and Actual Prices[a] of Basic Foods in Mexico City, 1960-79.[b]

Year	General Index	Corn	Tortillas	Bread	Milk	Beef
1960	25.7	1.044	0.925	2.946	1.780	13.341
1961	26.6	1.110	0.920	2.980	1.845	14.392
1962	26.6	1.100	0.920	3.023	1.853	14.352
1963	26.5	1.112	0.920	3.000	1.863	14.378
1964	27.7	1.173	0.937	3.027	1.910	14.770
1965	28.1	1.201	1.199	3.000	1.939	15.485
1966	29.2	1.263	1.205	3.002	2.145	16.160
1967	30.0	1.293	1.210	3.000	2.250	16.962
1968	30.9	1.301	1.210	3.000	2.222	17.957
1969	31.4	1.309	1.210	3.000	2.250	18.211
1970	32.5	1.395	1.210	3.000	2.374	19.117
1971	34.2	1.416	1.210	3.000	2.450	20.840
1972	34.9	1.460	1.231	3.000	2.484	22.138
1973	39.8	1.562	1.435	3.050	2.764	25.883
1974	54.0	2.029	2.187	5.708	3.339	32.733
1975	61.2	2.765	2.559	6.782	3.699	35.600
1976	69.3	3.116	2.870	7.844	3.911	38.970
1977	86.0	3.716	3.579	9.630	4.894	45.400
1978	100.0	4.228	3.579	10.960	5.717	62.450
1979	119.3	4.486	4.177	12.240	5.991	86.180
% Total Increase	364.2	329.7	351.6	321.6	236.6	546.0

[a] Corn, tortillas, bread, and beef values are valued in pesos per kilo; milk is valued in pesos per liter.
[b] Source: Instituto Nacional de Estadística, Geografia e Informatica, *Estadísticas Hist Nacional de Est*, Tomo II (Mexico City: INEGI, 1990), 772.

for beef and dairy production from 1980 to 1988 (compare tables 4 and 5).[25] The lower input costs for beef production somewhat dampen the rise in the more labor- and technology-intensive dairy sector in the combined beef/dairy column of table 5. It is apparent that dairy farming profits have been eroding since the late 1970s, and this deterioration has become increasingly serious since 1982.

Higher costs and lower profits have led to lower production. Growth in the volume of livestock and agricultural production was rather anemic from 1975 to 1985, and there was little change in the production volume of either butter or cheese in Mexico from 1970 to 1986. Milk production did increase, however, even in the 1980s. Mexico did not export milk from the 1960s through the early 1980s, while the importation of powdered milk grew dramatically, indicating that demand far surpassed domestic production, and undoubtedly it will continue to do so (see table 6). The trend toward herd expansion in the 1970s began to reverse in the early 1980s, most likely in response to worsening economic conditions. A sharp drop in the number of cattle in 1984 was an expected response in view of the economic downturn experienced in 1982. The two-year lag probably was due to farmers waiting to see whether the economy would rebound. In 1987 and 1988 Mexican farmers were hard hit (refer to tables 1, 2, and 5) by the effects of the 17 December 1987, federal government hike in the price of basic commodities (gasoline, natural gas, electricity, and staple foods), raising prices an average of 87 percent before "freezing" those prices as part of the Economic Solidarity Pact designed to slow inflation. Farmers' reactions ranged from alarm, to terror, to resignation and disillusionment. Inflation had been slowed but not stopped by 1989-90 (refer to table 1).

TRENDS IN THE STATE OF GUANAJUATO

A 1986 report from the Guanajuato offices of the Secretary of Agricultural and Hydraulic Resources (SARH) showed that only 2.6 percent of the state's dairy farms were large and mechanized (more than 50 head of cattle and an average of 266 head), but these few farms produced 46.7 percent of the milk in the state. Mechanized medium-sized farms (minimum 31 head, average 43) represented 3.9 percent of all dairy farms and accounted for 9.5 percent of milk production. Farms of medium size (averaging 27 head) but with limited

Table 4.
Wholesale Price Index for Powdered and Fresh Milk in Mexico, 1984-88.

Year	General Index	Fresh Milk	Powdered Milk
1984	1,010.4	889.6	856.5
1985	1,551.6	1,320.6	1,207.1
1986	2,923.0	2,352.3	2,159.1
1987	5,244.9	4,766.3	-
1988	9,604.8	8,736.8	-
% Total Increase	-	979.7	920.0

Source: Banco de México, *Indicadores Economicos* (Mexico City: Banmex, 1990), III-H-32 (f-g, j-k); base year, 1978.

Table 5.
National Index of Costs of Production in Mexico, 1980-90.

Year	General Index	Increase (%)	Agri-culture	Increase (%)	Live-stock	Increase (%)	Beef and Dairy	Increase (%)
1980	100.0	-	100.0	-	100.0	-	100.0	-
1981	125.5	25.5	132.0	32.0	132.7	32.7	130.1	30.1
1982	197.7	57.5	177.0	34.1	187.3	41.1	204.7	57.3
1983	394.1	99.3	352.3	99.0	336.9	79.9	385.0	88.1
1984	644.8	84.7	611.8	73.7	656.3	94.8	727.0	88.8
1985	1,001.0	55.2	962.8	57.4	1,039.7	58.4	1,228.7	69.0
1986	1,796.7	79.5	1,847.2	91.9	1,660.0	59.7	1,947.0	58.5
1987	4,407.2	145.3	4,423.8	139.5	3,888.1	134.2	4,673.3	140.0
1988	8,783.7	99.3	9,417.0	112.9	8,734.4	124.6	10,237.2	119.1
1989	9,904.8	12.8	13,131.7	39.4	10,895.9	24.7	-	-
1990	12,571.7	26.9	18,409.9	40.2	12,941.9	18.8	-	-

Source: Banco de México, *Indicadores Economicos* (Mexico City: Banmex, 1990), III-28, III-30, and III-H-47(b,c).

or no mechanization accounted for 17.5 percent of all dairy farms and 21.8 percent of production. Finally, small-scale producers (fewer than 10 head, average 8) constituted the majority (76 percent), but produced only 22 percent of the state's milk. The overall trend between 1989 and 1992 was for increased milk production in the state (up 23 percent) and in the country (up 19.9 percent).[26] The SARH office in Guanajuato notes that although milk production continues to rise, it is increasingly concentrated in larger farms. It estimates that 40 percent of the dairy farms in the state went out of business in 1993 and 1994. These figures indicate that the dairy industry in Guanajuato is becoming centralized in larger-scale operations.

MEXICAN DAIRY FARMERS IN THE AGE OF NAFTA

Researchers examining the preliminary changes in Mexico's political-economic structure leading up to NAFTA agree that the treaty will simply accelerate and institutionalize changes already under way.[27] It is important to extend this argument, however, and ask how the opening of the economy, as orchestrated by NAFTA, is affecting different regions and sectors of the agrarian economy in Mexico. As previously discussed, government support since the mid-1960s for large-scale export agriculture at the expense of food self-sufficiency has left the country dependent on external sources for all of its basic foods. Peasant corn producers have suffered especially. Under pressure from inexpensive imports, particularly from the United States and Canada, many corn farmers have stopped producing for the domestic market.[28] Between 1982 and 1988 Mexican corn production dropped by 43 percent. In the same period, bean production in Mexico dropped more than 50 percent. As noted above, the dairy sector is also in competition with cheap imports, especially powdered milk, which Mexican processors can purchase from the government for 25-30 percent less than domestic fresh milk. At the same time, the average Mexican worker's buying power eroded by 65-70 percent from 1982 to 1994.[29] As a consequence, the consumption of milk and derivative products, never central to the Mexican diet, fell 78.3 percent between 1982 and 1989, and the American Farm Bureau estimates that fresh milk consumption in Mexico has declined by nearly 50 percent over roughly the same period.[30] It bears reiterating that

Table 6.
Importation of Dry Milk (thousands of tons) in Mexico, 1966-70,
1976-80, and 1981.

	Imports			Exports		
	1966-70	1976-80	1981	1966-70	1976-80	1981
Dry Milk	26	90	154	1	1	0
% Increase	-	246.2	71.1	-	0	-100
% Total Increase	-	-	492.3	-	-	-100

Source: James W. Wilkie, David E. Lorey, and Enrique Ochoa, *Statistical Abstract of Latin America*, vol. 26 (Los Angeles: UCLA Latin American Center Publications, 1988), 451; James W. Wilkie and Peter Reich, Statistical Abstracts of Latin American, vol. 20 (Los Angeles: UCLA Latin American Center Publications, 1980), 494-95.

these transformations were taking place before the implementation of NAFTA.

While NAFTA institutionalizes a set of new political-economic arrangements that were essentially already in place, it is an error to underestimate the importance of NAFTA for dairy farming in Mexico. As Isaac so astutely observes, "very often, the extent and severity of hardship resulting from economic structural change is a function of the speed of change: the faster it occurs, the greater the dislocations (e.g., hardship, suffering)."[31]

The *rate of change* is accelerated by NAFTA in all areas of Mexican domestic agriculture, but especially in the dairy sector. Whereas many crops, including corn, have phased in competition over 15 years, the dairy sector was left relatively unprotected under NAFTA. Schweikhardt and Yumkella note that Mexico imported, on average, 47,000 tons of powdered milk, 2,400 tons of cheese, and 6,000 tons of butter from the United States between 1988 and 1993. NAFTA will permit 40,000 tons of powdered milk to enter Mexico duty-free each year, an amount that will rise by 3 percent annually over 15 years;

portions above that quota will be assessed a 139 percent tariff.[32] In practical terms, there is little phase-in for the Mexican dairy industry. Farmers must adapt immediately to a new economic order or be driven quickly out of business.

Representatives of the Confederation of Ejidal Dairy Farmers, an organization within the National Confederation of Peasant Farmers (CNC), argue that by mixing fresh and powdered milk, processors are saving between 20 and 30 percent of their production costs. The use of imports is not just a cost-reducing measure, but is necessary because of low national production levels. Mexico produces about 15 million liters per day, while demand is 19-21 million liters per day. Not surprisingly, Mexico is the world's largest powdered milk importer, absorbing 46 percent of global exports.[33] The director of the National Confederation of Rural Producers (CNPR), Jesus Gonzalez, further notes that the import of cheap powdered milk amounts to little more than commodity dumping by the United States and the European Community, where farmers' subsidies range from 69-74 percent.[34] NAFTA has had an immediate effect on the Mexican dairy industry—competition with international producers of cheap, subsidized milk: the milk war. Declining average prices per liter for wholesale Mexican milk reflect the new reality: in 1989, $1.00 (US $0.36); 1990, $1.19 (US $0.41); 1991, $1.02 (US $0.34); 1992, $0.97 (US $0.31); 1993, $0.95 (US $0.30); and in 1994, $0.85 (US $0.26).

ADAPTING TO THE NEW ECONOMIC ORDER

"As soon as NAFTA took effect on January 1 [1994], American milk flooded across the Rio Grande."[35] Mexican dairy farmers have responded in a number of ways. Along the border, dairy states such as Chihuahua have raised taxes on imported fresh milk.[36] Trucks delivering fresh milk from El Paso to Juárez have been attacked, the drivers beaten and sent packing, and the trucks vandalized and sometimes burned.[37] It remains to be seen how nontariff barriers to trade and acts of resistance will be treated by international law, but it is likely that they will be seen as violations of the free-trade agreement.

Competition with imports is less obvious in the Mexican interior, where U.S. powdered milk is sold to processors by the Mexican government.[38] During interviews completed in the summer of 1994, a number of sources claimed that dairies were importing cheese and simply affixing their label to it as if it were produced in Mexico. Some farmers in Guanajuato have, for example, banded together and publicly dumped their product or given it to the poor (a powerful message in a country where at least half of the population does not consume milk or its byproducts), and others have publicly sacrificed calves.[39] Aside from these attempts to embarrass the government into increased support, three adaptive strategies are emerging among farmers in north-central Guanajuato as a response to NAFTA: some go out of the dairy business altogether, some remain independent, and some form cooperatives.

SARH officials argue that it is primarily the very small, undercapitalized dairy operations that are going out of business, as evidenced by the stable, if not slight increase, in fresh milk production in Guanajuato.[40] They further contend that this marks a transformation in and modernization of the industry as production begins to concentrate in larger, capitalized, and more efficient farms. Such an explanation may highlight the broad outlines of a changing rural economy, but does not capture the complexity of this process. Larger capitalized family farm operations are also getting out of the dairy business, although clearly they have far more options than do their smaller counterparts. Several Guanajuato farmers surveyed for this research had sold their herds in the past year and opted for contract farming in export vegetable crops, such as broccoli. According to Pancho Martínez, the former owner of 85 head of prime dairy cattle:

> My Father [who died in 1991] started this farm with nothing. But last year I could see that we were not making any money and that it would only get worse. It was the hardest decision I've ever made, but we sold the cows and some of the equipment. It's been a hard year, but I've got a contract with Birds Eye and Mar-Bran to grow broccoli and some other crops. These kinds of partnerships are the only way to survive.

Other farmers are attempting to adapt by forming cooperatives, a strategy being used by both large and small-scale operations in the region. For example, Ejido La Petaca has 36 farms that average ten cows each. As part of the Article 27 reform, *ejidos* are being encouraged to form associations and capitalize production (especially through the Solidarity Program, which makes credit and technical support available). Currently, La Petaca's farmers are making so little profit that they cannot maintain their equipment. One man pointed out that his milking machine had been idle for several months because he could not afford to repair it. Farmers here face two problems. Not only are their establishments small and undercapitalized, but also their herds are characterized by low production. Thus, to transform their farms into competitive enterprises, they will have to upgrade their herds, as well as invest heavily in other forms of infrastructure. As part of a privatized former *ejido*, they no longer can expect the government to absorb their debt, and failure means the loss of their land.

Another new regional cooperative, The Dolores Hidalgo, Guanajuato Milk Producers Association, has 22 members ranging from small-scale family farmers to large-scale capitalized enterprises.[41] The relatively small number of members, it was explained, was a conscious decision to reduce the likelihood of conflict and dissension. Partners contribute monthly toward the purchase of trucks to pick up the milk from participating farms and to construct a plant where the milk will be stored in cooling tanks and quality tested in an on-site laboratory.[42] The facility will also provide storage for jointly purchased equipment and other resources, such as fertilizers and animal feed. The group secured a large bank loan using one member's farm as collateral.

The formation of the cooperative is driven by three interrelated motives. Pancho Moreno, one of the farmers instrumental in its formation, noted that the most important issue was cutting out the middleman who resells the milk to various large processing plants.[43] "He is making a lot of money off the backs of farmers" by purchasing the milk at very low prices, storing it in his cooling tanks, and selling it to large processors when they need it. Pancho estimated that he was producing a liter of milk for about $90 new centavos in August 1994, but received only $85 new centavos per liter. The cooperative strategy is to eliminate the middleman and get $1.10 per liter of cooled milk (with $10 centavos going to maintenance of the cooperative and to pay off the loan).

The second motive is to achieve increased efficiency through economies of scale. For example, members will be able to purchase agricultural inputs such as fertilizers and medicines at lower cost. There are also plans to use a portion of the new plant to manufacture cattle feed with sorghum and other grains produced by members.

Third, the cooperative is considering adding yogurt and cheese operations. These elaborated products are very popular with a small but affluent elite. The key to this third goal, as the co-op members well understand, is finding a market for their product. The new cooperative has just begun to operate commercially and has yet to negotiate a contract with a large processor, such as Nestlé or Dannon Yogurt. Pancho noted that the biggest problem is to produce enough volume per day to secure a contract. Ultimately, they will be forced to add members and heighten the risk of dissension.

They face other risks as well. From a microeconomic perspective, the formation of a cooperative such as this one is a logical strategy for confronting increased international competition. In the past, wholesale prices and demand were such that farmers could make a profit, but that is increasingly not the case. Cheap imported powdered milk has depressed the price of fresh fluid milk. In response, farmers are seeking greater economies of scale, on the one hand, and are cutting out the middlemen who have historically made considerable profits from individual farmers, on the other.

From a macroeconomic perspective, however, this strategy may be doomed. Even without the middleman, farmers will receive only around $1.10 per liter of cooled milk, an increase of $25 new centavos. If we factor in $10 new centavos per liter for overhead and debt payment, that increase is pared down to $15 new centavos per liter—about US $0.04 per liter. If production costs continue to rise as they have over the past decade, then that thin buffer of profit will erode quickly. A continuing drop in milk prices will erode profits even more. If their variable rate loans readjust upward, they may be forced to default.[44] Thus, these heavily indebted farmers stand to lose everything, should the enterprise fail.

While the Dolores Hidalgo cooperative is at least momentarily surviving, others have not been so fortunate. The Northeast Guanajuato Milk Producers Union was initiated in 1993 with approximately 80 members who each made monthly contributions and purchased a plot of land for their plant. Due to dissension and mistrust when it came time to secure a bank loan for construction and equipment, rather than put up a single capital item, such as a farm, members chose to use small individual collateral (for example, a car or truck). When it came time to pool this collateral, only nine of the members participated, effectively killing the project.

Many farmers in north-central Guanajuato are remaining independent, either by choice or by lack of other options. While they are not taking the capital risk of the farmers forming cooperatives, they are also being forced toward the economic edge as they barely break even or lose money on their operations. A common response to this dilemma is to enter into a "discourse of efficiency" about their plight;[45] that is, to try to find new cost-effective methods. While these are experienced farmers, there are certainly areas in which they could improve. For example, in one north-central Guanajuato dairy community, irrigation ditches were replaced with a system of tubes to feed water to the fields and cut water loss. While farmers are trying to find ways to reduce costs and increase production, all may be in vain, given the lack of accessible credit and the speed of entry of international competition.[46]

In sum, the struggles and innovations of the dairy farmers in Guanajuato are mirrored on the national scene. Some are making a radical choice and selling out. Others are taking a conservative stance and remaining independent, hoping that some relief may come from the administration that took office in December 1994 led by Ernesto Zedillo. Still others are taking the middle road and forming cooperatives. Unable to transform their farms instantly into "modern" operations, they are attempting to alter their relationship to the market and thereby further rationalize distribution. As Cohen reminds us,

> Structural adjustment, whatever else it refers to, also includes the differentiation of the rural agricultural sector into a shrinking portion of overall production from the poorer small farms and the emergence and growth of a larger, commercial farm segment that will continuously expand its proportion of agricultural production in the next several decades.[47]

Farmers forming cooperatives achieve both horizontal integration (with fellow farmers) and vertical integration (with large dairy processors). Such a relationship is advantageous to both farmer and processor because it, at least hypothetically, reduces their risk in an otherwise unstable economic environment. This is what institutional economists refer to as an "embedded" transaction—exchange that is personalized through enduring social networks.[48]

Ironically, these entrepreneurial creators of cooperatives may be more vulnerable to failure than their more conservative counterparts who choose to remain independent. The co-op farmers made assumptions about the stability of variables beyond their control: the price of milk, the cost of credit, the rate of inflation, and their costs of production. The December 1994 peso devaluation, of course, proved those assumptions to be tragically wrong.

Although many farmers clearly understand the problems they face, the accelerated pace of economic change is such that they have do not have enough time to respond. Even before the peso devaluation, massive rural dislocation was being predicted by a wide range of researchers.[49] The speed of economic change, rapid displacement, and the possibility of further political instability in an already unstable situation will challenge Mexican agrarian policy throughout the 1990s.[50]

NAFTA AND DAIRY FARMING IN MICHIGAN

If the Mexican dairy industry is effectively driven to extinction by NAFTA and the rapid entry of U.S. competition, then it would seem that the U.S. dairy industry will benefit from access to this new and potentially large market.[51] Yet many dairy farmers in Michigan and throughout the Midwest have been very critical of NAFTA.[52] To consider the reasons for this apparent irony, we must first consider the structure of the U.S. dairy industry.

In the 1940s and 1950s, the U.S. dairy industry completed many of the structural adjustments just now being experienced in Mexico. New legislation designed to improve sanitary conditions in the production process forced farmers to capitalize their operations or fold. In California's Central Valley, for example, the new laws and an increasingly competitive market put 2,864 dairy farms out of business during the 1950s. Production became centralized among a shrinking number of larger farms, although the average dairy farm in 1959 still had only 89 cows.[53] The data from contemporary Guanajuato seems to parallel the experience of U.S. farmers 35 years ago.

The structural adjustment has been ongoing since the 1950s and represents one of the last arenas in U.S. agriculture where large and small capital are still struggling to prevail. Most other sectors are now dominated by large agribusinesses. While dairy farms were forced to expand and capitalize in order to stay competitive, they nonetheless remained family owned. A major change over the past three decades has been their size. In California's Central Valley, for example, dairy farms grew from 249 cows in 1970 to 401 in 1982.[54] Other farms in California, Texas, Florida, and Kansas have more than 1,000 head, with plans for dairies in excess of 3,000 head.[55]

In the process, U.S. dairy farms have become increasingly factory-like. Since the 1970s, much of the reason lies in agricultural tax codes with a number of features favoring agribusiness: corporate tax rates, cash accounting, capital gains, investment tax credit, and accelerated depreciation. The 1986 revised agricultural tax code provided some relief to small-scale farmers, but critics contend that large corporate farms remained disproportionately advantaged. Tax advantages, economies of scale, and massive technological inputs have given these large operations a major advantage over small-scale farms. As a result, one-third of U.S. dairy farms shut down during the 1980s, with more than 21,000 going out of business in Wisconsin and Minnesota alone.[56]

Michigan dairy farmers are similarly threatened. The average dairy farm in the state is still small, averaging 74 head (including dry cows). From 1967 to 1987, herd size decreased by 29.6 percent (the U.S. average was a drop of 24.5 percent), while milk output rose by 47.6 percent. Since 1977, the number of active dairy farmers in the state has declined by about one-quarter. Compared to the rest of the Midwest, Michigan has the largest average herd size (74) and the highest percentage of farms (24.8 percent) with 100 head or more, while the "traditional" dairying states of Minnesota and Wisconsin average only 51 and 55 head, respectively. Individually owned farms tend to produce less milk on average than larger operations. While 71.7 percent of farms are still individually owned in Michigan, this proportion is the second lowest in the Upper Midwest, behind Indiana, underscoring Michigan's movement toward economies of scale. Furthermore, Michigan has the highest average production per cow and the fewest farms (14.7 percent) producing less than 10,000 pounds of milk per year, a group that accounts for only 6 percent of total production. Consequently, it seems that the state's dairy industry has already made at least a partial adjustment toward larger and more efficient enterprises.[57]

Although Michigan is one of the leading dairy producers in the Midwest, it ranks only seventh in the nation. The regions with the greatest increase in milk production between 1977-79 and 1984-86 were the Northwest (up 38 percent), the Southwest (up 35 percent), and the Southern Plains (up 25 percent). The largest dairies are in California, Texas, Florida, and Kansas.[58] In California, for example, the average dairy has 475 cows. As the U.S. population center shifts toward the Southern Plains and the West, lower production and transportation costs also increase the profitability of the large corporate dairies being developed in those regions. In Texas, for example, it was estimated that production costs in 1986 were $0.50 less than those in the Upper Midwest,[59] and wholesale prices were higher by $1.50 per hundredweight, suggesting that it was $2.00 per hundredweight more profitable to produce in Texas than in the Upper Midwest.[60] Additionally, milk marketing orders established in 1937 to ensure production and availability of milk outside of the Midwest determine how much processors pay farmers for raw milk. Regional pricing involves a complex alchemy that includes how far a farm is from Eau Claire, Wisconsin, and ensures that producers in Texas or California receive a higher price per hundredweight than midwestern farmers.

Michigan family dairies thus face two different struggles. First, there is competition within the state between larger and smaller operations, with the trend toward the slow domination of larger operations. Second, there is competition between the relatively small Michigan farms and their larger and more profitable corporate competitors in the West and Southern Plains. Michigan dairy farmers and their counterparts in the Midwest have been confronted with greater corporate centralization and concentration in the industry over the past 30 years, but especially since the mid-1970s.

In this context, the entrenched opposition to NAFTA by Michigan dairy farmers seems counterintuitive. Mexican dairy farmers were already being forced out of business by the withdrawal of subsidies and other forms of agricultural support in anticipation of NAFTA, and research concurs that the U.S. dairy industry will easily out compete the unprotected Mexican industry with the implementation of NAFTA.[61] If the Mexican economy can recover from the past twelve years of eroding worker buying power, then U.S. farmers will have a large new market with demand unmet by domestic sources.[62] Yet, dairymen in the Upper Midwest claim that U.S. corporate dairies will simply relocate to Mexico and that NAFTA will force the removal of subsidies they argue are necessary to remain profitable.[63] While Michigan dairy farmers generally acknowledge that their Mexican counterparts will be unable to compete with U.S. imports, they also understand that large capital is fairly mobile and will relocate to wherever labor and production costs are lower.

> American agriculture need only look at industry to imagine the con-
> sequences of a free-trade pact with Mexico. Some 2,000 plants have
> relocated below the border, with hundreds of thousands of jobs lost in
> the U.S. Even before the Mexican trade pact is near agreement, Cargil
> and Con-Agra, two giants in the meat industry have rushed to purchase
> meat packing facilities in Mexico. Their objective is not to sell meat in
> Mexico . . . but rather to send the boxed product to the U.S.[64]

The fears expressed by farmers about lost subsidies and industrial relocation articulate concerns broader than NAFTA and are related to trends in the global economy. Agricultural competition with the European Community and Canada,[65] both of which have heavily protected and subsidized agricultural sectors, has intensified, as evidenced by the GATT disputes. In contrast, Mexico, has removed most subsidies from the agricultural sector, with only corn and beans remaining protected during a 15-year phaseout.[66] Consequently, Mexican farmers (in all but a few specialized agricultural sectors, such as cut flowers and winter vegetables and fruits) will find it almost impossible to compete with their more efficient and capitalized neighbors to the north. At the same time, reduction in U.S. subsidies will make U.S. farmers more vulnerable to the competition of their heavily subsidized European counterparts, who have historically been large suppliers of powdered milk to Mexico, but will have little direct effect on our agricultural relationship with Mexico itself.

The second major concern about industrial relocation to take advantage of cheaper Mexican labor reflects the historical struggle between large and small capital in agriculture. Farmers are protesting the "broader political-economic processes that favor the centraliza-tion of agricultural production" that have been occurring in the dairy sector over the past several decades.[67] NAFTA may stimulate this process, but it is likely to have little direct effect on the Michigan dairy industry. The U.S. industry is highly localized, forming a number of regional "milksheds" that produce and process for local consumption. Prices, too, are set regionally. While it costs Michigan farmers more to produce milk than in the U.S. South or West, and while they receive less per hundredweight for their product, this has no connection with NAFTA. In many ways, then, it makes little difference to Michigan dairy farmers whether their counterparts in the southern and western United States are able to take advantage of potential markets in Mexico. Nevertheless, NAFTA has become a convenient vehicle for articulating fears about a rapidly globalizing economy in which the family farmer is becoming increasingly threatened and obsolete.

CONCLUSION

Analysis of the Michigan dairy industry reveals an interesting paradox: many farmers are critical of NAFTA in the face of expanded market opportunities. While NAFTA may have little or no direct effect on Michigan dairy farmers, their fears about NAFTA merit attention. They, like their counterparts elsewhere in the United States, have a deep-seated sense of the zero-sum nature of competition. If Mexico imports more milk from the United States and it does not come from Michigan, then this is interpreted as a real loss in opportunity, if nothing else, and competitive advantage goes to dairy producers in the West and Southwest. Recalling the quotations at the beginning of this chapter, although Stewart Huber criticizes the apparently contradictory rhetoric of NAFTA, given the reality of the current downturn in dairy exports to Mexico—a combined result of the peso devaluation in December 1994 (making U.S. products 35-40 percent more expensive) and regulatory intervention by local governments in Mexico (such as the Chihuahua tax on imported fluid milk from the United States)—most analysts still believe that the prospects for U.S. dairy exports are quite good in the medium to long term.

If we agree, for the moment, that Mexico represents an expanding market for the United States, there are still ways in which Michigan farmers can be hurt by a boom in the dairy industry's Mexican market share. Under new federal agricultural tax codes that favor the formation of corporate dairies nationwide, Michigan farmers may find further threats to their livelihood as large-scale production leads to declining milk prices. While the Michigan industry has already gone through a phase in which smaller operations have gone out of business, leaving only larger operations as viable producers, its farms are still quite small when compared to corporate dairies in California and Texas. This is particularly problematic since it already costs more to produce milk in Michigan than in warmer climates. The case of the Land O'Lakes Dairy, one of the largest cooperatives in the Upper Midwest (and one of the country's major milk processors), clearly underscores the problems facing the region's farmers when they are forced to compete nationally and internationally.[68] Land O'Lakes is not limited to the local market, but sells in all 50 states. In 1993, it paid its farmers $12.90 per hundredweight, compared to the $12.00 paid by Seattle's Darigold Dairy to its farmers. Land O'Lakes faces stiff competition for market share in the nation's grocery stores and cannot raise its prices. The result is eroding corporate profits.

National competition, which could turn into international competition as the Mexican market opens, will further stimulate the formation of large dairies using new and sophisticated technology. The introduction of bovine growth hormone (rBGH), for example, has received negative responses from many farmers in Michigan. Some promote themselves as organic or alternative dairies, but attempts to label milk as rBGH-free have come under legal attack from large dairies.

A further threat to Michigan farmers is the possibility of surplus generated in more competitive dairy regions. New technology for storing and shipping milk could result in those surpluses flowing into less competitive regional milksheds, such as the Upper Midwest as well as Mexico. DuPuis has examined whether states have either protected their small-scale farm sector or encouraged corporate farms, and she found that those in the Upper Midwest generally adopted the former strategy, while western states such as California chose the latter.[69] She notes that truck hauling dissolved geographical boundaries between regional milksheds as early as the 1920s. While state-level milk price regulation has protected these milksheds, it is clear that less competitive regions are extremely vulnerable, especially if farmers are not well organized or have little political power at the state level.

While NAFTA may not be directly related to the transformation of the Michigan dairy industry, it encourages a number of historical trends in farm size, technology, and transportation that may lead to heightened competition among dairy regions. The Upper Midwest, with its small to medium size farms, is particularly vulnerable to competition from large corporate operations in the Southwest and West. As noted earlier, since Michigan already has experienced more concentration into larger farms than have other Upper Midwest states, it is in a somewhat better position than many of its neighbors (some of whom, such as Minnesota, have state laws against corporate farms). If Michigan follows their lead and attempts to ban the use of bovine growth hormone or outlaw corporate land ownership, it runs the risk of diverting capital to states such as California or Texas. Yet Michigan must weigh the health and social costs of not banning such practices as its farmers struggle to survive in a national and global market.

NOTES

1. Stewart Huber, president of the Farmers Union Milk Marketing Cooperative, cited in *Thumb Farm News*, 13 February 1995.
2. Allen R. Myerson, "New Limits Are Seen to Freer Trade: Taxes and Strife in the Mexico Border Area," *New York Times*, 6 September 1994, C1.
3. "No Problema Lechero," *El Sol del Bajío*, 7 May 1993, 1A.
4. This is especially true of the "new internationalization of agriculture" school. For a general introduction to this approach, see David Barkin, *Distorted Development* (Boulder, Colo.: Westview Press, 1990); Stephen E. Sanderson, *The Transformation of Mexican Agriculture: International Structure and the Politics of Rural Change* (Princeton, N.J.: Princeton University Press, 1986). Useful correctives to this approach come from Laura T. Raynolds, David Myhre, Philip McMichael, Vivian Carro-Figueroa, and Frederick Buttel, "The 'New' Internationalization of Agriculture: A Reformulation," *World Development* 21, no. 7 (1993): 1101-21; David Goodman and Michael Watts, "Reconfiguring the Rural or Fording the Divide?: Capitalist Restructuring and the Global Agro-Food System," *Journal of Peasant Studies* 22, no. 1 (1994): 1- 49.
5. Raynolds et al., "'New' Internationalization," 1106.
6. *Ejidos* are peasant farming communities created as part of the land reform mandated in Article 27. Large estates and haciendas were expropriated by the state, and the land was redistributed to peasant groups. In the vast majority of these *ejidos*, peasants received use rights to a plot of land, which they worked individually. Far fewer in number and generally less successful are collective *ejidos*, in which land was worked communally. In

either case, title to the land was kept by the state. See Billie R. DeWalt, Martha W. Rees, and Arthur D. Murphy, *The End of Agrarian Reform in Mexico: Past Lessons, Future Prospects* (San Diego: Center for U.S.-Mexican Studies, University of California, 1994).

7. Casio Luiselli, "Agricultural Dilemmas of Mexico: Reflections of a Policy Maker," in *Food and Farm: Current Debates and Policies*, Christina Gladwin and Kathleen Truman, eds. (Lanham, Md.: University Press of America, 1989), 85-98.

8. Judith Adler Hellman, *Mexican Lives* (New York: New Press, 1994), 116.

9. Ibid., 117.

10. David Barkin and Timothy King, *Regional Economic Development: The River Basin Approach in Mexico* (New York: Cambridge University Press, 1970).

11. See, for example, ibid.; David Barkin and Billie R. DeWalt, "Sorghum and the Mexican Food Crisis," *Latin American Research Review* 23, no. 3 (1988): 31-32; José Luis Calva, "El Eventual Tratado de Libre Commercio y sus Posibles Impactos en el Campo Mexicano," *México* 22, no. 87 (1991): 27-32; Hellman, *Mexican Lives*, 119; and Aaron E. Zazueta, "Agricultural Policy in Mexico: The Limits to a Growth Model," in *State, Capital and Rural Society*, Benjamin S. Orlove, Michael W. Foley, and Thomas F. Love, eds. (Boulder, Colo.: Westview Press, 1989), 122-26. Barkin and DeWalt observe (32), in addition, that from 1940 to 1979 between 70 and 99 percent of government spending on agriculture was on irrigation projects, especially in the northern states of Sonora, Sinoloa, and Tamaulipas.

12. David Barkin, Rosemary L. Batt, and Billie R. DeWalt, *Food Crops vs. Feed Crops: Global Substitution of Grains in Production* (Boulder, Colo.: Lynne Rienner, 1990), 33.

13. Hellman, *Mexican Lives*, 120-21.

14. Ibid., 121-22.

15. PROCAMPO is a program of unlinked subsidies, the only type allowed under the new GATT rules, to producers of basic grains.

16. James H. McDonald, "NAFTA and Basic Food Production: Dependency and Marginalization on Both Sides of the US/Mexico Border," *Research in Economic Anthropology* 15 (1994): 129-43.

17. Carlos Acosta and Guillermo Correa, "Se Busca Manipular Electoralmente a los Más Pobres, Denuncian Campesinos e Investigadores," *Proceso* 884 (1993): 28-30.

18. Ibid., 30.

19. McDonald, "NAFTA"; Calva,"El Eventual Tratado"; Barkin, *Distorted Development*; Zazueta, "Agricultural Policy"; Lois Stanford, "Transitions to Free Trade: Local Impacts of Changes in Mexican Agrarian Policy," *Human Organization* 53, no. 2 (1991): 99-109; Lois Stanford, "Peasant Resistance in the International Market," *Research in Economic Anthropology* 13 (1994): 67-91; Kirsten Appendini, *De la Milpa a Los Tortibonos* (Mexico City: El Colegio de México, 1992); Cynthia Hewitt de Alcántara, *Restructuraci: El Colegio de México, 1992); Cyn*(Mexico City: El Colegio de México, 1992); Blanca

Suárez, "La Modernizacirnational Market," f Changes in Mexican Agrarian Policy," " serve (32), in addition, that from 1940 to 1979 between 70 and 99 percent of government spending on agriculture was on irriSelf-Sufficiency in Mexico," *Latin American Perspectives* 14, no. 3 (1987): 271-97.

20. Barkin, "End of Food Self-Sufficiency," 286.

21. Jeffrey Bortz, "The Development of the Quantitative History of Mexico," in *Statistical Abstract of Latin America*, James W. Wilkie and Enrique Ochoa, eds. (Los Angeles: UCLA Latin American Center Publications, 1989), 1108-27, and other researchers have pointed out that the quality of the Mexican data is often questionable. I do not attempt to construct my entire argument around these data; rather, I use them to provide a macroeconomic backdrop for my local study. The Mexican statistics do provide insight into broad economic trends in the country, and this is sufficient for the purposes of this analysis. The political nature of "official" macroeconomic data is well known; see, for example, Mary E. Hawkesworth, *Theoretical Issues in Policy Analysis* (Albany: SUNY Press, 1988). I would argue that if the data are biased in a consistent direction, it is toward minimizing the severity of the current economic crisis.

22. James W. Wilkie, "From Economic Growth to Economic Stagnation in Mexico: Statistical Series for Understanding Pre- and Post-1982 Change," in *Statistical Abstract of Latin America*, James W. Wilkie, David E. Lorey, and Enrique Ochoa, eds. (Los Angeles: UCLA Latin American Center Publications, 1988), 913-36.

23. Ibid., 925.

24. For a more complete listing of foods under government price control, as well as foods considered part of Mexico's *canasta básica* (staple foods), refer to Sergio Estrada-Berg, "Processed Foods Reflect a Changing Lifestyle," in *Business Mexico,* John H. Christman, ed. (Mexico City: American Chamber of Commerce in Mexico, 1981), 230, 232.

25. Tables 4 and 5 have different base years (1978 and 1980, respectively). Were the base years the same, the gap between the wholesale price of milk and costs of production would be even more pronounced.

26. Javier Mojarro, SARH, Celaya, Guanajuato, personal communication, August 1994.

27. Appendini, *De la Milpa*; Barkin, "The End of Food Self-Sufficiency" and *Distorted Development*; Calva,"El Eventual Tratado"; Hewitt de Alcántara, *Restructuracive*; McDonald, "NAFTA"; Stanford, "Transitions" and "Peasant Resistance"; George A. Collier, *Seeking Food and Seeking Money: Changing Relations in a Highland Mexican Community* (Geneva: United Nations Research Institute for Social Development, 1990); George A. Collier, "Reforms of Mexico's Agrarian Code: Impacts on the Peasantry," *Research in Economic Anthropology* 15 (1994): 105-28; Barry L. Isaac, "Introduction," *Research in Economic Anthropology* 15 (1994): 1-12; James H. McDonald, "Corporate Capitalism and the Family Farm in the U.S. and Mexico," *Culture and Agriculture* 45/46 (1993): 25-28; and José Luis Sosa,

"Dependencia Alimentaria en México," *El Cotidiano* 34 (1990): 39-43.

28. Armando Sepúlveda Ibarra, "No se Embargará al Ejido por Deudos con Bancos: Hank G.," *Excélsior*, 15 November 1991, 1.

29. Tom Barry, "The Economy," in *Mexico: A Country Guide*, Tom Barry, ed. (Albuquerque: Inter-Hemispheric Education Resource Center, 1992), 97; and Anthony DePalma, "Mexico's Pact for a Stable Economy," *New York Times*, 27 September 1994, sec. C, 1, 8.

30. Suárez, "La Modernizaci, 1, 8.r-Hemispheric EducaNAFTA: *Effects on Agriculture* (Washington, D.C.: American Farm Bureau Foundation, 1992).

31. Isaac, "Introduction," 7.

32. David B. Schweikardt and Kandeh Yumkella, *The North American Free Trade Agreement and Agricultural Trade: Dairy Products* (East Lansing: Department of Agricultural Economics, Michigan State University, 1993).

33. Guadalupe Rodríguez Navarrete, "Productores de Leche: En Situaci University, 19*Peacenet*, 13 May 1994.

34. Raul Adorno Jimenez, "Acuerdo de Ganaderos con SARH and SECOFI," *Peacenet*, 13 May 1994.

35. Myerson, "New Limits . . . ," C1.

36. In Chihuahua, a 9 percent tax was levied on imported fresh milk. The legality of this move under both GATT and NAFTA trade rules is questionable, but the United States has yet to file a formal complaint with the World Trade Organization.

37. Myerson, "New Limits . . . ," C1.

38. U.S. Department of Agriculture, "In Focus: NAFTA, in Dairy Situation and Outlook Report (Washington, D.C: USDA, 1993).

39. Adorno Jimenez, "Acuerdo."

40. Javier Mojarro, Personal Communication, August 1994.

41. The Dolores Hidalgo Cooperative (Union de Productores de Leche de Dolores Hidalgo, Gto.) has the following membership and share structure:

	Shares/Cows Owned		Shares/Cows Owned
Antonio Bortoloti	110/180	Candido Cárdenas	8/8
Antonio Cuellar	15/15	Rodolfo Cuellar	65/20
Alfredo Frena	34/34	Cosme Gonzalez	7/7
Elias Jimenez	110/100	José Jimenez	45/40
Manuel Mancera	17/15	Cruz Martínez	12/12
David Moreno	25/25	Francisco Moreno	54/54
Miguel Mueno	25/25	Francisco Moreno	54/54
Adan Rodríguez	5/8	Arturo Rodríguez	6/6
Bonifacio Rodríguez	10/50	Donato Rodríguez	44/44
Rafael Rodríguez	15/15	Jesus Sanchez	34/34
Pablo Sanchez	10/10	Juan Vallejo	90/70

Note: In cases where farmers bought more shares than they have cows, they are planning to augment their herd in the future. Those with fewer shares than cows usually are committed to selling part of their daily production of milk elsewhere.

42. Recent reports suggest that 70 percent of the milk produced in Mexico is deficient in one way or another in terms of sanitary standards. This is a clear concern for dairy processors that is being shifted downward to direct producers, who will be required to meet increasingly high sanitary standards. See Ruth E. Salgado, "70% de 66 Marcas de Leche Registran Deficiencias en su Elaboraciards.*Peacenet*, 13 May 1994.

43. In the State of Aguascalientes, for example, the wholesale price of milk is $75 centavos (U.S. $0.23) per liter, and the retail price for fresh milk is $1.75 (U.S. $0.53) per liter. See Adorno Jimenez, "Acuerdo."

44. The peso devaluation has driven interest rates to 80 percent on mortgages, 100 percent on personal loans, and 120 percent on credit cards. How these farmers are coping with this crisis or whether they have even survived it will require further field research.

45. For an example from other regions of Mexico, see Guadalupe Rodríguez Gges, 100 percent on personal loans, and 120 percent on credit cards. How these farmers are coping with this crisis or w*Sistemas de Trabajo en la América Indígena*, C. Esteva Fabregat, ed. (Ecuador: Editorial Abya Ayala, 1994).

46. One farmer claimed that he had attempted to get a loan in 1993 through a government source, FIRCO, to expand his dairy herd and buy new equipment. He was told that dairy farms were high-risk loans and that the bank believed the dairy industry would be destroyed within two years. He has since sold his herd. For those who could secure credit in the summer of 1994, interest rates ranged around 30 percent annually.

47. Ronald Cohen, "Growth Is Development, Distribution Is Politics," *Research in Economic Anthropology* 15 (1994): 15-37.

48. Mark Granovetter, "Economic Action and Social Structure: The Problem of Embeddedness," *American Journal of Sociology* 91 (1985): 481-510, and "The Nature of Economic Relations," in *Understanding Economic Process*, Sutti Ortiz and Susan Lees, eds. (Lanham, Md.: University Press of America, 1992); James M. Acheson, *Anthropology and Institutional Economics* (Lanham, Md.: University Press of America, 1994).

49. McDonald, "NAFTA."

50. For example, El Barzy Press of America, 1994).

51. American Farm Bureau, *NAFTA*; U.S. Department of Agriculture, "In Focus: NAFTA"; Congressional Budget Office, *Agriculture in the North American Free Trade Agreement* (Washington, D.C.: CBO Papers, 1993); U.S. International Trade Commission, *Potential Impact on the U.S. Economy and Selected Industries of the North American Free-Trade Agreement*, Publication No. 2596 (Washington, D.C.: USITC, 1993).

52. Michigan Farmers Union, *Policy Statement* (Hastings, Mich.: MFU, 1993); Carl McIlvain, president of the MFU, personal communication, July 1993.

53. Mark Friedberger, *Farm Families and Change in Twentieth-century America* (Lexington: University of Kentucky Press, 1988), 42.

54. Ibid., 43

55. McDonald, "Corporate Capitalism"; "California Visionaries Looking to Kansas," *Salina Journal*, 30 June 1994, 3.

56. Marty Strange, *Family Farming: A New Economic Vision* (Lincoln: University of Nebraska Press, 1989); and Sharon Schminkle, "Move on over Wisconsin: Upper Midwest Is Slipping as Leading Milk Producer," *Chicago Tribune*, 22 March 1992, C4.

57. Larry R. Borton, Larry J. Connor, Larry G. Hamm, Bernard F. Stanton, Jerome W. Hammond, Myron Bennett, Wiliam T. McSweeney, John E. Kadlec, and Richard M. Klemme, *Summary of the 1988 Northern U.S. Dairy Farm Survey*, Research Report No. 509 (East Lansing: Agricultural Extension Service, Michigan State University, 1990).

58. Brian P. Crowley, *The National Dairy Program Hearing* (Washington, D.C.: U.S. Government Printing Office, 1988), 198.

59. This reduction in costs has to do with the warmer climate in southern and western states.

60. Edward V. Jesse, *The National Dairy Program Hearing* (Washington, D.C.: U.S. Government Printing Office, 1988), 40-41.

61. McDonald, "NAFTA."

62. The Mexican dairy industry has never been able to meet a historically increasing demand. In the 1980s, demand dropped off when worker buying power declined. If the Mexican economy is revitalized and buying power is reestablished, then we can assume there will be very high demand for milk and an elastic market. See James H. McDonald, "The Emergence of Inequality among Capitalizing Family Farmers in Mexico," (Ph.D. diss., Arizona State University, 1991).

63. "Sugar, Dairy Producers Hit Proposed Free Trade Pact," *Flint Journal*, 5 September 1992, A5.

64. Carl McIlvain, president of the Michigan Farmers Union, personal communication, July 1993.

65. It should be remembered that Canada kept its dairy sector out of the NAFTA negotiations.

66. Calva, "El Eventual Tratado"; McDonald, "Emergence of Inequality."

67. McDonald, "NAFTA," 136.

68. William M. Stern, "Land O'Low Returns," *Forbes*, 15 August 1994, 90.

69. E. Melanie DuPuis, "Sub-National State Institutions and the Organization of Agricultural Resource Use: The Case of the Dairy Industry," *Rural Sociology* 58, no. 3 (1993): 440-60.

III.
Economic and Public Policy Dimensions of NAFTA

Antidumping Laws and NAFTA:
What Can We Expect?

Corinne M. Krupp

In Michigan, participation in international commerce is a critical source of sales, growth, and income for many firms. Exports in 1989 accounted for 14.31 percent of the gross state product. Michigan is home to four members of the list of 50 largest U.S. exporters and ranks fourth nationally with 5.04 percent of total U.S. merchandise exports.[1] Due to the relative significance of international trade in the state's economy, especially with the two most important U.S. trading partners, Canada and Mexico, Michigan companies must be knowledgeable about trade policy, and policy makers must be aware of the real market effects of the measures they implement.

Since World War II, most nations have participated in multilateral tariff reduction under the auspices of GATT. These negotiations, or rounds, have led to major decreases in the average tariff rates among GATT participants, the indirect result of which has been a dramatic increase in the use of nontariff barriers. These include a wide array of trade-impeding instruments, such as quotas, voluntary export restraints, export subsidies, countervailing duties, and antidumping laws. They have become popular tools for governments to promote exports and protect domestic firms from import competition.

One of the most popular forms of nontariff barriers is to penalize foreign dumping in the domestic market. Under international trade law, dumping refers to selling a foreign good in a domestic market at a price below "fair" or "normal" value. Fair value is defined slightly differently in various countries' antidumping laws, but Article VI of GATT states that it is either the price at which the good is sold in the foreign market, the fully allocated cost of production, or the price at which the good is sold in a third-country export market.[2] Thus, the primary difference in the definitions is the benchmark price against which fair value is determined. In the first definition, the foreign seller's export price is compared to the average home market price. In the second, also known as sales below cost, the export price is compared to the seller's ex-factory cost of production plus a markup for profits. The third compares the foreign seller's export price to a third-country export price and is used when the seller does not have an adequate home market for comparison purposes.

In order for duties to be imposed on dumped imports, it must be shown that the domestic industry has suffered material injury due to dumping, and there must be evidence of a positive dumping margin (the percentage difference between the fair value price and the export price). A foreign seller cannot be penalized for dumping unless a clear linkage is established between this action and material injury to the domestic industry. Some of Michigan's largest and most important firms have filed antidumping cases against foreign competitors in the United States. In 1993, a high-profile suit against minivans from Japan was initiated on behalf of General Motors, Ford, and Chrysler. Other cases involving Michigan producers include iron construction castings from Canada (1985), tapered roller bearings from Hungary, Italy, Japan, China, Romania, and Yugoslavia (1986), forged steel crankshafts from Germany and the United Kingdom (1986), and tart cherry juice from Germany and Yugoslavia (1991), to name a few.

This chapter briefly reviews the antidumping procedures in the United States, Canada, and Mexico in force prior to the U.S.-Canada Free Trade Agreement and NAFTA, and points out similarities and differences among them. This is followed by a discussion of how these agreements affect the application of antidumping laws in the three countries and what changes will be implemented. Finally, some of the problems that have arisen among the three countries in their use of antidumping laws in the past will be examined, and some current proposals for radically changing the antidumping rules and procedures will be presented. The implications of these changes for Michigan industries and policy makers also will be addressed.

POLICY QUESTIONS

The primary focus of this chapter is a clear comparison of the differences in antidumping laws and procedures in the United States, Canada, and Mexico, both before and after NAFTA, with the express purpose of informing Michigan policy makers and business leaders about the nature of these laws and their enforcement. In particular, the following key issues arise:

- How open are the procedures for investigation and government decision making in the three countries? Can an industry expect to receive a fair hearing and a ruling based upon the facts of the case, or do politics strongly influence the final outcome?
- Are there major differences in investigative procedures, data requirements, and criteria for an affirmative material injury finding among the countries?
- What are the provisions for settling disputes about antidumping case procedures or outcomes among the countries?
- How have the two trade agreements affected the way in which countries can use their antidumping laws? Also, how was the GATT Antidumping Code amended in the Uruguay Round, and how do these changes affect the United States, Canada, and Mexico in terms of the antidumping provisions of NAFTA?
- What issues in the use and enforcement of antidumping law were left unresolved by GATT, and what are some of the current suggestions for antidumping law reform?

The answers to these policy questions are very important for Michigan producers who export to Mexico or Canada. Knowledge of the circumstances under which a firm may be accused of dumping and how an investigation is likely to proceed will enable firms to respond more effectively to such charges. Likewise, if a Michigan firm believes it has been injured by foreign dumping, it needs to know how the U.S. procedures work. These policy issues will be discussed in the following general overview of antidumping laws in the three NAFTA countries.

BACKGROUND

The antidumping code became part of GATT during the Kennedy Round (1964-67) and was altered during the Tokyo Round (1973-79). Attempts were made during the Uruguay Round (1986-93) to discourage and restrict the use of antidumping laws worldwide, and the code was strengthened in some ways. The issue has a much longer history than this, however. Canada's first antidumping legislation dates to 1904, and the U.S. Revenue Act of 1916 had provisions making it illegal to dump with the intention of injuring, destroying, or preventing the establishment of a U.S. industry.[3]

While the first U.S. legislation was concerned with predatory dumping, the current procedure does not require exposure of any such intent, and it has become much easier to use the law as a weapon against import competition, whether unfair or not. In fact, there is evidence that industries can and do use or threaten to use the law to harass importers or persuade them to collude in raising prices.[4] Many believe that the law and investigative procedures are biased in favor of domestic industry.[5]

Since the 1980s, antidumping regulations have become the most frequently used nontariff barrier. The increased number of filings in the NAFTA countries are an example. During the 1950s and 1960s 12 antidumping petitions were filed in the United States against Canadian imports, none against Mexican imports. In the 1970s, there were twice as many antidumping investigations of Canadian imports and 6 of Mexican imports. By the 1980s, the respective numbers had risen to 27 and 8. In only the first two years of the 1990s, 4 cases against Canada and 3 against Mexico were filed.[6] Since 1970, U.S. investigations have also been initiated in greater numbers against Japan (119 cases), Germany (32 cases), China (28 cases since 1980), and South Korea (34 cases).

Canadian and Mexican producers have also become increasingly active in their use of antidumping laws. From 1980 to 1988, 319 investigations were initiated in Canada, 55 against U.S. imports. In Mexico during that period, 30 procedures were initiated, 14 against U.S. imports. In comparison, the 409 antidumping filings in the United States during the same period were second only to the 465 such filings in Australia.[7]

COMPARISON OF NORTH AMERICAN ANTIDUMPING LAWS

Under the GATT code, two primary criteria must be met before imposing antidumping duties—proof of dumping and material injury—and investigations into each charge are usually conducted by separate agencies. The petitioner must show that the foreign exporter has sold the product at a dumped price and must demonstrate that the dumping is causally linked to a material injury it has suffered. In the first instance, the dumping margin is calculated as the percentage gap between the foreign firm's export price and its ex-factory home price of the good in question. To show material injury, the domestic industry usually develops a trend analysis using data on its sales, financial performance, investment and employment, and price pressures as a result of the dumping. Several important deadlines must be met in an antidumping case, and these are usually strictly defined by statute. As a first step, within 20 days of the filing, both investigative agencies examine the antidumping petition to ensure that the claims are not frivolous or unfounded. Next, within 45 days of the filing, the agency investigating the material injury claim makes a preliminary decision about the nature and extent of injury. If material injury is attributed to the dumped imports, then the other agency completes its simultaneous investigation of the dumping margin. If that reveals a positive margin, then the first agency conducts a more comprehensive injury investigation. The case culminates with the imposition of antidumping duties on the import shipments if the final material injury decision is affirmative.

The U.S. and Canadian antidumping laws and procedures can be directly compared, since they are quite similar in most respects, whereas the Mexican law will be analyzed separately due to procedures that differ in many important ways. The United States and Canada are in complete compliance with the GATT antidumping code, the broad aspects of which were discussed previously, and have similar procedural methods and criteria. In both countries, two separate agencies conduct the material injury and dumping margin investigations. In the United States, material injury is handled by the U.S. International Trade Commission (USITC), whose counterpart is the Canadian International Trade Tribunal (CITT). Dumping margin determinations are made, respectively, by the International Trade Administration (ITA), an arm of the U.S. Department of Commerce, and by the Deputy Minister of National Revenue for Customs and Excise (DMNR).

There are basically two areas in which the Canadian and U.S. laws differ. The first is the way in which material injury and the allegedly dumped imports are linked. In Canada, the imports must constitute an "important," "significant," or "direct" cause of injury to the domestic industry. The USITC requires only that the imports contribute to the material injury suffered by the domestic industry; they need not be the main or even a substantial cause. This makes it easier for U.S. industries to clear this hurdle in U.S. antidumping cases.

The other important difference is the way in which the effect of the antidumping outcome on the public is considered. In Canada, the CITT can impose antidumping duties only after determining whether they are in the public interest. If they will cause more harm than benefit, then this must be reported to the Ministry of Finance, which then can reduce the duties or remove them altogether. The United States has no such provision.[8]

Mexican antidumping laws are relatively new and are still being amended to comply with the antidumping code in GATT, which Mexico joined in 1986.[9] The country's basic antidumping and countervailing duty procedures are contained in the Foreign Trade Regulatory Act of 1986 and the Regulations Against Unfair International Trade Practices of 1988.[10]

Prior to NAFTA, two basic conditions had to be satisfied in order to petition successfully for antidumping relief in Mexico: proof of an "unfair international practice" and of injury or threat to cause injury to the domestic industry. After 1986, Mexican law was largely in compliance with Article VI of GATT, except for its material injury test, which required only proof that the imports caused or threatened material injury to the domestic industry, not that any injury actually existed or had occurred during the time in which the case was being considered. The very broad language of the injury criteria made proof very easy to show: "loss or reduction or deprivation of any legal or normal profits that one or some national producers suffer or will suffer . . . [including] impediments to the establishment of new industries or the development of the existing ones."[11]

Unlike the U.S. and Canadian situation, in which two separate agencies handle the material injury and dumping margin determinations, a single Mexican agency is responsible for the entire investigation. This agency is the Secretariat of Commerce and Industrial Development (SECOFI), and it also has the power to initiate antidumping cases.[12] In fact, in the five years since the Mexican law was enacted, SECOFI has filed nearly half of the 75 petitions.[13] Another difference is a more restrictive standing requirement than in either the United States or Canada. In order for a domestic industry to file a case in Mexico, at least 25 percent of the industry must support the petition.[14]

The primary differences between U.S. and Mexican law are the time frame for deciding cases, injury criteria, standing, and the transparency of the procedure itself. Before passage of NAFTA, SECOFI could impose provisional antidumping duties immediately after a filing, well before any reasonably comprehensive investigation could be completed, if there was preliminary evidence of dumping and material injury. In some cases, the alleged dumpers were not even aware of the petition when they were informed of the duties. The second provisional duty determination was to be made 30 days after the first, but it usually occurred five months later. The entire investigation and final duty determination were supposed to be completed within six months of the filing, but the statutory time limitations were frequently violated, and cases tended to average 18 months.[15]

Prior to NAFTA, in addition to the broad injury criteria under Mexican law, there were no public hearings, and SECOFI was not required to consider all of the submitted evidence, but only what it deemed relevant to the case.[16] Finally, Mexico still does not have a reputation for conducting antidumping and countervailing duty investigations in any sort of a quasi-judicial manner, although judicial review of administrative decisions is currently available. The lack of procedural transparency was one of the more troubling aspects of Mexico's antidumping law before passage of NAFTA.

POLICY OPTIONS: CHANGES UNDER NAFTA AND PROPOSALS ON THE HORIZON

Preferential trade agreements have proliferated during the last two decades in Europe, Asia, and North America, a trend that appears to be continuing and that raises several questions. How does increased integration among countries affect their trade policies? How have

NAFTA changes in antidumping law affected the three partners? What are the pros and cons of fundamental reform in global antidumping laws, which are likely to be a major issue for the World Trade Organization in the near future?

Two popular types of preferential trade arrangements are free-trade areas and customs unions. In the former, members eliminate trade barriers among themselves over time, but maintain existing barriers and policies toward nonmembers. A customs union is more integrated, as members not only eliminate barriers among themselves, but also agree on uniform tariffs and policies toward nonmembers.

Along with integration comes a tendency to reduce nontariff barriers, such as antidumping laws and subsidies (countervailing duties). While countries retain the right to use these measures against partners as well as nonmembers, one of the world's most integrated trading areas, the EEC, recently has discussed replacing antidumping laws with a harmonized antitrust code applicable to all members.[17]

In the case of North America, U.S. and Canadian antidumping laws have remained essentially unaltered, but major changes were made in the Mexican law in 1993 to bring it into compliance with GATT and NAFTA. Procedures are much more transparent; decisions are to be based upon all the facts in the administrative record; the length of the investigation has been extended, allowing adequate time for responses to requests for information, and explicit timetables have been set; there are clear guidelines as to the timing of decisions, appeals, and the rights of both petitioners and respondents in a case; SECOFI must provide a detailed statement of its reasons and a legal basis for its decisions; and the former practice of imposing duties before issuing a preliminary determination is no longer permissible.

SECOFI has adhered to the statutory timetables in conducting investigations and making its rulings. Public hearings are a regular feature of the process, as are disclosure conferences in which SECOFI presents its decisions, reasoning, and methodology. These changes have made Mexican practices more comparable to those in the United States and Canada.

During the NAFTA talks, both Canada and Mexico campaigned vigorously for fundamental changes in U.S. antidumping law, but their requests were rebuffed. The U.S. government insisted that any fundamental changes should be made on a multilateral basis under the auspices of GATT. Thus, while passage of the U.S.-Canadian Free

Trade Agreement (FTA) in 1989 and the more recent adoption of NAFTA in 1994 did not significantly alter antidumping procedures in North America, several important developments merit discussion.

In particular, a new method for settling disputes among members that was negotiated under the U.S.-Canadian agreement was extended to Mexico under NAFTA. Under the FTA, a binational panel of five (two chosen by each country and one chosen by mutual agreement) may review, at the request of either country, administrative antidumping or countervailing duty rulings made in Canada or the United States. This review replaces other domestic judicial reviews, and its primary focus is on whether national laws were properly applied. Both countries agreed to accept its decisions as binding. Since implementation of the FTA, the panel has received 17 requests for administrative review, all but two brought by Canada. An outside evaluation found that the panel review is shorter than the previous domestic judicial reviews by the U.S. Court of International Trade, that the panel has provided well-reasoned decisions, and that both sides perceive this dispute resolution mechanism as working fairly and efficiently.[18]

Under NAFTA, a binational panel of five representatives from the two countries in dispute is authorized to review less-than-fair-value decisions made in the FTA countries. The partners keep their pre-NAFTA antidumping laws, and if any amendments are made, the other partners must be notified and consulted far in advance of the implementation date. In addition, amendments must be consistent with the GATT code and "with the object and purpose of NAFTA."[19]

During the Uruguay Round, and more recently, there has been general discussion about replacing antidumping laws with cross-border competition laws. The rationale is the failure of antidumping laws to distinguish between two types of price discrimination (dumping): predatory pricing to eliminate competition or to deter entry versus procompetitive pricing to establish a toehold in a new market, unload perishable or obsolete goods, or meet lower-cost competitors. Predatory behavior is illegal under U.S. antitrust laws, but the second type of competition, at least if conducted in the United States by domestic firms, is perfectly legal. If the competitor is foreign, however, the same behavior is illegal under the antidumping law.

Competition policy, including antitrust and merger guidelines, establishes the rules for market rivalry among domestic firms and distinguishes between these types of pricing, yet antidumping laws penalize international price discrimination no matter why it occurs, as long as material injury by reason of the dumped imports is demonstrated. Some argue that the law should be applied only in cases of predatory dumping, while procompetitive pricing between domestic and foreign firms should be permissible, as it is under domestic competition laws. Others argue that proving predatory dumping is nearly impossible since it requires knowledge of the firm's intent to destroy its competition or to keep potential entrants out of the market. Thus, restricting the definition of dumping to predatory pricing may render the antidumping law toothless.

During the FTA negotiations, the two countries agreed to assess their domestic competition legislation in order to consider how to replace antidumping laws with competition laws. The five major findings of the technical group assigned this task were: (1) existing laws on predatory pricing require little change to address cross-border violations; (2) price discrimination laws, which would be better substitutes for antidumping laws than predatory pricing laws alone, would require some changes to be made applicable to cross-border discrimination; (3) new rules governing forum choice (the country in which the investigation is conducted) are required to avoid parallel litigation and/or forum shopping; (4) the treble damage rule under U.S. antitrust law is a serious obstacle to enforcement of remedies in cross-border cases; and (5) special rules may need to be developed to address third-country dumping (transshipment through a member country in order to dump in the trade region).

In essence, the technical group found that competition policy could largely replace antidumping laws in application, as long as the U.S. and Canadian competition laws were harmonized. The major stumbling block is the difference in the two countries' use of subsidies and countervailing duty laws.[20] Since antidumping and countervailing duties are closely related (both are classified as "less-than-fair-value" cases), the countries must harmonize their very different views about what constitutes a subsidy and when it constitutes unfair trade promotion for the domestic industry.

The technical group was given seven years to devise an implementable plan, but no provision was made for such a group under NAFTA. In chapter 19 of NAFTA, the parties agreed "to consult on the potential to develop more effective rules and disciplines concerning the use of government subsidies; and [to consult on] the potential for reliance on a substitute system for dealing with unfair transborder pricing practices and government subsidization."[21] Thus, while the question of replacing antidumping laws with a harmonized domestic competition policy has been investigated and is a topic of ongoing discussion at the World Trade Organization, there is no indication that implementation of such a change is forthcoming soon. What is now relevant to firms and policy makers is the current state of the GATT antidumping code, now that the Uruguay Round has concluded and the NAFTA countries have accepted the agreement.

REVISIONS IN THE GATT ANTIDUMPING CODE

The future of global antidumping laws depends upon ongoing negotiations within the World Trade Organization. As mentioned before, the Uruguay Round resulted in a few changes to the code but not a complete rewriting, despite dogged attempts at reform by many countries.[22]

Two of the changes concern the resolution of international disputes. First, a "standard of review" was adopted by which GATT countries are required to review antidumping determinations. Second, a new dispute settlement mechanism requires countries to resolve less-than-fair-value disagreements by binding decisions subject to this standard of review. This will make it harder for GATT panels to second-guess antidumping determinations made by the United States and other countries. These changes do not affect current antidumping laws in the United States, Canada, and Mexico, but others do.

One of the new provisions concerns the calculation of dumping margins, an extremely complicated affair.[23] The best and most fair ("apples-to-apples") comparisons between foreign and export prices are recognized to be on the basis of individual-to-individual sales price, or average-to-average price. Previously, countries were permitted to compare average foreign market values to individual export sales prices, thus biasing the procedure toward finding a positive dumping margin. That is no longer permitted.[24] In addition, the use of constructed value for calculating dumping margins has been expanded to include circumstances under which home market sales comprise less than 5 percent of sales to the importing country. This obviates the need to use much less accurate third-country sales prices in these situations.

GATT also established a new lower bound for dumping margins and dumped imports: margins below 2 percent will be ignored, and investigations will not be initiated if dumped imports comprise less than 3 percent of total imports or if cumulated imports represent less than 7 percent of total imports. In addition, the new rule regarding standing in filing a petition requires at least 25 percent of the industry to support the filing, and more of the industry must support or be neutral to the petition than oppose it.[25]

Countries are also required to make antidumping procedures more transparent (that is, to follow specified time frames, incorporate due process, publish decisions and explain them based upon the evidence contained in the administrative record, and so forth) This ruling applies specifically to countries whose antidumping procedures are still secretive and mysterious. Finally, the new sunset provision states that for each antidumping order on the books, a five-year review is required after the order is issued. If there is no review or if the review shows dumping is not present or likely to resume, the order is to be terminated.

A particularly vexing issue left unsolved by the Uruguay Round regards circumvention of antidumping orders. Specifically, since these orders apply to very specific products from a particular country or countries, foreign producers can avoid paying dumping duties by exporting an unfinished version of the product or one slightly different from the offending product. The GATT code is silent on how to deal with this matter, although it now explicitly recognizes the problem and the authorities' right to address it. This is one aspect of antidumping that the World Trade Organization will address in the future.

CONCLUSION AND POLICY IMPLICATIONS FOR MICHIGAN

Dumping can be a particularly damaging way for an import competitor to gain market share. Especially in sectors requiring continuous research and development expenditures and capital investment to stay competitive, foreign dumping can damage not only current, but also future profits and a firm's market viability. Michigan has many industries in this category, including chemicals, automobile manufacturing, and industrial machinery, many of which have already had firsthand experience with the antidumping law. A number of economists and policy makers believe that the current law provides an invaluable recourse for industries beleaguered by foreign dumping. Conversely, others believe that antidumping laws are misused to fend off import competition, and view this as a troubling development in world trade, particularly because the procedures sanctioned by GATT are skewed toward the domestic industry filing the case. The recent changes to the code will not have a major effect on the propensity to use this nontariff barrier; more drastic changes are needed. Until a full accounting of the net costs and benefits of imposing antidumping duties is made within each investigation, these measures will probably continue to increase in popularity.[26]

Trade policy is made at the federal level, but this does not imply that Michigan has no role to play in influencing the effective use of antidumping laws and their reform. Assistance through a general "trade policy information clearinghouse" at the state level could be provided to firms either contemplating a petition or facing an investigation abroad. Such assistance could include basic information about how the law works and the requirements for filing, the pros and cons of using the antidumping law and other options available, and the names of contacts in the Washington legal community for advice and further help if the case goes forward. While large firms such as General Motors and Dow Chemical may be able to obtain this kind of information easily from their own extensive networks, smaller firms may find such assistance invaluable.

Finally, Michigan policy makers can and should become involved in the antidumping versus competition policy debate, since it appears likely that a decision will be made by the World Trade Organization in the not-so-distant future. While antidumping laws can offer valuable protection, especially in industries characterized by long-term research and development and product innovation, there is also the risk of increased filings against U.S. firms abroad for procompetitive behavior (such as meeting local price competition). Given the relative importance of international trade in Michigan's economic base and the multinational focus of many of its important industries, the state's policy makers must actively participate in the debate in order to influence U.S. negotiators when the World Trade Organization tackles this important issue.[27]

NOTES

1. U.S. Bureau of the Census, *Statistical Abstract of the United States: 1995,* 115th ed. (Washington, D.C.: U.S. Government Printing Office, 1995), 816, table 1338.
2. "Agreement on the Implementation of Article VI of the General Agreement on Tariffs and Trade" (Geneva: GATT, 1979).
3. Jacob Viner, *Dumping: A Problem in International Trade* (New York: Augustus Kelley Publishers, 1966), 242-54.
4. John Michael Finger, "Dumping and Antidumping: The Rhetoric and the Reality of Protection in Industrial Countries," *World Bank Research Observer* 6, no. 2 (1992): 121-43; Mark Herander and J. Brad Schwartz, "An Empirical Test of the Impact of the Threat of U.S. Trade Policy: Antidumping Duties," *Southern Economic Journal* 51, no. 1 (1984): 59-79; and Corinne Krupp and Patricia Pollard, "Market Responses to Antidumping Laws: Some Evidence from the U.S. Chemical Industry," *Canadian Journal of Economics* 29, no. 1 (1996): 199-227.
5. Robert Boltuck and Robert Litan, eds., *Down in the Dumps* (Washington, D.C.: Brookings Institution, 1990).
6. See annual reports from the International Trade Commission for evidence.
7. John Jackson and Edwin A. Vermulst, eds., *Antidumping Law and Practice* (Ann Arbor: University of Michigan Press, 1989), 15, table 2.
8. According to Presley. Warner, "Canada-U.S. Free Trade: The Case for Replacing Antidumping with Antitrust," *Law and Policy in International Business* 23, no. 4 (1992): 812, the Canadian provision is rarely used and is perceived by some to have been a failure.
9. All countries, in order to become contracting parties to GATT and to receive the associated benefits of membership, must comply with all of the GATT codes.
10. Neil Longley and Terry Wu, "Mexican and U.S. Antidumping and Countervailing Duty Policies: Issues in the Free Trade Negotiations," *Law and Policy in International Business* 23, no. 4 (1992): 894. In 1993, Mexico allegedly passed a revised version of its antidumping law and regulations. These changes will be discussed later.
11. Peter McLaughlin, "Mexico's Antidumping and Countervailing Duty Laws: Amenable to a Free Trade Agreement?" *Law and Policy in International Business* 23, no. 4 (1992): 1025.
12. Similar power resides with the respective agencies in Canada and the United States, but such initiations are rare.
13. McLaughlin, "Mexico's Antidumping," 1027.
14. Under U.S. law, the petitioner must be a manufacturer, an association of manufacturers, or a labor group from the affected industry; there is no threshold percentage of the industry that must back the petition, although if majority support cannot be shown, the investigation will be halted. In

Canada, the DMNR actively investigates whether the petitioners represent a "significant" proportion of Canadian production. Complainants representing 44 percent of the industry have had standing to file cases, so the threshold for "significant" is vague. See Warner, "Canada-U.S. Free Trade," for more references on this issue

15. Longley and Wu, "Mexican and U.S. Antidumping," 902-3.

16. McLaughlin, "Mexico's Antidumping," 1028, 1039.

17. The European Free Trade Association (EFTA) also has been considering such a move. See Michael Hart, "Dumping and Free Trade Areas," in Jackson and Vermulst, *Antidumping Law and Practice*, 326-42.

18. McLaughlin, "Mexico's Antidumping," 1036-37.

19. Paul, Hastings, Janofsky, and Walker, *NAFTA: Summary and Analysis* (Washington, D.C.: Matthew Bender and Associates, 1992), 106-7.

20. Countervailing duty laws apply when a domestic industry suffers material injury due to subsidized import competition. Duties may be imposed on the import prices to offset the unfair beneficial effect of the subsidies.

21. "Chapter 19: Review and Dispute Settlement in Antidumping and Countervailing Duty Matters," *North American Free Trade Agreement* (Washinton, D.C.: Executive Office of the President, 1993), 11.

22. David Mueller, "Antidumping," *Business America* 115, no. 1 (January 1994): 15-16.

23. See Boltuck and Litan, *Down in the Dumps*, for an illuminating look at the complexity of this part of the antidumping procedure.

24. The exception is spot-dumping by a foreign seller to particular customers or in a particular region.

25. Another technical change to dumping margin calculations is that below-cost sales may be disregarded as long as they comprise less than 20 percent of sales, but there are special allowances when a producer is in a start-up phase. Profits for use in constructed value calculations must be based on above-cost profits by the producer of the dumped product, and if these are not available, then the authorities must either use average profits on all sales of the same product by other producers, or average profits on different products made by the same producer. In addition, actual general expenses must be used, not a 10-percent-of-costs figure, as applied by the United States. This will likely reduce the dumping margin, since the higher the cost figure, the easier it is for the domestic industry to show foreign sales below cost and, thus, dumping.

26. See Gary Horlick, "How the GATT Became Protectionist: An Analysis of the Uruguay Round Draft Final Antidumping Code," *Journal of World Trade* 27, no. 5 (1993): 5-17; and John Michael Finger, *Antidumping* (Ann Arbor: University of Michigan Press, 1993), chap. 4, for extensive discussions on reforming antidumping laws.

27. I wish to thank Tom Graham and John Greenwald for sharing their legal knowledge about the Mexican system, and Maura Binley and Sandy Maclaren for providing information about the Canadian antidumping laws.

Trends in Manufacturing Employment in the NAFTA Region: Evidence of a Giant Sucking Sound?

David D. Arsen, Mark I. Wilson, and Jonas Zoninsein

The debate on NAFTA's employment effects has focused alternately on the issues of investment displacement and trade creation. Ross Perot gave graphic expression to the fears of U.S. workers with his prediction that NAFTA would generate a "giant sucking sound" of U.S. jobs migrating to Mexico.[1] Other critics, less nationalistic in perspective, stressed NAFTA's unfavorable effects on income distribution and labor and environmental standards in all three countries. They also predicted U.S. job losses, arguing that, between 1992 and 2000, due to the cumulative shift of investment from the United States to Mexico, 260,000 to 439,000 U.S. jobs would be lost.[2]

Most economists supported NAFTA and predicted modest employment gains among all three partners. According to free trade theory, NAFTA would encourage member countries to specialize in producing the goods and services they make most efficiently and to export these in exchange for imports of goods and services made more efficiently elsewhere, thereby raising productivity, income, and employment in each country. The most publicized technical report supporting the agreement argued that in the short run NAFTA and related Mexican reforms would help maintain a sizable U.S. trade surplus with Mexico, thereby generating the net creation of about 170,000 U.S. jobs by 1995 (using 1990 job figures as a base).[3]

These opposing projections are premised on necessary but tenuous assumptions concerning the modeling of economic forces and the course of uncertain future events. Clearly, the recent peso devaluation and resulting Mexican government commitment to fiscal and monetary austerity have dramatically undermined employment benefits predicted by NAFTA proponents. But another drawback of such forecasting exercises is that they ignore important evidence on actual employment trends.

This chapter adopts an alternative approach to examining NAFTA's regional employment effects, one that implicitly encompasses both the trade and the investment effects. We examine the historical evidence on manufacturing employment before NAFTA's passage, from 1978 to 1992, when Mexico's economic reforms gained momentum and the Canada-U.S. Free Trade Agreement went into effect. Although NAFTA included negotiated settlements on a wide range of technical issues, it essentially locked in policy reforms adopted by Mexico since 1985 to liberalize its trade and investment.[4] Consequently, while our explicit objective is not prediction, we assume the relevant trends during that period will continue under NAFTA's implementation.

Our results show a more complex picture than the one suggested by the studies mentioned above. Economic liberalization in the NAFTA region has not caused a net loss of U.S. manufacturing jobs to Mexico. Trade and investment liberalization, however, have contributed to very interesting changes in industry-level competitive advantage that have more in common with the predictions of NAFTA critics than supporters. These results are obtained from a shift-share analysis. The chapter also considers the effects of NAFTA on Michigan's economy.

AGGREGATE MANUFACTURING EMPLOYMENT TRENDS

Table 1 summarizes manufacturing employment trends in the NAFTA region from 1978 to 1993, using data from the International Labour Office.[5] There was a net reduction in manufacturing employment in the region of 10.3 percent, or 2.3 millon jobs. This trajectory of regional loss is punctuated by cyclical fluctuations, notably the recessions of the early 1980s and 1990s and the 1983-89 expansion. Yet, the downward long-run trend is revealed in a peak-to-peak comparison of 1979 and 1989. Despite the 1980s expansion, the 22.4 million manufacturing jobs in 1989 were still roughly a million shy of the 1979 level. Also, regional manufacturing employment continued to fall in 1993, the first year of the present expansion, to its lowest level in 16 years.

This gradual loss occurred in conjunction with shifts in the distribution of manufacturing jobs across the three countries. Over the period covered by table 1, there was a modest decline in the U.S. share, from 90.6 percent in 1978 to 87.9 percent in 1992. Canada's share increased gradually until 1989, but most of this relative gain was lost to the United States during the initial years of the FTA. Mexico's share nearly doubled between 1978 and 1992, rising from 2.3 percent to 4.4 percent.

Table 1.
Manufacturing Employment in the NAFTA Region, 1978-1993.

	Employment (000's)	Growth Rates (%)	U. S.	Regional Share Canada	Mexico
1978	22,642.0	. . .	90.6	7.2	2.3
1979	23,261.5	2.74	90.4	7.2	2.4
1980	22,524.4	- 3.17	90.1	7.3	2.6
1981	22,445.9	- 0.35	89.8	7.4	2.8
1982	20,886.4	- 6.94	89.9	7.2	2.9
1983	20,727.3	- 0.76	89.0	8.4	2.6
1984	21,599.8	4.21	89.7	7.8	2.5
1985	21,937.6	1.56	87.8	7.8	4.4
1986	21,664.4	- 1.25	87.5	8.1	4.4
1987	21,860.2	0.90	87.1	8.6	4.3
1988	22,203.3	1.57	87.1	8.6	4.3
1989	22,396.8	0.87	86.8	8.9	4.3
1990	21,955.7	- 1.97	85.2	8.5	4.4
1991	21,083.0	- 3.97	87.5	7.9	4.5
1992	20,695.7	- 1.84	87.9	7.7	4.4
1993	20,317.8	- 1.83	....	...	...

Source: International Labour Office, *Yearbook of Labour Statistics* (Geneva: ILO), various years.

This sharp rise requires closer consideration, since most of the growth occurred in 1984 and 1985, with Mexico's employment share remaining stable for the remainder of the period. Indeed, there was virtually no change in the distribution of manufacturing employment across the three countries between 1985 and 1992. The ILO data indicate an extraordinary 76.4 percent increase in Mexican manufacturing jobs between 1983 and 1985. Mexico's significant and continuing moves toward economic liberalization began with changes made between early 1983 and June 1985 during the de la Madrid administration.

It is inviting to attribute Mexico's rapid increase in regional employment share around 1985 to early returns from its economic reforms, but other factors likely were at play, particularly in view of the stable Mexican share as liberalization continued. We believe that the sharp rise in Mexico's regional employment share in 1985 primarily reflects nonreported revisions in the data collection and classification methodology of Mexican institutions in charge of employment statistics (for instance, changes in the size of manufacturing establishments included in the samples). While the magnitude of this possible influence cannot be precisely assessed, insofar as it is relevant, the series before and after 1985 are not strictly comparable.

Nevertheless, other indicators suggest significant development of the Mexican manufacturing sector around this time. Between 1983 and 1985, Mexican imports of intermediate and capital goods increased by 71.4 and 78.8 percent, respectively.[6] Moreover, among foreign enterprises operating in Mexico, exports rose by 105 percent and imports by 200 percent in the same period.[7] The growth of foreign enterprise imports in Mexico was primarily composed of intermediate inputs and capital goods for setting up production facilities. These data suggest that, starting around 1985, Mexico experienced a sharp increase in manufacturing jobs in establishments operated by TNCs. Yet, as Mexican employment associated with this foreign direct investment has continued to grow up to the present, it has merely displaced existing manufacturing employment in smaller and less efficient firms previously operating in Mexico. Hence, Mexico's share of regional manufacturing jobs has remained constant for nearly a decade, despite a cumulative process of liberalization and important development of its manufacturing sector.

INDUSTRY TRENDS IN MANUFACTURING EMPLOYMENT

This section offers an initial examination of manufacturing employment trends at the three-digit industry level. The primary focus is on the relative significance of two distinct elements of employment change within each of the NAFTA countries: (1) industry growth or decline across the region as a whole, and (2) employment change due to shifts in production among the three partners. The analysis focuses on peak-to-peak trends from 1978 to 1989. Data for 1992, the most recent year available, are also presented for comparison purposes. Despite the recession that year, 1992 data reveal continuity with industry trends over the preceding period.

We classify the 28 ILO manufacturing industries into three groups. Group I industries are those in which the number of jobs declined steadily over 1978-89 for the region as a whole. Group II industries are those in which regional employment levels increased steadily over the period. Group III industries had regional employment levels that were either roughly stable or did not follow a monotonic trend.

Table 2 presents employment in the NAFTA region according to our classification scheme. Half of the manufacturing industries fall into Group I, and they represent roughly half the manufacturing jobs in the region, falling from 53 percent in 1978 to 46.4 percent in 1989. In Group I alone, regional employment dropped by 1.7 million over the period, a decrease of 14.2 percent.

The six industries in Group II together increased their share of total manufacturing employment from 30.7 percent to 37.1 percent from 1978 to 1989, generating a net growth of 1.3 million jobs (a robust 19 percent increase). With the exception of food manufacturing, where U.S. employment fell slightly, job growth in each Group II industry was shared by all three countries. Group III is comprised of eight industries with a stable share of total employment, slightly more than 16 percent during the period.

We now consider the extent to which industry-level job loss in the United States can be attributed to employment gains in Mexico or Canada. It is important to recognize that shifts from the United States to the other NAFTA countries are only one of several possible sources of U.S. job loss. Employment declines also may be attributable to slow growth in product market demand, to labor-saving technological change, or to growth in production at sites outside the NAFTA region.

Table 2.
Employment by Industry in the NAFTA Region, 1978, 1989, and 1992.

Industry	1978 Employment (000s)	Share (%)	1989 Employment (000s)	Share (%)	1992 Employment (000s)	Share (%)
Group I						
Tobacco products	84.3	0.4	60.2	0.3	58.7	0.3
Textiles	1,038.6	4.6	75.7	3.9	783.4	3.8
Apparel	1,419.9	6.3	1,202.7	5.4	1,123.1	5.4
Leather products	95.4	0.4	58.0	0.3	56.5	0.3
Footwear	184.9	0.8	108.3	0.5	93.6	0.5
Petroleum refineries	175.3	0.8	132.0	0.6	132.1	0.6
Glass products	189.3	0.8	138.8	0.6	129.5	0.6
Nonmetallic mineral products	545.9	2.4	482.3	2.2	430.7	2.1
Iron and steel	960.0	4.2	523.4	2.3	451.1	2.2
Nonferrous basic metal	476.5	2.1	412.9	1.9	379.1	1.8
Fabricated metal products, except machinery	1,822.3	8.0	1,642.3	7.4	1,504.0	7.3
Machinery (excl. elec.)	2,407.2	10.6	2,295.4	10.3	2,071.5	10.0
Electrical machinery	2,151.7	9.5	1,963.1	8.8	1,757.9	8.5
Other manufacturing	482.4	2.1	427.4	1.9	418.1	2.0
Subtotal	12,033.7	53.0	10.322.5	46.4	9,389.3	45.4
Group II						
Food manufacturing	1,732.5	7.7	1,753.4	7.9	1,766.6	8.5
Printing and publishing	1,268.5	5.6	1,717.2	7.7	1,661.3	8.0
Other chemicals	576.9	2.5	627.0	2.8	679.4	3.3
Plastic products	485.7	2.1	723.7	3.2	711.1	3.4
Transport equipment	2,215.3	9.8	2,390.0	10.7	2,141.2	10.4
Scientific equipment	669.9	3.0	1,060.5	4.8	973.0	4.7
Subtotal	6,948.8	30.7	8,271.8	37.1	7,932.6	38.3
Group III						
Beverages	320.4	1.4	303.5	1.4	288.5	1.4
Wood products	858.5	3.8	880.2	4.0	785.3	3.8
Furniture and fixtures	529.0	2.4	597.7	2.7	515.3	2.5
Paper products	852.6	3.8	853.3	3.8	821.6	4.0
Industrial chemicals	661.8	2.9	672.0	3.0	592.0	2.9
Miscellaneous petroleum and coal products	58.7	0.3	46.0	0.2	42.6	0.2
Rubber products	327.1	1.4	285.9	1.3	268.2	1.3
Pottery and china	51.4	0.2	50.3	0.2	46.7	0.2
Subtotal	3,659.5	16.2	3,688.9	16.6	3,360.2	16.3

Source: International Labour Office, *Yearbook of Labour Statistics* (Geneva: ILO), various years.

Table 3 presents employment change from 1978 to 1989 for each partner in only those industries in which the United States evidenced a clear pattern of job loss. Most of these U.S. losses (roughly 92 percent) occurred in Group I industries—that is, in those industries whose regional share declined. In eight of these industries Canada also lost employment. While Mexican jobs increased in all but one of these industries (iron and steel), the magnitude of that growth falls far short of matching the U.S. losses.

Overall, of the approximately 2 million manufacturing jobs lost by the United States in Group I industries during 1978-89, Mexico absorbed at most 350,000 and Canada another 50,000. In other words, the combined effects of trade dislocation and investment displacement within the region account for no more than 20 percent of the U.S. loss in manufacturing jobs. This calculation is an upper bound for the employment shift and certainly overstates it on several counts. First, the actual net displacement of U.S. jobs to Mexico and Canada was less insofar as nonmanufacturing industries in the United States experienced job growth through trade with these countries. Second, this calculation implicitly attributes to North American trade the effects of any other factors that independently generated manufacturing employment growth in Mexico and decline in the United States. Third, it is striking that Mexico's entire job gain is less than the mysterious jump of 425,000 jobs reported for Mexico in the ILO data between 1984 and 1985. This suggests that this estimate of an employment shift is probably a statistical artifact of revisions in data collection and reporting by Mexican government agencies. For this reason, the more refined methodology for assessing employment shifts developed in the following sections will be applied only to the 1985-92 period.

The combined effects of slow economic growth, globalization of production beyond the NAFTA region, and technical progress, therefore, must represent the main factors behind U.S. employment loss.[8] There is, however, one potential caveat to this conclusion of a virtually inaudible "sucking sound." It turns on the possibility, suggested earlier, that an investment shift by TNCs from the United States to Mexico actually displaced extant Mexican employment while simultaneously reducing U.S. employment. It is not essential from this viewpoint to demonstrate that foreign direct investment somehow caused existing Mexican employment to decline. To preserve the possibility of the investment displacement effect, one merely needs to

Table 3.
Employment Change in Selected Manufacturing Industries, 1978-89 (in thousands).

Industry	U.S.	Canada	Mexico
Group I			
Tobacco products	-21	-3.3	0.2
Textiles	-178	-2.4	17.5
Apparel	-243	3.0	32.8
Leather products	-34	-3.4	0.0
Footwear	-87	-3.5	13.9
Petroleum refineries	-47	3.9	0.0
Glass products	-52	-0.6	2.0
Nonmetallic mineral products n.e.c.	-70	-7.6	14.0
Iron and steel	-380	-50.2	-6.4
Nonferrous metals	-62	-5.6	4.0
Fabricated metal products	-223	22.8	20.2
Machinery (excl. elec.)	-196	49.5	34.7
Electrical machinery	-259	16.3	54.1
Other manufacturing	-69	4.4	9.6
Subtotal	-1,921	23.3	196.6
Group II			
Food manufacturing	-31	10.8	32.1
Group III			
Beverages	-42	-0.4	25.5
Industrial chemicals	-92	9.3	92.9
Subtotal	-134	8.9	118.4
Total	-2,086	52.0	347.1

Source: International Labour Office, *Yearbook of Labour Statistics* (Geneva: ILO, various years).

assert a counterfactual world in which Mexican employment would have fallen absolutely in the absence of this foreign investment.

SHIFT-SHARE ANALYSIS

There is a systematic technique for assessing the sources of employment change in the NAFTA region, one that permits the isolation of industry-level changes in each country's competitive position within the region. Shift-share analysis disaggregates employment change into components reflecting national, industry-specific, and local competitive forces. So we assess national employment change by industry, against the experience of the three NAFTA countries combined. The shift-share technique divides manufacturing employment change in each nation into three components: national share (NS), industry mix (IM), and competitive shift (CS).

By definition, the total change in manufacturing employment in each country equals the sum of these three components.[9] The NS effect controls for the pace of regional manufacturing employment change by indicating the change for each country if it had changed at the same rate as aggregate manufacturing employment in the region. IM reflects employment change due to the industrial composition of each country's manufacturing sector. Essentially, it measures a country's concentration in industries that are growing relatively rapidly or slowly at the regional level. A positive IM indicates relative concentration in industries with employment growing at least at the aggregate regional rate, while a negative IM indicates concentration in manufacturing industries growing slowly (or declining) at the regional level. CS measures a country's deviations from the employment change expected if employment in each industry changes at the regional rate for that industry. This component is usually interpreted as an indicator of competitiveness. A positive CS implies competitive advantage, since a country's employment in a particular industry is growing more rapidly than the regional rate for that industry. A negative CS identifies industries and countries with slower growth rates than expected.

Despite its simplicity, shift-share analysis is a useful way to account for the nature of employment change within the NAFTA region.[10] In particular, it permits an assessment of a key concern raised by NAFTA, namely, whether trade and investment liberalization is producing systematic shifts in competitive position (job growth) across countries. This should be revealed in the results for the CS effect, once the effects of aggregate employment growth and industrial structure are controlled in the NS and IM variables.

On the one hand, if NAFTA critics associated with the "giant sucking sound" prediction are right, then we should observe a substantial negative competitive shift effect in the United States (and perhaps Canada), while Mexico should enjoy a substantial positive competitive shift. An additional proposition suggested by some critics is that the industries most vulnerable to employment loss should be those with highest U.S. production worker wages. If true, the competitive shifts by industry should be inversely related to average wage rates across U.S. manufacturing industries.

On the other hand, NAFTA proponents' prediction of increased economic specialization and trade across countries implies that each country should experience competitive shift losses in some industries and offsetting gains in others, but no clear pattern of aggregate competitive shift at the national level.[11] This prediction can be made more precise, since NAFTA proponents explicitly anticipated a specific pattern of competitive shifts across industries. In particular, following traditional notions of comparative advantage based on factor proportions, the United States and Canada should experience competitive shift gains in capital- and technology-intensive (high-wage) industries and competitive shift losses in labor-intensive and standardized- or low-technology (low-wage) industries. Mexico, meanwhile, should experience competitive shift gains in labor-intensive, low-tech, and low-wage industries and competitive shift losses in capital-intensive, high-tech, and high-wage industries.

SHIFT-SHARE RESULTS FOR EMPLOYMENT IN THE NAFTA REGION

The shift-share analysis was performed on the ILO data for 1985-92. As a starting year, 1985 has the twofold advantage of marking the beginning of concerted Mexican liberalization and of avoiding the changes in Mexican industrial classifications noted previously.

Summary shift-share results for the region are presented in table 4. A more refined presentation is offered in appendix A, which shows each of the three effects for each country at the industry level. Each country lost manufacturing jobs during 1985-92, as aggregate manufacturing employment in the region declined by 6.8 percent. The NS columns in tables 4 and appendix A simply allocate this employment loss across industries in the three countries in proportion to their 1985 employment levels.

Table 4.
Shift-Share Analysis for the NAFTA Region, 1985-92, Summary Results (employment change in thousands).

Country	Employment Change (000s)		NS	IM	CS
Canada	-137.2	=	-116.2	+14.1	-35.0
Mexico	-48.4	=	-65.7	-16.4	+33.7
United States	-1305.1	=	-1308.7	+2.3	+1.3

Source: Authors' calculations.

The rate of employment change associated with the IM effect is the same across the three countries for any given industry and is calculated as the product of these rates and 1985 industry employment by country. Regionally, only five of the industries experienced employment growth from 1985 to 1992: other chemicals (18.3 percent), plastic products (12.2), printing and publishing (6.9), food manufacturing (5.3), and paper products (0.2). Another five experienced employment declines of less than 6.8 percent. Industries with the sharpest regional job loss were iron and steel, tobacco products, footwear, and leather products, for which declines ranged from 21 to 54.2 percent.

Table 4 shows that, on balance, Canada benefited from its concentration in industries growing relatively rapidly at the regional level, producing a modest increase of 14,100 jobs. Mexico was relatively concentrated in declining industries, generating a negative IM effect of 16,400 jobs. The IM effect produced significant employment gains and losses in individual U.S. industries, primarily those with the fastest and slowest aggregate growth, but they basically offset each other to produce a negligible net increase of 2,300 jobs.

The most interesting results are found in the CS effect, which indicates each country's industry-level employment growth relative to the corresponding regional rate. Since, for each industry, the CS effect necessarily sums to zero across countries, these results reveal emerging patterns of industry-level competitiveness or comparative advantage among the three nations. The summary CS effect in table 4 flatly rejects the notion of a systematic employment shift from the United States to its partners. On balance, the main shift is Mexico's gain of 35,000 jobs at Canada's expense. The United States has maintained an essentially stable competitive position within the region. Consistent with the position of NAFTA supporters, trade and investment liberalization since 1985 thus far has not generated a decline in the regional comparative advantage of U.S. manufactures.

U.S. industry-level employment trends are far more sensitive to factors affecting industry growth as a whole than to factors affecting shifts in the relative competitiveness of the NAFTA nations. Results in appendix A indicate that, for the United States, the IM effect in most industries (24 of the 28) dominates the CS effect (that is,| IM | > |CS|). This is partly a consequence of the fact that the United States comprises a large share of regional manufacturing employment. Also, in all but four U.S. industries, the directional change in employment is the same as the IM effect. The CS effect plays a relatively greater role in Mexico and Canada than in the United States, but it still tends to be secondary to the IM effect.

Although the aggregate CS results are broadly consistent with the predictions of NAFTA supporters, the pattern of competitive shift across industries is less compatible with their sanguine projections. In several industries there were significant variations in the pace of employment change across countries. Yet, one does not observe the supporters' predicted pattern of positive competitive shifts for high-tech and high-wage industries in the United States and negative competitive shifts in U.S. low-tech and low-wage industries. Indeed, the results indicate just the opposite: The U.S. experienced a substantially negative, and Mexico a substantially positive, competitive shift in high-tech industries. Moreover, the sharpest U.S. employment loss associated with declining regional competitive advantage came in very capital-intensive and high-wage industries.

Table 5 identifies those industries with the largest positive and negative competitive shifts in the United States. It is striking that the greatest U.S. gains in regional competitive advantage came in relatively low-tech industries: textiles, food manufacturing, iron and steel, and paper products. Mexico and Canada experienced negative competitive shifts in each of these industries. The largest declines in U.S. regional competitive advantage occurred in two large, capital-intensive, and high-tech industries: electrical machinery and transport equipment, whereas Mexico and Canada each posted gains in both of these industries.

Table 5.
Competitive Shifts in Selected Industries in the NAFTA Region (employment change in thousands).

Industry	United States	Canada	Mexico
Largest U.S. gains			
Textiles	34.7	-26.3	-8.4
Food manufacturing	30.6	-27.3	-3.4
Iron and steel	24.5	-9.1	-15.3
Paper and paper products	15.8	-14.5	-1.3
Other chemicals	14.3	-15.8	1.5
Plastic products	13.1	-5.4	-7.7
Nonmetallic mineral products	10.3	-8.9	-1.4
Rubber products	7.4	-7.4	0.0
Largest U.S. losses			
Electrical machinery	-40.4	34.0	6.4
Transport equipment	-35.9	22.0	13.9
Other manufacturing	-20.8	18.5	2.2
Industrial chemicals	-16.4	-0.4	16.9
Beverages	-15.3	-6.7	22.1
Footwear	-9.4	3.9	5.5
Printing and publishing	-5.5	7.1	-1.2

Source: Authors' calculations, see Appendix A.

These conclusions are reinforced and strengthened by evidence presented in table 6, which shows competitive shifts in seven high-tech industries. These were selected based on Tyson's survey of alternative classification schemes for high-tech industries.[12] Nearly all manufacturing activities generally classified as high-tech fall within these seven industries, although at the three-digit ISIC level each includes some activities that are not high-tech. Plastic products (ISIC 356) includes polymers and synthetic resins and fibers. Other chemicals (352) includes pharmaceuticals, antibiotics, and medicines. Machinery except electrical (382) covers office machinery, computers, and computer-controlled machine tools. Electrical machinery (383) includes electronic components, telecommunications equipment, and integrated circuits. Transport equipment (384) incorporates aerospace and auto assembly. Scientific instruments (385) includes optical instruments, electronic measuring and controlling instruments, and particle accelerators. The United States enjoyed a positive competitive shift within the NAFTA region in only two of these, other chemicals and plastic products. In aggregate, for the seven high-tech industries, the United States suffered a competitive shift decline of 72,000 jobs, while Canada and Mexico gained 39,000 and 34,000, respectively.

Table 6.
Competitive Shifts in High-Tech Industries in the NAFTA Region (employment change in thousands).

Industry	U.S.	Canada	Mexico
Electrical machinery	-40.4	34.0	6.4
Transport equipment	-35.9	22.0	13.9
Industrial chemicals	-16.4	-0.4	16.9
Other chemicals	14.3	-15.8	1.5
Plastic products	13.1	-5.4	-7.7
Scientific equipment	-3.6	3.6	0.0
Machinery (excl elec.)	-3.5	0.9	2.6
Total	-72.4	38.9	33.6

Source: Authors' calculations, see Appendix A.

Industry-level competitive shifts in the United States are also inversely correlated with industry wage levels. We examined U.S. Bureau of Labor Statistics data on average production worker wages for 1988, the midpoint of the period covered in the shift-share analysis. The average hourly wage in U.S. industries experiencing competitive shift gains was $9.26, compared to $10.05 in industries experiencing competitive shift losses. This result is reinforced by a calculated correlation coefficient between industry wage and competitive shift of -0.15. An estimate of the average wages of U.S. manufacturing jobs gained and lost as a result of competitive shifts in the region can be obtained by weighing industry wages by the number of jobs lost or gained through competitive shifts. This calculation indicates that the average job gained paid an hourly wage of $9.22, while the average job lost paid $9.84.

In sum, results of the shift-share analysis are consistent with some and inconsistent with other claims of both critics and supporters of NAFTA. Thus far, regional trade and investment liberalization has not generated a giant sucking sound of employment shifts from the United States to Mexico. Trends in U.S. manufacturing employment are determined primarily by regional trends in industry employment. There is, however, evidence that Mexico has achieved modest gains at Canada's expense. Yet, the pattern of industry-level shifts in national competitiveness within the region is not consistent with the projections of some NAFTA supporters and is much closer to the critics' position. In general, the United States has lost competitive advantage in knowledge-intensive industries that provide good jobs, offset by competitive gains in less technologically progressive industries that offer lower wages.

These conclusions should be viewed in light of two limitations. First, the evidence concerning emerging trends in industry-level competitive advantage within the region is premised on relatively aggregate industrial classifications. Any three-digit industry comprises a range of activities spanning a more or less broad spectrum of technical sophistication, wage rates, capital-labor ratios, and so on. An analysis of four-digit ISIC classifications might temper or strengthen the patterns observed at the three-digit level.

Second, the shift-share analysis is necessarily retrospective, not predictive. We have suggested, however, that employment trends over 1985-92 constitute a useful indicator of future trends. They are, in any case, clearly superior to the highly optimistic employment forecasts of "authoritative" economic analyses in the years leading up to NAFTA's passage. Yet, while the precise pattern of long-run development in the region remains uncertain, relevant consequences of the peso devaluation over the medium term are now clearly in view.

The Mexican financial crisis produced a 50 percent depreciation of the peso against the dollar and forced draconian macroeconomic policies that raised Mexican interest rates to nearly 100 percent. Austerity is designed to contract domestic income to limit imports and to moderate inflationary pressures greatly aggravated by the rising peso price of foreign imports. These developments have crushed the Mexican market for U.S. and Canadian consumer goods. The demand of Mexican firms for foreign intermediate and capital goods also has been sharply constrained. At the same time, the dramatic fall in the dollar price of Mexican labor, coupled with NAFTA's elimination of restrictions on foreign investment, has created a powerful incentive for TNCs to shift production to Mexico to serve the U.S. market.

How will these developments modify future employment trends portrayed in the shift-share analysis for the 1985-92 period? Slow (indeed, presently negative) growth of the Mexican economy will constrain aggregate employment growth in the region, which will be reflected in national shares. Future competitive shifts will be affected by two offsetting forces. On the one hand, recession will reduce employment in domestic Mexican firms, reducing Mexico's share of regional jobs. On the other hand, the likely shift of investment from the United States and Canada to Mexico will generate Mexican employment gains relative to the other two nations. The balance of these two opposing effects cannot be known in advance. There remains in any case a renewed possibility for a future sucking sound (however large), even if such an effect is not evident in the data thus far. Given the current recession in the Mexican economy, however, this effect will not be unambiguously isolated in a shift-share analysis, even after future employment data become available.

IMPLICATIONS FOR MICHIGAN MANUFACTURING

Canada and Mexico are Michigan's top two foreign export markets, and each has accounted for a growing share of the state's exports in recent years. Michigan sends two-thirds of its exports to Canada, $14 billion out of $21 billion in 1991. Michigan's $1.6 billion in exports to Mexico in 1991 are barely one-tenth of the volume exported to Canada, but this flow has grown rapidly in recent years.[13]

The structure of the Michigan economy makes it a particularly interesting case for the study of NAFTA's employment effects. Michigan will be a laboratory for some of the most important, contentious, and unresolved employment consequences of the agreement. Our finding that North American trade and investment liberalization has not generated net manufacturing employment displacement from the United States to Mexico still leaves open the possibility that it has caused significant net employment gains or losses in particular subnational areas. Michigan's economic base is heavily concentrated in transport equipment and capital goods. This proud legacy now gives the state a dubious distinction: Michigan's top three manufacturing industries are experiencing not only employment declines, but also competitive shift employment losses to Mexico and Canada. Future employment effects of NAFTA on Michigan will depend critically on the foreign investment and sourcing decisions of the state's corporations.

Table 7 shows Michigan's manufacturing employment by industry and includes concentration ratios comparing the industrial structure of state employment in each industry to that of the United States as a whole.[14] A ratio greater than one indicates an industry in which the state is relatively concentrated, while a ratio of less than one indicates underrepresentation in Michigan relative to the entire country. With 178,000 jobs, the transport equipment industry (car and truck assembly and most vehicle parts) is by far the state's leading source of manufacturing jobs. Other major industries in Michigan are machinery (excluding electrical) and fabricated metal products, each with more than 100,000 employees.[15] These three industries alone account for more than 54 percent of the state's manufacturing employment. In addition, Michigan has high concentration ratios (but lower employment levels) in iron and steel, furniture, and plastic products.

The auto and truck industry continues to assume a central role in Michigan's economy, both through its direct employment effect and through its demand for vehicle parts, capital goods, and a range of producer services. The transport equipment industry is also responsi-

Table 7.
Michigan Manufacturing—Concentration and Employment by Industry, 1991.

Industry	Concentration Ratio (U.S. = 1.0)	Employment
Plastic products	13.023	39,875
Transport equipment	3.19	178,270
Fabricated metal products	2.55	104,392
Iron and steel	2.38	27,108
Furniture and fixtures	2.17	30,187
Machinery (excl. electrical)	2.02	118,498
Glass and glass products	1.72	7,250
Leather products	1.31	2,158
Nonmetalic mineral products n.e.c.	1.27	2,894
Nonferrous metals	1.26	11,017
Other chemicals	1.03	24,706
Printing and publishing	1.01	46,194
Paper and paper products	0.99	20,548
Industrial chemicals	0.89	7,759
Food and kindred products	0.77	34,632
Other manufacturing	0.70	7,918
Rubber products	0.70	5,232
Lumber and wood products	0.65	13,676
Scientific equipment	0.53	15,431
Beverages	0.48	2,627
Apparel	0.45	14,310
Electrical machinery	0.45	21,567
Petroleum and coal products	0.35	1,672
China and pottery	0.26	537
Footwear	0.25	499
Textiles	0.05	1,053

Sources: U.S. Dept. of Commerce, *County Business Patterns, 1991* (Washington, D.C.: GPO, 1991); U.S. Bureau of Labor Statistics, *Employment and Earnings, 1991*, (Washington, D.C.: GPO, 1991).

ble for more than half of the state's exports to both Canada and Mexico. Yet, in terms of employment, it is declining both in Michigan and in the United States as a whole. Much of the recent domestic employment loss in this industry has come through impressive gains in labor productivity and trade with nations outside NAFTA. However, regional trade has augmented net U.S. job losses in the transport equipment industry. One indication of this augmentation is the fact that in recent years the United States has maintained substantial trade deficits with both Mexico and Canada in both road vehicles and parts. Indeed, the deficit with Mexico in vehicle parts is only slightly smaller than the U.S. deficit in this category with Japan, which has been the subject of so much political friction lately. As the shift-share analysis reveals, these job losses and trade imbalances reflect shifts in production to Mexico and Canada, both of which experienced absolute increases in transport equipment employment during 1985-92.

Clearly, employment in Michigan's transport equipment industry remains vulnerable to significant competitive challenges from Canadian and especially Mexican production sites. While the state's total exports to Mexico increased by 51 percent between 1987 and 1991, exports of transport equipment declined,[16] and the peso crisis will aggravate this trend. The possibility that NAFTA could stimulate Michigan transport industry employment always rested on the prospect that the accord would stimulate rapid growth in Mexican income, which in turn would raise Mexican demand for Michigan-produced vehicles.[17] For the time being, this market has collapsed, despite lower Mexican tariff barriers under NAFTA, while the incentive to shift vehicle assembly from Michigan to Mexico to serve the North American market has increased significantly.

A key variable affecting the employment trajectory of Michigan's transport equipment industry will be the extent to which producers of vehicle parts continue to move production to Mexico to supply Mexican and U.S. assembly operations. Apart from the peso depreciation's incentive for such movement, if just-in-time production systems now in vogue in the auto industry are to be fully adopted in Mexico, then the auto companies will likely seek to source parts from sites in or much closer to Mexico than Michigan.

The employment implications of NAFTA for Michigan's two other largest manufacturing industries, fabricated metal products and machinery, are more ambiguous. North American trade in these industries has produced net U.S. job gains, but in recent years the U.S. competitive position relative to Canada and Mexico has eroded. Again, employment in both of these capital goods industries is declining both in Michigan and in the United States. The shift-share analysis indicates that from 1985 to 1992 both Canada and Mexico enjoyed competitive shift employment gains at the expense of U.S. jobs. Yet this accounted for only a small portion of U.S. employment loss in these industries, 6.7 percent in fabricated metals and only 1.4 percent for machinery (excluding electrical). Still, the United States continues to maintain trade surpluses with Mexico and Canada in these categories. Michigan, in particular, has benefited from growing exports in both industries to Canada and, more dramatically, to Mexico. The state's exports of fabricated metal products to Mexico grew from a low base by nearly 600 percent between 1987 and 1991, while exports of industrial machinery roughly doubled. By 1991, Michigan's combined exports to Mexico in these two industries represented 45 percent of the value of the state's exports of transport equipment to that country.[18]

A rise in U.S. foreign investment in Mexico need not curtail, and may increase, Michigan employment in fabricated metal products, machinery, and other capital goods industries, since they produce items used in the establishment of new plants and equipment. Greater foreign investment in Mexico is more likely to enhance the state's employment in capital goods industries if, (1) it represents an expansion of investment rather than a shift of investment that otherwise would have been placed in the United States, and (2) capital goods producers in the state elect to serve the Mexican market from Michigan rather than relocate south of the border. Orders for capital goods tend to be lumpy and irregular. Rather than a steady stream of output for the same clients or general retail markets, capital goods tend to be sold in spurts to a constantly changing range of businesses, as they invest in new plants and equipment. After a sale, there may be no orders from a given customer for an extended period, while the next sale is made to a firm on the other side of the continent. Given the nature of the market, in addition to skilled labor requirements, Michigan's capital goods producers may be less prone to shift operations to Mexico than, for instance, auto suppliers, although there are incentives for doing so, and these may grow.

So far, most Michigan producers of consumer goods have been slower to shift production to Mexico. The pace of future Mexican income growth is especially important for the state's consumer goods industries, including cereal, furniture, baby food, pharmaceuticals, household appliances, and plastic products. This also applies to such Michigan-based retailers as K-Mart Corporation and F & M Distributors, as well as Michigan medical equipment and supplies firms.

It should be recognized that even if NAFTA contributes to net employment loss in certain Michigan industries, it still may benefit Michigan firms in those industries. Sourcing production from Mexico can be expected to lower costs, enhancing market share and profits. Also, while such shifts will decrease the number of domestic production jobs in some industries, they may buttress white-collar and professional employment, which tends to remain at headquarters. Some of these jobs are classified outside manufacturing. Indeed, even in the case of Michigan auto and capital goods firms with production operations in Mexico, most continue to rely on the services of Michigan engineering, design, consulting, and construction firms with which they have established relations. Of course, these favorable developments, coupled with the loss of production jobs, are consistent with the possibility that NAFTA will heighten income inequality in the state.

The net employment effect of NAFTA has always turned on the balance between the potential stimulus to domestic employment from increased access to and growth of the Mexican market, on the one hand, and the threat of job losses associated with the shift of production to Mexico, on the other. Over the medium term, the Mexican financial crisis has severely constrained the former and strengthened the latter influence. Given the dominant role of transport equipment in Michigan's economy and trade with Mexico, the immediate employment effect of North American trade and investment liberalization for Michigan will likely be negative. If and when the Mexican economy resumes sustained growth, however, these setbacks will start to be offset by employment gains.

CONCLUSION

NAFTA represents a significant step in a broad process of economic globalization that encompasses productivity gains due to production specialization, increasing returns to scale, and mechanization of the

labor process. Our analysis indicates that regional trade and investment liberalization have not yet generated net manufacturing
employment displacement from the United States to Mexico. U.S.
manufacturing employment trends are determined primarily by factors that affect regional trends in industry employment, not shifts in
job location within the region. Yet, the pattern of industry-level shifts
in national competitiveness raises concerns about NAFTA's effect on
the quality of available jobs. In general, the United States has lost
competitive advantage in knowledge-intensive industries that provide
good production jobs, while gaining in less technologically progressive industries with lower wages. This, coupled with the differential
effect of NAFTA on production and professional jobs within industries, means that the key issue becomes the distribution of the productivity gains achieved by trade and investment liberalization.

Given the size of the U.S. economy and the relatively small volume of international trade relative to total output, job creation
depends primarily on the rate of economic growth and the characteristics of technical progress. This suggests that policy to improve
employment conditions in the U.S. labor market should target
domestic factors affecting the volume and allocation of industrial
investment. Opposition to trade liberalization is obviously a poor
substitute for strengthening domestic investment. Yet, distributional
issues associated with international economic forces matter. For trade
liberalization not only extends markets and promotes productivity
growth, as business interests are prompt to note, but also undermines
the bargaining position of workers and subnational governments in
their negotiations with firms, and generates uneven spatial patterns
of economic gains and losses.

It is important, therefore, that international public policy initiatives explicitly shape the process of globalization in the direction of
reducing income inequality, disseminating high labor standards, protecting the environment, and creating a strong regime of human
rights both within countries and internationally. On this issue a wide
range of economists, including both NAFTA supporters and opponents, can agree. Indeed, it was NAFTA's alleged weakness on these
counts (not a giant sucking sound) that constituted the most compelling criticisms of the accord all along. Whenever countries with
significantly different levels of economic and political development
embark on trade accords to coordinate public policies and regula-

tions, an opportunity is created for the dissemination of democratic practices and the establishment of an international regulatory system focused on counterbalancing the degenerative and destabilizing effects of a global market economy.[19]

NOTES

1. See Ross Perot, with Pat Choate, *Save Your Job, Save Our Country: Why NAFTA Must Be Stopped—Now!* (New York: Hyperion, 1993).
2. The rationale for this anticipated investment displacement effect was that NAFTA would both spur growth in the Mexican economy and reduce the risk that future Mexican governments would depart from liberalization, thereby increasing the attractiveness to U.S. firms of hiring low-wage Mexican labor to serve both the domestic and export markets. This approach assumes that the increase in U.S. foreign direct investment in Mexico represents a decline of investment in the United States, instead of being partially financed by a shift of U.S. investment from other countries to Mexico. See Timothy Koechlin, Mehrene Larudee, Samuel Bowles, and Gerald Epstein, "Estimates of the Impact of the Free Trade Agreement on Direct U.S. Investment in Mexico," Summary of Testimony to the U.S. Trade Representative Public Hearings on NAFTA, Boston, Mass., 11 September 1991; and Timothy Koechlin and Mehrene Larudee, "The High Cost of NAFTA," *Challenge* (September/October 1992): 19-26.
3. Employment projections from a range of studies are summarized by Congressional Budget Office, *Estimating the Effects of NAFTA: An Assessment of the Economic Models and Other Empirical Studies*, CBO Papers (Washington, D.C.: CBO, June 1993); and Gary C. Hufbauer and Jeffrey Schott, *NAFTA: An Assessment* (Washington, D.C.: Institute for International Economics, 1993). A number of these studies, while supportive of NAFTA, predict no net employment changes. Hufbauer and Schott's employment projections drew criticism when it was revealed that their model's long-term forecast of no net U.S. employment gains was deleted from the published manuscript. The difference between their short-run and long-run predictions turned on the expectation that Mexico's heavy dependence on U.S. factory equipment and other exports would fade over the long term, thereby balancing imports and exports and eliminating the net employment gains by 2010. See Keith Bradsher, "Trade Pact Job Gains Discounted: Forecasters See Just a Short-Term Rise," *New York Times*, 22 February 1993. Of course, this now seems an irrelevant academic quibble in light of the fact that the U.S. trade surplus with Mexico was transformed to a deficit of $15 billion just 18 months after NAFTA went into effect.
4. Mexico's significant moves toward economic liberalization were initiated between 1983 and early 1985. In addition to severe macroeconomic

adjustment (IMF-mandated austerity in the wake of Mexico's international debt crisis) imposed to cut domestic absorption of current production, Mexico also began trade liberalization (reductions in import tariffs and the removal of import licensing), a devaluation of the peso, a move toward greater flexibility in the rules affecting foreign investment, and the selling or closure of a large number of state-owned enterprises. The emphasis on liberalization measures was renewed after July 1985 and again after November 1988. The negotiations leading to NAFTA were part of the third stage in this process of Mexican economic reform. By the time of NAFTA's passage in the fall of 1993, the average level of Mexican tariffs on U.S. goods had fallen to less than 10 percent. The sequencing, scope, and effect of economic reforms in Mexico during the 1980s are discussed in Wilson Peres Nuñez, *Foreign Direct Investment and Industrial Development in Mexico* (Paris: OECD, 1990); Rogelio Ramirez de la O, "Mexico: Economic Outlook in the 1990s," in Sidney Weintraub, Rubio F. Luiz, and Alan D. Jones, eds., *U.S.-Mexican Industrial Integration: The Road to Free Trade* (Boulder, Colo.: Westview Press, 1991); and Jaime Zabludovsky, "Trade Liberalization and Macroeconomic Adjustment," in Dwight S. Brothers and Adele E. Wick, eds., *Mexico's Search for a New Development Strategy* (Boulder, Colo.: Westview Press, 1990).

5. International Labour Office, *Yearbook of Labour Statistics* (Geneva: ILO, 1978-95).

6. See Sidney Weintraub, *Transforming the Mexican Economy: The Salinas Sexenio* (Washington, D.C.: National Planning Association, 1990).

7. See Peres Nunez, *Foreign Direct Investment*.

8. A straightforward calculation demonstrates that U.S. manufacturing job losses are due to strong labor productivity growth coupled with slower growth in output demand. Labor productivity (P) is defined as output (Q) per labor hour (L), that is, $P = Q/L$. Expressing this equation in terms of employment (E) gives: $E = Q/P$. Transforming this expression to growth rates, where lowercase letters represent the annual growth rate of the respective variable, gives $e = q - p$. For the U.S. manufacturing sector between 1978 and 1989, the growth rates of these variables were: employment (labor hours) = -0.4 percent, output = 2.9 percent, and labor productivity = 3.3 percent. (Calculations are based on data in the *Economic Report of the President* [Washington, D.C.: U.S. Government Printing Office, various years])

9. Shift-share analysis is usually applied to the analysis of subnational areas compared to national economic trends. For this international application, we have followed revisions developed by Balbir S. Sihag, and Carol C. McDonough, "Shift-Share Analysis: The International Dimension," *Growth and Change* 20, no. 3 (1989): 80-88. The change in manufacturing employment comprises three factors: national share (NS), industry mix (IM), and competitive shift (CS), and can be represented as

Employment Change$_j$ = NS$_j$ + IM$_j$ + CS$_j$

The notation used to define these three effects is given below, with superscripts referring to periods (year 1 and year 2) or, in the empirical application that follows, 1985 and 1992:

n = total NAFTA manufacturing employment;

e_i = NAFTA employment in industry i;

e_j = manufacturing employment in country j; and

e_{ij} = employment in manufacturing industry i in country j.

The formulation of each of the three components is:

National share$_j$ = $[e_j^1(n^2/n^1)] - e_j^1$;

Industry Mix$_j$ = $[e_{ij}^1 (e_i^2/e_i^1 - n^2/n^1)]$; and

Competitive Shift$_j$ = $\{e_{ij}^2 - (e_{ij}^1[e_i^2/e_i^1])\}$.

10. Some methodological concerns have been raised regarding shift-share analysis. Technical problems such as bias introduced by choice of beginning and end years, the sensitivity of the analysis to choices regarding employment category disaggregation, and insufficient attention to the technique's theoretical underpinnings have been noted by Stephen Fothergill and Graham Gudgin, "In Defense of Shift-Share," *Urban Studies* 16, no. 2 (1979): 309-19; and Benjamin H. Stevens, and Craig L. Moore, "A Critical Review of the Literature on Shift-Share as a Forecasting Technique," *Journal of Regional Science* 20, no. 4 (1980): 419-37. Approaches that minimize some of the most common criticisms are addressed by Richard A. Barff, and Prentice L. Knight, "Dynamic Shift-Share Analysis," *Growth and Change* 19:1-10, who design a dynamic method that avoids the problem of uneven employment changes between chosen periods, and by Stephen D. Casler "A Theoretical Context for Shift and Share Analysis" *Regional Studies* 23, no. 1 (1989): 43-48, who develops the theoretical foundation of the approach. For an international application such as ours, however, it should be noted that the shift-share technique is not directly rooted in factor price equalization theory. An excellent overview is provided by John A. Dawson, *Shift-Share Analysis: A Bibliographic Review of Technique and Applications* (Monticello, Va.: Vance Bibliographies, 1982). Most of the suggestions to improve the technique cannot be used in the present application, given data limitations mainly pertaining to Mexico.

11. Orthodox trade theory assumes balanced trade. Yet, a clear pattern of aggregate competitive shift gains or losses in a country's manufacturing sector is not necessarily inconsistent with the theory, since these gains or losses may be offset by competitive shifts in trade of nonmanufactured goods and services.

12. See Laura Tyson, *Who's Bashing Whom? Trade Conflict in High-Technology Industries* (Washington, D.C.: Institute for International Economics, 1993).

13. See U.S. Department of Commerce, *U.S. Exports to Mexico: A State-by-State Overview, 1987-1991*, (Washington, D.C.: U.S. Government Publications Office, July, 1992).

14. Concentration ratios compare the industrial structure of Michigan's manufacturing employment to that of the United States as a whole. For each industry i,

$$\text{Concentration ratio}_i = (e_i^{mi}/e^{mi})/(e_i^{us}/e^{us}).$$

15. The composition of the industry designated machinery (excluding electrical), ISIC 382, is sometimes the subject of confusion. It does not refer to machines that do not use electrical power, but instead to those that are not electric motors, generators, electrical transmission and distribution equipment, and telecommunications equipment. Machinery (excluding electrical) includes the manufacture of engines, agricultural machinery and equipment, metal- and woodworking machines, and office computing and accounting machinery.

16. See U.S. Department of Commerce, *U.S. Exports to Mexico*.

17. Some projections by NAFTA proponents were, in retrospect, wildly off the mark. The Hudson Institute, for example, predicted that the Mexican market for vehicles would grow from 300,000 to at least one million in the first year after NAFTA implementation. See Alan Reynolds, "Opposition to Free Trade Hurts U.S. Industry: Comment," *Detroit News*, 7 April 1991, 3B.

18. See U.S. Department of Commerce, *U.S. Exports to Mexico*.

19. The authors wish to acknowledge the excellent research assistance of Jessica Davis, Vince Frillici, and Karla Simon.

Appendix A.
Shift-Share Analysis for the NAFTA Region, 1985-1992 (employment change in thousands).

Industry	United States			Canada			Mexico		
	NS	IM	CS	NS	IM	CS	NS	IM	CS
Food manufacturing	-94.3	167.7	30.6	-13.2	23.5	-27.3	-6.5	11.6	-3.4
Beverages	-14.5	-6.1	-15.3	-2.2	-0.9	-6.7	-4.9	-2.1	22.1
Tobacco products	-4.3	-10.0	-0.6	-0.5	-1.1	-0.4	-0.4	-0.9	1.0
Textiles	-47.7	-11.0	34.7	-5.3	-1.2	-26.3	-5.1	-1.2	-8.4
Apparel	-76.2	-31.3	4.5	-5.9	-2.4	-3.7	-2.4	-1.0	-0.8
Leather products	-4.0	-33.5	-2.1	-0.4	-3.8	2.1	0.0	0.0	0.0
Footwear	-7.2	-54.4	-9.4	-1.0	-7.7	3.9	-1.1	-8.5	5.5
Wood products	-48.4	24.8	-1.4	-6.4	3.3	2.7	-0.4	0.2	-1.3
Furniture and fixtures	-33.6	1.8	2.7	-3.3	0.2	-3.0	-0.5	0.0	0.3
Paper products	-45.6	46.7	15.8	-7.9	8.1	-14.5	-2.2	2.2	-1.3
Printing and publishing	-97.0	195.9	-5.9	-7.8	15.7	7.1	-0.8	1.5	-1.2
Industrial chemicals	-36.2	-28.3	-16.4	-2.1	-1.6	-0.4	-7.5	-5.9	16.9
Other chemicals	-34.7	128.4	14.3	-4.1	15.4	-15.8	-0.1	0.5	1.5
Petroleum refineries	-9.6	-16.9	1.5	-1.5	-2.6	-1.5	0.0	0.0	0.0
Misc. petroleum and coal products	-2.6	0.6	1.9	-0.1	0.0	-0.9	-0.3	0.1	-1.0
Rubber products	-18.5	-8.9	7.4	-1.8	-0.9	-7.4	0.0	0.0	0.0
Plastic products	-37.2	104.1	13.1	-2.6	7.2	-5.4	-3.3	9.3	-7.7
Pottery and china	-2.6	1.3	-0.6	-0.2	0.1	-0.8	-0.4	0.2	1.4
Glass products	-7.3	-0.7	0.0	-0.8	-0.1	-2.9	-1.5	-0.1	2.8
Nonmetallic mineral products	-28.0	-11.3	10.3	-2.1	-0.8	-8.9	-2.3	-0.9	-1.4
Iron and steel	-30.2	-63.3	24.5	-4.1	-8.6	-9.1	-4.6	-9.6	-15.3
Non-ferrous metals	-24.7	-15.9	4.6	-3.0	-1.9	-3.2	-1.3	-0.8	-1.4
Fabricated metal products	-99.5	-21.8	-8.7	-8.8	-1.9	8.4	-3.1	-0.7	0.2
Machinery (excl. electrical)	-149.2	-97.3	-3.5	-6.6	-4.3	0.9	-2.7	-1.8	2.6
Electrical machinery	-126.4	-144.2	-40.4	-7.4	-8.5	34.0	-6.0	-6.8	6.4
Transport equipment	-133.2	36.1	-35.9	-12.3	3.3	22.0	-7.6	2.0	13.9
Scientific equipment	-71.0	-27.4	-3.6	-2.0	-0.8	3.6	0.0	0.0	0.0
Other manufacturing	-24.9	-122.3	-20.8	-2.8	-13.6	18.5	-0.8	-3.9	2.2

Source: Authors' calculations using International Labour Office statistics.

NAFTA's Meaning for Michigan: Transnational Integration and Local Competitive Strategies

Richard Child Hill and Kuniko Fujita

What does NAFTA mean for Michigan? NAFTA encourages cross-national relations among companies and local areas in the United States, Canada, and Mexico. Public officials in all three nations will increasingly calculate comparative advantage and economic progress by the trade and production status their local industries achieve in the North American regional economy. The policy challenge is finding the right framework for sustained and equitable growth among North American localities, given trends toward transnational regional integration. Our research on local Japanese political-economic ties to the East Asia region leads us to believe Michigan would benefit from a North American linkages strategy.

GLOBALIZATION

The world political economy is reorganizing from Cold War bipolarity to a multilateral system of regional blocs. Clusters of adjacent nations are reducing barriers among themselves to facilitate trade, investment, and labor flows.[1] Regional agreements enable transnational corporations (TNCs) to further integrate economic production across national borders. Forty percent of world trade now takes place inside TNCs.[2]

Globalization is occurring around three regional poles with many subregional cross-border networks. The United Nations Centre for Transnational Corporations (UNCTC) has examined the emerging triad organization of the world economy as revealed in patterns of foreign direct investment (FDI). U.S. companies target FDI to Latin America and the Caribbean, with lesser flows to Asia and Africa. Japan's FDI flows mainly into East Asia. European Community firms dominate FDI in Central and Eastern Europe and Africa, with lesser participation in Latin America, Asia, and the Pacific.[3]

REGIONAL DIVISIONS OF LABOR

Ideally, transnational divisions of labor should complement and strengthen comparative advantage among all participants in a regional commodity chain. Cross-national regional investment should upgrade the industrial structure in host and home localities and accelerate trade among them. A core-periphery division of labor based upon hierarchical, nonreciprocal relationships among localities does not meet the complementarity criterion. Less developed areas, dependent on core TNCs for all factors of production save cheap labor, are constrained from moving to higher levels of industrialization by technological weakness and small domestic markets.[4]

A competitive regional division of labor—when countries, regardless of development level, attempt to move into the same capital- and technology-intensive manufacturing activities while simultaneously protecting their mature sunset industries—also fails the complementarity test. TNCs promote this kind of zero-sum specialization when they simultaneously produce the same products and competing models in several regions.[5] This practice weakens the logic of comparative advantage, generates excess capacity, and deepens economic friction among localities.

THE LOW AND THE HIGH ROAD

The division of labor among areas in a region—whether complementary, competitive, or dependent—shapes possibilities for local development. Two paths can be identified.[6]

The high road is a complementary regional division of labor. It expands trade and investment, thereby providing the wherewithal for upgrading worker skills and the technical capacities of small supplier firms. Mass production is jettisoned in favor of flexible specialization that helps to integrate forward and backward production linkages, boost productivity, and raise wages and incomes.[7] Most workers and suppliers are included in efforts to improve quality and create new products and processes.

The low road is a competitive or dependent regional division of labor. It generates uneven investment, geographically dispersed forward and backward production linkages, and contracts markets. It results in lower growth in productivity, wages and incomes, and it provides less incentive for innovation.

Herzenberg has outlined two scenarios for the North American auto industry.[8] His high-road vision forecasts integrated concentrations of high-tech, high-skill assembly and supplier plants in Ontario, the north-central and southern United States, and northern Mexico and the Mexico City area. U.S. auto assemblers and suppliers experience stable employment and modest wage growth. Mexico's employment also grows, with rising wages and an expanding domestic market. Enhanced North American performance reduces the trade deficit with Japan.

In the low-road model, Mexico becomes a low-wage, low-skill production base. Company relocation to Mexico, or the threat of it, thwarts efforts to shift to flexible production and more cooperative relations among U.S. assemblers, suppliers, and workers. The intense wage competition spreads to Canada. New assembly plants in all three nations become high-tech islands surrounded by smaller supplier firms competing on low compensation costs. The trade deficit with Japan persists, particularly in high-value parts. Low productivity growth limits wage increases throughout North America, thereby limiting market expansion in Mexico. Limited markets and import competition reduce North American auto employment.

DYNAMIC COMPARATIVE ADVANTAGE

Regional industrial organization is shaped by combined business-government strategies. The UNCTC has investigated the effect of global markets and integrated international production on local competitiveness.[9] In a closed economy, firm traits determine competitiveness. In an open, arm's length trading economy, national capabilities determine competitiveness. In a world economy characterized by integrated international production, the competitiveness of a firm depends on the combined locational advantages of each of the nations in which it has affiliates. Therefore, the competitiveness of companies and governments becomes increasingly interdependent.

Virtually every activity along a TNC's value chain—finance, parts production, research and development, accounting, procurement, training, distribution—can be performed in a different geographical location, depending upon what configuration contributes most to the profitability of the entire corporate system. Ford Motor Company's plant in Hermosillo, Mexico, is an example. Ford, in association with Mazda, created the product in its world design studio, trained the Mexican workers in Spain and Japan, and markets the car in the United States.[10]

As enterprise expansion brings previously distinct production activities and geographical units in two or more countries under one corporate roof, competition centers upon government policies and local institutions directly affecting the production process, as revealed, for example, in the recent U.S.-Japanese Structural Impediments Initiatives. Upgrading auto workers' skills and the technical capacities of smaller suppliers can best be achieved through regionally coordinated trade, investment, and industrial relations policies. Otherwise, progress in industrial relations, sourcing, and network building may be confined to a few large assembler and supplier companies.

EAST ASIA'S FLYING GEESE

The world's closest approximation to a complementary regional division of labor is found in East Asia, in relationships among Japan, the Asian NICs (South Korea, Taiwan, Hong Kong, and Singapore), and the ASEAN Four (Thailand, Malaysia, Indonesia, and the Philippines). East Asian national economies continue to grow at a rapid pace despite the economic slowdown in the rest of the world. The region's growth rate will likely double the average of the industrialized world over the last quarter of this century.[11]

A variety of research suggests that East Asian countries are linked, like geese flying in V formation, by innovation and catch-up product cycles and by stages of specialization among and within product sectors.[12] Japan is now the center of product and process innovation in sophisticated, knowledge-intensive manufacturing; the Asian NICs are engaged in a catch-up product cycle, importing advanced manufacturing from Japan and exporting simpler manufacturing to the ASEAN Four. The latter are lower-rung players in the catch-up product cycle, importing capital-intensive manufacturing from Japan and the Asian NICs and exporting primary commodities and light manufacturing.[13]

As Japanese firms develop new products, they shift domestic production to the higher value-added innovations to maintain a leading market position. They simultaneously use their electronic and process technologies to continuously improve production organization. Product diversification broadens the range of consumer choices, rising productivity reduces prices, and both stimulate domestic demand and new export markets. More mature technologies are transferred to the Asian NICs and the ASEAN countries. Japan's domestic demand for the products of transferred technology are met by imports. This division of labor, flying geese analysts argue, is promoting industrialization in the Asian NICs and ASEAN countries while enabling Japan to maintain a leading economic position in the region.[14]

Product cycle sequences and development stages are guided by potential comparative advantage. National governments intervene in the market to guide production indirectly through taxes and subsidies and directly through public enterprises and local content legislation, and they learn from one another's industrial policy experiences.[15]

Advocates of the flying geese model acknowledge that it is based upon unequal technological capacities among nations, but they argue that the flying geese approach offers the best hope for negotiating competing national interests and stabilizing relations among economies that are unequal in size and stage of development through a system of "agreed specialization." This view further assumes a strong state in relation to transnational corporations and selective controls over direct investment outflow that encourage trade.[16]

OSAKA'S ASIA LINKAGES

Our recent field research in the City of Osaka and Osaka Prefecture (the closest Japanese approximation to state government) indicates that Japanese officials formulate local development policies with flying geese divisions of labor in mind.

Energy crises and currency appreciation have repeatedly threatened Japan's economy since the 1960s. Yet most localities have reorganized their industries and prevented the withering of their manufacturing base. The City of Osaka, Japan's second largest manufacturing economy, maintained a steady level of employment between 1975 and 1990. While manufacturing jobs declined slightly, from 31.5 percent to 25.5 percent of total employment, jobs in services rose to compensate.[17]

Osaka's successful restructuring strategy is based upon investigations of the city's changing position in the international division of labor and Japan's changing geopolitical role in the world system. Osakans believe their comparative advantage now lies in deepening their historic ties with Pacific Rim nations. The industrial strategies of the city and prefecture target the problems facing small- and medium-sized producers and are framed within a more encompassing national development model.

The Japanese view their nation as a tapestry of regional economies, each radiating out from a city or network of cities. Each region possesses a historically unique mix of industries, worker skills, and educational institutions. As globalization of the Japanese economy progresses, and as cross-national competition among regions intensifies, local areas are developing industrial strategies targeted to their regional strengths.

Manufacturing still matters in Japan. Osaka's officials are as preoccupied with industrial policies as they are with land use and the built environment. They expend an uncommon amount of effort thinking through and articulating an economic vision for their city. In their view, Osaka's continued economic vitality is linked to East Asian regional integration. Their Asian linkages strategy differs from, yet complements, that of other major urban areas in Japan and stakes out their city's comparative advantages in the world economy.

Economic restructuring is done by private firms, but because the Japanese are great believers in following the product cycle, government officials fashion policies to help local businesses trade and invest abroad and upgrade their product and process technologies at home. City bureaucrats routinely survey, think through, disseminate information about, and develop policies to improve the functional and spatial linkages among businesses that compose their industrial base.

Osaka's industrial strategies target small- and medium-sized businesses (SMBs).[18] Since most of the components assembled by larger firms into final products are produced by SMBs, the international competitiveness of Osaka's big companies depends directly on the performance of local SMBs. With the transition from mass production to flexible specialization, more initiative in developing new product and process technologies is now passing to small companies.[19]

Japanese SMBs, like those in other nations, tend to pay lower wages, have less access to capital, possess less managerial depth, marshall fewer resources for research and development, and have more limited marketing ability than do large companies. Core manufacturing technologies, including CNC machine tools, computer-aided design, and modern methods for quality management, production planning, and inventory control, are less widely deployed among SMBs than among large companies.

Development officials in Osaka are attempting to narrow the gap between large and small companies by helping SMBs become more network oriented, high-value oriented, research-and-development oriented, and globally oriented. In league with trade associations, Osaka's local officials are fostering networks of SMBs by bringing them together around shared services: market forecasting, quality control, training, materials purchasing, and information technologies, including how to set up and run in-house and intercompany information networks.[20]

Networks help SMBs continuously improve their competitive edge.[21] Networks also help anchor SMBs to the city. When firms rely on the public provision of networking services, their survival depends upon community prosperity, and they are more likely to identify with the local political community.[22]

Strong institutional ties, encapsulated in third-sector organizations and study commissions, bind together private industry, various levels of government, and universities. The Osaka Prefectural Institute for Advanced Industry Development regularly surveys local companies and monitors local industries' changing niche in the international division of labor. The institute also surveys current and planned FDI by city firms and anticipates its effect on local SMBs.

The Osaka Prefectural Institute for Advanced Industry Development exemplifies the blurred boundaries among government, business, and the third sector, which facilitates institutional coordination in Japan.[23] The institute conducts basic research on industrial policy for the prefectural government, but it is housed in the Chamber of Commerce and Industry, a third-sector organization. Sixty people work for the institute, 40 on a permanent basis, 20 on temporary appointment from the government.[24]

Institute findings help city officials decide upon financial assistance and networking policies to help SMBs make transitions to higher-value production. During the period of our field research, institute researchers were conducting a study of the international division of labor between Osaka and other East Asian locales in the metal and machinery industries, focusing particularly on the effect on Osaka SMBs of organization and location changes in the production of bicycles, bicycle parts, spectacle parts, and screws.[25]

The city also facilitates international business networking through annual conferences on global business opportunities. These information-oriented trade fairs encourage local imports and manufacturing investments in other countries by matching up business interests. Most participants are small, independent companies. Those foreign firms participating are usually seeking Japanese technology and investment partners.[26]

In contrast to Western industrial localities, Osaka's manufacturing FDI has not hollowed out the city's industrial base. Japanese FDI has been accompanied by a "conscious and concentrated policy of upgrading the industrial and technological structure of Japan's economy."[27] The Japanese have played the game of catching up with the more advanced industrial countries, and they are acutely aware of their own vulnerability to competition from other nations on the Asian Pacific Rim. Unlike their Western counterparts, Osaka development officials take it for granted that transfer of capital and technology overseas must be connected to a strategy of industrial restructuring at home.

WHITHER MICHIGAN?

Parallels to Japanese economic strategizing exist in the United States, of course. The neo-Progressive wing of the Democratic Party has favored small business modernization policies since the early 1980s.[28] Michigan has been a leader in that regard. During Governor James Blanchard's administration, the state formulated an industrial strategy to deploy new technology to smaller manufacturing companies in industries linked to automobile production, such as plastics, primary and fabricated metals, and machinery.[29] To help SMBs adopt advanced manufacturing technologies and procedures, the state's Department of Commerce created a comprehensive industrial extension agency, the Michigan Modernization Service (MMS). It was subsequently housed in Ann Arbor in a new third-sector think tank, the Industrial Technology Institute (ITI), devoted to industrial modernization.

The Engler administration eliminated the MMS, and the ITI now survives in a more privatized form. Concerns about industrial modernization continue unabated, however. Doug Ross, who headed the Michigan Department of Commerce during the creation of MMS and ITI, is now formulating vocational training programs for the Clinton administration. National groups like the Modernization Forum organize constituencies and lobby for policies to modernize small firms. Congress has funded several regional technology deployment centers (one is housed in ITI) through the National Institute for Standards and Technology (NIST). There is no shortage of people, ideas, and practical wisdom to draw upon in the United States.

The United States differs from Japan, however, in this regard: local industrial strategies are still in the experimental stage, and organizations advocating industrial modernization still have the look and feel of social movements. In Japan, the need to mount local industrial strategies is taken for granted. Mechanisms for marshalling information and financial resources in support of local industrial objectives are in place. Policy coordination among levels of government and between government and business is institutionalized. Industrial policies are routinely applied and evaluated.

Michigan's economic future still hinges on manufacturing. The state could do worse than take a cue from Osaka by emphasizing industrial as well as land-use and built environment policy; by formulating local industrial strategies connected to analyses of potential comparative advantages in the North American division of labor; by promoting SMB modernization through the provision of hub services that help SMBs form networks to share resources and risks, as well as upgrade their product and process technologies; and by establishing advanced urban industrial research institutes that continuously survey, analyze, and publicize changing local business practices and needs and help SMBs keep in touch with changing regional markets.

There are major barriers to this kind of approach in the United States, of course, not the least of which is the legacy of U.S. hegemony in the world, including a preoccupation with geopolitics over economic interest, and a laissez-faire rather than an economic strategy outlook.[30] International competition is pressuring the United States to become more in step with Japan and the EC; eventually, a new partnership among federal, state, and local governments will be required. In the future, while the federal government engages in macroeconomic fiscal and monetary policy, more states and localities will likely be engaging in microeconomic intervention with regional comparative advantage in mind.

NOTES

1. More than one hundred cross-national regional pacts have been identified recently. See Klaus Schwab and Claude Smadja, "Power and Policy: The New Economic World Order," *Harvard Business Review* 72, no. 6 (1994): 40-52.
2. Dennis Encarnation, *Rivals beyond Trade* (Ithaca, N.Y.: Cornell University Press, 1992).
3. United Nations Centre for Transnational Corporations (UNCTC), *World Investment Report 1991: Transnational Corporations and Integrated Production* (New York: United Nations, 1991); also see Kenichi Ohmae, *Triad Power* (New York: Macmillan, 1985).
4. Gary Gereffi, "Capitalism, Development and Global Commodity Chains," in Leslie Sklair, ed., *Capitalism and Development* (London: Routledge, 1994), 211-31.
5. General Motors, for example, simultaneously produces the Chevrolet Celebrity in Oklahoma City; Ramos Arizpe, Mexico; and St. Therese, Quebec. The Ramos Arizpe plant has a unit cost advantage of $700-$1,000 over the other plants, putting pressure on U.S. and Canadian workers to conform to production conditions in the Mexican plant. See Stephen Baker, David Woodruff, and David and Elizabeth Weiner, "Detroit South: Mexico's Auto Boom: Who Wins, Who Loses," *Business Week*, 16 March 1992, 98-103.

6. Commission on the Skills of the American Workforce, *America's Choice: High Skills or Low Wages?* (Rochester, N.Y.: National Center on Education and the Economy, 1990).

7. Mass production methods lower costs by minimizing product diversity and maximizing economies of scale. Flexible specialization—the production of high-quality models in relatively low volumes—achieves efficiencies through spatial agglomeration and just-in-time (JIT) delivery logistics. Greater flexibility in deployment of equipment and labor improves quality. JIT synchronization of delivery to the assembly line enhances productivity by reducing inventories, waste, plant size, and energy costs. See Michael Cusumano, *Manufacturing Innovation and Competitive Advantage: Reflections on the Japanese Automobile Industry* (Cambridge, Mass.: Sloan School of Management, 1988).

8. Stephen Herzenberg, "Continental Free Trade and the Future of the North American Auto Sector: Regionally Integrated High Wage Production or Islands of Automation Amid a Sea of Low Wage Production?" (Washington, D.C.: Bureau of International Labor Affairs, U.S. Department of Labor, 23 July 1991).

9. UNCTC, *World Investment Report 1993: Transnational Corporations and Integrated Production* (New York: United Nations, 1993).

10. Louis Uchitelle, "Northern Mexico Becomes a Big Draw for High-Tech Plants—and U.S. Jobs," *New York Times*, 21 March 1993, sec. F, pp. 1, 14.

11. Thomas Duesterberg, "Trade, Investment, and Engagement in the U.S.-East Asia Relationship," *Washington Quarterly* 17, no. 1 (1993): 73-90.

12. See, for example, Bundo Yamada, *International Strategies of Japanese Electronics Companies: Implications for Asian Newly Industrializing Economies* (Paris: OECD, 1990); Ministry of International Trade and Industry, *White Paper on International Trade* (Tokyo: MITI, 1992); Richard F. Doner, "Japanese Foreign Investment and the Creation of a Pacific Asian Region," in Jeffrey A. Frankel and Miles Kahler, eds., *Regionalism and Rivalry: Japan and the United States in Pacific Asia* (Chicago: University of Chicago Press, 1993), 159-214; Richard Child Hill and Yong Joo Lee, "Japanese Multinationals and East Asian Development: The Case of the Automobile Industry," in Leslie Sklair, ed., *Capitalism and Development* (London: Routledge, 1994), 289-315.

13. Hirohisa Kohama, "Japan's Economic Development and Foreign Trade," in Chung H. Lee and Ippei Yamazawa, eds., *The Economic Development of Japan and Korea* (New York: Praeger, 1990), 3-18.

14. Ippei Yamazawa, *Economic Development and International Trade: The Japanese Model* (Honolulu: The East-West Center, 1990).

15. See, for example, Edward K. Y. Chen, "Foreign Direct Investment in East Asia," *Asia Development Review* 11, no. 1 (1993): 24-59; and Ryuichiro Inoue, Hirohisa Kohama, and Shujiro Urata, eds., *Industrial Policy in East Asia* (Tokyo: Japan External Trade Organization, 1993).

16. Kiyoshi Kojima, *Japan and a New World Economic Order* (Boulder, Colo.: Westview Press, 1977).

17. Osaka City, *The Contemporary Situation of Osaka City* (Osaka: Mayors Office, 1992), 14.

18. The Ministry of International Trade and Industry (MITI) is responsible for national industrial policy. City governments and prefectures usually focus on small-business policies, including various kinds of loans and subsidies. Interview with Asuo Kawasaki, Professor of Economics, Yokkaichi University, and former Osaka Prefecture development official, Osaka, 1 October 1992.

19. Tadao Kiyonari, "Restructuring Urban-Industrial Links in Greater Tokyo: Small Producers' Responses to Changing World Markets," in Kuniko Fujita and Richard Child Hill, eds., *Japanese Cities in the World Economy* (Philadelphia: Temple University Press, 1993), 141-58.

20. The experience of Japanese cities corroborates findings from Western Europe that small firms can escape the limitations of size when they collaborate in networks and combine into industrial districts. See Charles Sabel, "Flexible Specialization and the Reemergence of Regional Economies," in *Reversing Industrial Decline? Industrial Structure and Policy in Britain and Her Competitors*, Paul Hirst and Jonathan Zeitlin, eds., 17-70 (Oxford: Berg, 1989).

21. Small suppliers in large Japanese cities faced a crisis after the steep currency appreciation in 1985 drove up land prices and encouraged the outsourcing of parts. Many big companies moved mass-production facilities abroad and concentrated on new product development in Japan. Production of standardized parts also was shifted to the Asian NICs. Networks help small businesses meet the new product development challenge through continuous upgrading, while continuous improvement protects the small producer from international competition. Interview with Takashi Murakoso, Associate Research Director, Osaka Prefectural Institute for Advanced Industry Development, Osaka, 15 October 1992. This feature of the Japanese production system is often overlooked in discussions of Japanese-style capitalism.

22. Sabel, "Flexible Specialization," 17-70.

23. Daniel Okimoto, *Between MITI and the Market* (Stanford, Calif.: Stanford University Press, 1989).

24. Interview with Yasuda Yutaka, Section Chief, Planning, Osaka Prefectural Institute for Advanced Industry Development, 1 October 1992.

25. Interview with Takashi Murakoso, cited in note 21 above.

26. The Osaka Chamber of Commerce and Industry has been holding these meetings since 1983. The 1992 conference attracted 870 people from 44 countries along with 3,000 Japanese companies. Interview with Sugimoto Michio, Director, Osaka Chamber of Commerce and Industry, 5 October 1992.

27. Tessa Morris-Suzuki, "Reshaping the International Division of Labor: Japanese Manufacturing Investment in Southeast Asia," in *Japan and the Global Economy*, Jonathan Morris, ed., 135-55 (London: Routledge, 1991).

28. David Osborne, *Laboratories of Democracy* (Boston, Mass.: Harvard University Business School Press, 1988).
29 State of Michigan, *The Path to Prosperity* (Lansing: Michigan Department of Commerce, 1984).
30. Clyde V. Prestowitz, Jr., and Robert B. Cohen, *The New North American Order* (Washington, D.C.: The Economic Strategy Institute, 1991).

Free Trade, Social Policy, and Family Policy: A Michigan Perspective

Lynn Duggan

Although predictions of welfare state retrenchment have been hotly debated within the political science field since the early 1970s, only recently have social expenditure reductions gained enough momentum for this trend to be documented. Developments in the United States, Canada, New Zealand, Australia, and Great Britain leave little doubt that retrenchments have occurred, although the duration and extent of this trend remain unclear.[1]

Within economics the literature on welfare states has focused increasingly on the question of what types of policy are "affordable" now that the older industrial countries, loosely termed "the North," must compete with newly industrial countries in the East and South. National social policies, defined here as those designed to change the distribution of resources that would be generated by free markets, are essentially believed to be in competition. Countries with policies that foster high levels of productivity and earnings, and that attract corporate investment, "win" in this competition.

Among economists, neoclassical theorists exclude questions of political power from their cost-benefit models, while political economists maintain, as this author does, that a society's understanding of affordability is shaped by the relative power of its diverse groups. Social policy structures income and power relationships among market actors and between the market and nonmarket spheres of a society. The resulting distributions influence future policy options.

The decisions of social policy makers are based on assumptions as to which individuals or groups should be allowed to carry out which transactions at the expense of other individuals or groups (measured in goods, services, and relative power). The chosen policy mix determines which "growing pains" of marketization and globalization will be redistributed and whether redistribution will take place at the local, regional, national, or trade bloc level.

Economists of all persuasions agree that national borders have become increasingly irrelevant to production, trade, and, especially, finance, resulting in an effective "globalization" of nations into one large market in which actors are increasingly rewarded for economically "rational" behavior.[2] Economists disagree, however, on the inevitability of this trend. Some believe that states determine the form, direction, and fact of the globalization of economies, while others regard the market as a natural entity, above governments.

If states are curtailing and dismantling social programs, ostensibly to increase their competitiveness, this disassembly process will not be the exact inverse of the procedure that put such policies in place. In order to evaluate likely outcomes of the subtle processes in play, it is essential that policy makers begin as early as possible to chart the course of apparent trends.

This chapter sketches the history of social spending in welfare states and describes mechanisms through which globalization of national economies may affect the curtailment of social programs. It outlines changes in incomes and social spending along age and gender lines and summarizes current trends in labor markets and families. The effectiveness of social policy must be measured in relation to these trends.

In the absence of information regarding the duration of current trends and the future of social policy, we may be able to gain insight by looking at the apparent policy drift of regions that have experienced substantial economic restructuring due to competition from abroad. To this end, this chapter includes a brief case study of the state of Michigan. The world's foremost automobile-producing region until the 1970s, Michigan has been substantially affected by global competition, with automobile industry employment reduced by more than 25 percent since the late 1970s.[3] This massive restructuring of Michigan's economy has been accompanied by substantial changes in social policy, including reform of welfare (Aid to Families with Dependent Children) and reductions in other programs. Social policy as currently practiced in Michigan may be a precursor of the new trend in U.S. as well as global social policy.

It has been widely argued that national regulation of market economies must be replaced by international regulation. While I agree with this, I maintain here that effective policy for market regulation, whether national or global, requires a more thorough analysis of the relationship between market and nonmarket production.[4]

FREE TRADE, COMPETITIVENESS, AND SOCIAL POLICY

A long line of interdisciplinary thinkers in the tradition of Karl Polanyi has argued that economies cannot be separated from their social and cultural contexts. Instead of viewing government intervention as external to an economy, advocates of this approach assert that laws as well as social and political norms provide the framework within which market forces operate and are regarded as legitimate, as these establish the latitude of economic actors to engage in self-interested behavior. Along these lines, Reinicke asserts that international competition to reduce production costs does not represent a globalization of market economies, but only a globalization of production.[5] A global economy would require international agreement on social and legal norms and mechanisms, political forces and institutions, and ecological and resource constraints that would structure exchanges of labor, products, and resources. Free trade and capital mobility are just two of the myriad changes necessary in order to transform many national economies into a global one.

In the absence of such international agreements to define boundaries for the spread of markets, nation-states' integration into global markets has brought with it at least three phenomena that curtail governments' ability to pursue social policy objectives. First, dramatically intensified international competition in production has resulted in new systems of manufacturing that have reduced many older industrial nations' exports relative to imports. Lower demand for products and technological change that is in part a response to international competition has resulted in mass layoffs in previously well-paid jobs. Governments' income and payroll tax revenues are reduced, while the need for assistance grows among those affected by restructuring.

Second, the lifting of controls on financial capital and foreign exchange has increased the ease with which capital may exit a nation's economy in anticipation of rising inflation or falling interest rates, not to mention lower profit rates.[6] Consequently, greater capital mobility and currency speculation have reduced governments' ability to use expansionary fiscal policy.[7] The result is a worldwide "deflationary bias." Individual governments are forced to err on the side of lower spending in order to avoid debt and inflation, with the result of yet more unemployment and less social spending.

Third, competition among national and regional governments for corporate investment (to provide employment) has resulted in a tendency for jurisdictions to offer increasingly lucrative subsidies and tax exemptions to firms; this downward pressure on tax revenues means that less funding is available for social policy. As Bowles and Gintis point out:

> The result of a successful implementation of the global liberal model is a competition among dozens of nation-states, each seeking to maintain employment and promote economic growth, and each thus constrained to promote a favorable business climate in order to attract international capital. The state is thereby reduced to the equivalent of the perfectly competitive firm in neoclassical economics.[8]

This brings us to the main concern of this chapter. As borders become increasingly permeable, industries and whole economies restructure in response to new competition and export advantages, resulting in new pressures for governments to buffer vulnerable groups from undesirable effects of globalization.[9] Yet governments are less able to respond to these groups with protective policies or programs because of the downward pressures on social policy that globalization brings with it. It is governments' responsibility, however, to decide when and how to redistribute the costs and benefits that follow from the opening of national borders. This responsibility entails decisions concerning the degree to which domestic nonmarket actors should be protected from international market actors.

Western European countries view social protection as an inherent aspect of their integration into the European Union (EU), the trade bloc of 15 nations that aims eventually to become one economy with a single currency. To avoid competition among EU members for mobile corporate activities, the European Commission has set a ceiling on public expenditures that its member states may offer to firms.

The EU's Social Charter sets a floor for working conditions, and European Commission directives require members to provide, for example, 14 weeks of paid maternity leave and to undertake pay equity adjustments.

The Europeans are not immune to the pressures of free trade on social policy, however. The Maastricht Treaty's condition of financial discipline introduces a deflationary bias in macroeconomic policy (similar to that described above) that will continue after the monetary union is in place, due to the pressures of world financial markets. Member nations will only qualify for core European Monetary Union membership if they reduce their budget deficits to below 3 percent of Gross Domestic Product and cut government debt to less than 60 percent of GDP. In order to meet these conditions, European governments have implemented tax increases and have sold government-owned enterprises, but these measures will not reduce budget shortfalls permanently.[10] Due to a lack of public support for social policy cuts, France and Great Britain each ran deficits amounting to 6 percent of GDP last year, twice the Maastricht goal.[11] Western European governments are gradually trimming social policy at the margin and drifting toward privatization of service delivery and pensions.[12]

A social charter similar to Europe's is not on the agenda for the NAFTA countries.[13] In fact, although Canadians are increasingly concerned about their government's waning commitment to social entitlement programs, discussion of government's role in evening the playing field among economic actors is largely missing in the United States. When it takes place, it focuses mainly on the need to retrain manufacturing workers, the old and mostly male "labor aristocracy" that enjoyed extensive social insurance in the primary welfare tier. The mainstream U.S. media provide little or no discussion of international or interregional floors and ceilings for tax rates and government subsidies to firms.

It is precisely in the United States, among states and other tax jurisdictions, that the competition for corporate investment projects, noted above, has become prevalent. Economists of diverse political and theoretical biases, including Paul Krugman and John Kenneth Galbraith, disapprove of this practice, whether it is regional or international. Krugman notes its distortionary effects on resource allocation, and Galbraith laments its restraining effect on government redistributions and activity in general.[14] Although the lucrative incentives packages offered by governments to firms are reported to play a minor role in firms' location decisions, they often swing final decisions among firms' top geographic choices. Most important, they are believed to do so.[15] Capital is viewed as coming from outside tax jurisdictions, to be wooed in, or as requiring persuasion to remain in a state.

Economic theory has not yet developed tools to analyze this growing problem, but concepts found in the literature on corporate bidding for government contracts may be useful in analyzing government bids for corporate investment. One such concept, the notion of the "winner's curse," holds that the winning bid for a contract often exceeds the true value of the contract.[16] Government is, moreover, not subject to a hard budget constraint in contrast to firms, as its capacity to pay is limited only by its ability to tax the populace. If most of that constituency sees corporate investment as the key to its region's economic dynamism, the result is a reversal of power from governments to corporations. According to Chuck Collins, whereas corporate taxes made up one-third of U.S. tax revenues in 1953, they account for less than 10 percent of revenues today.[17]

A look at the trend in recent automobile investment projects shows a rapid escalation since 1980 in states' recruitment costs. According to Milward and Newman, who studied six of the largest recruiting targets, both the costs of industrial recruitment and the number of states offering incentives to new auto assembly facilities have risen rapidly. In 1980, the Nissan project that Tennessee "won" cost $11,000 in public funds (including tax exemptions) per job that the project created. Tennessee's recruitment of the Saturn Corporation five years later cost $26,000 per new job.[18] By 1993, Mercedes Benz agreed to locate operations in Alabama at a cost to that state of $150,000 to $200,000 per job.[19] South Carolina recently paid $110,000 per job for the BMW plant in Spartanburg.[20]

It is no simple task to assess the costs of states' competition for investment, as only half of them require "tax expenditure" budgets to be compiled. In addition, only about a dozen of these budgets provide sufficient information to calculate the amounts given away to business through tax incentives.[21] The federal Office of Management and Budget estimates that credits, deductions, and exemptions for corporations and wealthy individuals will cost $440 billion to all levels of government in fiscal 1996.[22]

Reminiscent of Krugman's focus on the distortionary effects of bidding, Melvin Burstein and Arthur Rolnick, of the Minnesota Federal Reserve Bank, assert that states' incentive packages to particular firms result in nonoptimal allocations of resources; ultimately, the average state gives away a portion of its tax revenue to local businesses, leaving fewer resources for public goods in the country as a whole.[23] A recent United Nations report asserts that nations' programs to attract certain industries have likewise grown so fast that governments are "overbidding." In response to this report, the UN has called for curbs on the use of incentives to woo multinational employers.[24]

In theory, the threat of "rate-busting," or offering corporations the lowest taxes or highest subsidies, by individual states or nations gives jurisdictions an incentive to engage in noncompete agreements to increase their power vis-à-vis corporations. But such agreements create an incentive for individual states and nations to cheat. Consequently, social agreements must take place at least one level higher, spatially, than the level at which regions are integrating into trade blocs. Hence, the Minnesota Federal Reserve Bank calls for Congress to "end the economic war among the states" by invoking the Commerce Clause of the Constitution.[25] There is no international government, however, to invoke such a clause in response to the UN call.

HOUSEHOLDS, STATES, AND MARKETS

In order to assess the merits of different social policy options, it is essential to understand the effects of markets on nonmarket processes and outcomes. Unfortunately, economic theory has little to say about unpaid production, most of which is household production. Until the 1960s the entire discipline, from Marxian to neoclassical economics, dismissed the need for concerted research on households in general. That sphere was viewed as part of the realm of nature, in which exogenous and vaguely defined biological imperatives and social norms dictate actions and determine outcomes. Markets were seen as evoking rational behavior that could be summarized in models. The study of households was relegated to departments of sociology and social work.

In the late 1960s, neoclassical economics spawned a field that analyzed unpaid as well as paid work, using mathematical models. Yet, although the "New Home Economics" defines household work as productive activity rather than leisure, using neoclassical concepts, this field focuses only on the dimension of exchange. Power is left out of the picture, in the neoclassical tradition. In these models, men and women choose freely between labor force and household work. As the contexts of these choices are exogenous to the models, outcomes are (tautologically) deemed Pareto-efficient. Government policy is regarded as distortionary, except in strictly defined cases of market failure.[26] Since insufficient parental time to care for children is not seen as a market failure, financial subsidies to single parents are regarded as distortionary and are believed to encourage an excess number of births to unmarried mothers.[27]

New Home Economics models of the household usually model children as a type of "consumer durable good" that parents "demand" based on relative prices, income, and preferences. This perspective leads to social policy that penalizes young parents for giving birth to offspring they are not able to support. An alternative to this analysis of children might view them as economic actors who are affected by the choices of society and their parents. According to this approach, social policy provides a framework for parents' choices, which in turn provides a framework for their children's own choices.[28]

An alternative to the New Home Economics analysis of households is feminist economic theory, which analyzes not only the technical efficiency of but also the power dimension within household divisions of labor. According to Nancy Folbre,[29] husbands' and fathers' control over the labor of women and children played a crucial role in cottage industries and farms in the United States and Europe. Control over wives was ensured by laws limiting women's property rights and options outside marriage, while control over children depended in part on their material interest in inheriting their father's land. Land ownership declined in importance when industrialization gained momentum, increasing children's access to labor force earnings and correspondingly reducing the fathers' power over their offspring.

As industrial jobs absorbed farmers, large families lost many of their advantages. Norms and institutions gradually shifted custody rights and responsibility for children to women in the event of divorce. Women slowly gained access to higher education, property rights, and a wider range of occupations, which made life outside marriage feasible for them and laid the foundation for the financial responsibility for children to be transferred from fathers to mothers.

However, while women's access to and entry into the labor force grew apace, men's transition into household work did not. As a result, the relative power of men remains greater. Because women are assumed to be the primary parent in families, employers have an incentive not to hire them. The "model employee" remains male.

As market economies and industrialization gradually altered familial power relations so that biological families were no longer compelled to behave as units of production and consumption, welfare states came into existence, responding to the need for nonfamily-based systems of insurance. But despite women's lower access to the labor market, such social insurance focused on wage replacement in the event of worker disability, retirement, and untimely death. Public assistance to mothers without male partners amounted to only a fraction of the social insurance program for members of the work force. In the United States, the state-level Mothers' Pensions programs and the federal Aid to Dependent Children program that followed these included substantial employment disincentives; if mothers made use of this assistance, they did so at the cost of most of the labor force income they might have been able to earn.[30]

U.S. FAMILIES: THE CURRENT PICTURE

Women now comprise 45 percent of the paid U.S. labor force, up from 35 percent in the early 1960s and slightly above the percentage for most industrial countries. They earn about 70 percent of what males earn in full-time, year-round employment.[31] The escalation in female labor force participation is in part a response to falling real wages for males since 1973, which not only increased families' need for an additional income, but also reduced women's financial incentives to marry. There are now twice as many single-mother households as there are breadwinner-housewife families. As Folbre notes, this trend is driven partly by social norms related to men's lesser stake in the labor of their wife and children and by male unemployment. Boys and girls growing up in industrial countries in the late twentieth century suffer from shortages of assets in the form of property, cash inheritance, human capital, and parental time.

As households have changed, so has the nature of employment in industrial countries. Rising female labor force participation has shifted much work previously performed in the household to the market, and contingent and low-paid service sector jobs have increased relative to manufacturing jobs.[32] Contingent workers receive lower wages and benefits than comparably employed non-contingent employees. During the 1980s, the proportion of U.S. employed household heads with full or partial health insurance coverage fell by 20 percent.[33]

Concomitant with the changing nature of labor markets and families, inequality has risen in the United States. A striking trend is the growing poverty among young parents and children; since male wages began to decline, poverty rates have fallen for the elderly but risen precipitously for the poor and young, particularly women and children.[34] According to Marian Edelman, from 1973 to 1990, the median earnings of U.S. heads of household under age 30 with children fell by 44 percent. Even children living with married parents under 30 were two and one-half times more likely to be poor in 1990 than such children were in 1973.[35] One-quarter of U.S. children under age six are now poor.[36] For African Americans under age 18, the poverty rate is about 47 percent, and for Hispanic children it is about 40 percent. Female-headed households make up about 52 percent of all poor families.[37]

The shifting of poverty toward children, youth, and women in the United States can be interpreted to mean that the metaphorical "last generation of patriarchs" has maintained its relative income (formerly legitimized as necessary to support wives and children). Women and children are left in a limbo somewhere between control by individual men and devaluation by society and in the market.

As adults, today's poor young mothers and fathers embody the above trends of relative asset impoverishment, a trend that had begun by the time they were born. The rise in single motherhood is related to falling real wages in the 1970s and rising inequality in the 1980s, which diminished poor men's ability to conform to the gender role norm for fathers—to support families.

These changes in labor markets and families have reduced parental time available for household work and child rearing. Women's growing employment and the rise in female headship mean that a greater number of families must purchase childcare services, but incomes of poor families are insufficient to procure quality daycare. Hence, there is a growing need for public childcare and other services to address this problem.

WOMEN-FRIENDLY STATES?

Until somewhat recently, feminist theorists tended to view the state as inherently patriarchal, with good reason. Laws gave men power over women, effectively sanctioning male violence against women and children. When labor force work drew men out of household-based agricultural and craft production in the nineteenth century, European and U.S. census bureaus categorized those engaged in household work as "dependents"; public policy and taxation were based on the idea that such work was not as productive as men's work.[38]

Despite the problematic gender foundations of the welfare state, women have been able to push for policies that increased their access to education and the labor force. To varying degrees, European women benefit from highly subsidized childcare, family allowances, and paid maternity leave, and U.S. women from affirmative action and enforced nondiscrimination. On both continents the state's role in protecting women from male violence has grown, although only slowly. In the last 20 years a gender voting gap has developed in the United States and Western Europe, with women supporting public expenditures on human services more often than men.[39] Caring for young children has become grounds for a supplementary pension in Sweden and Norway, although these nations' social security systems still privilege labor force work over caring work.[40]

But in the United States women's growing power via labor force and political participation has not prevented, and perhaps has given rise to, the emergence of a bipartisan consensus on the need to revive "family values." A "welfare reform" package will soon be passed in Congress that will force most recipients of AFDC to perform labor force work, with the clear implication that poor single parents will have less time to spend with and care for their children.

The new "workforce" programs vary, depending on the extent to which AFDC clients' individual needs are taken into consideration, but a "work first" approach is coming to exemplify current policy.

This provides AFDC parents with no new skills and simply helps them find low-wage jobs in the existing labor market. In recent years, although approximately 70 percent of AFDC recipients have left the rolls within the first two years of receiving benefits, most of them have fallen back on AFDC within the next five years. Robert Moffitt estimates that 95 percent of AFDC recipients would have earnings below the AFDC eligibility cut-off if they were employed.[41]

Many U.S. jobs lack health insurance benefits and pay wages so low that full-time work does not provide an income above poverty level for a worker with one or more children to support. Forty percent of poor persons worked for pay in 1992, and 9 percent had full-time work year round.[42] Young and less-educated single mothers tend to be among employers' least preferred workers and earn correspondingly low wages. They also tend to have the least seniority and are less likely to get the flexible work schedules necessary to meet their children's needs.

The new direction the United States has chosen for assistance to single parents exemplifies the dearth of economic theory on reproductive work, in that it fails to acknowledge the time necessary to rear children and hence penalizes children.[44] Single mothers on public assistance are the poorest group of parents, yet they are currently being forced to put their children's cash needs before their (parental or other caregiver) time needs, even though their low wages mean they must exchange large amounts of time for very little income. Precisely those mothers who are the least productive in the workforce—those with the least education and lowest skills—are forced to find employment. As Rebecca Blank summarizes the situation, the move toward workfare for poor mothers will increase their paid work, but may not improve their economic position and may, in fact, worsen it.[43]

Two opposite approaches to family policy can be identified, based on contrasting views of the household-labor force dichotomy. Feminist economists assert that free markets do not allocate enough time and income to child rearing, for which women are held responsible. As a result, women and men do not have equal access to the labor force and to human capital. Proponents of the second type of policy, a "free market" approach, believe that the demands of reproduction threaten the basis of production and must be strictly confined. Labor markets should reward labor based on productivity, and those who are not burdened by children's time needs are most productive. Despite adherence to neoclassical theory, this approach romanticizes domestic work. Women are believed to choose domestic work freely, to supply their family with the "labor of love" that markets cannot provide.

A government's choice of position on the continuum between these two poles of family policy depends in part on its constituency's understanding of and belief in the need for gender-equalizing policy, which is influenced by the relative power of men, women, and other groups in the society. Social policy conditions not only male-female bargaining strength within households but also men's and women's goals, as well as their respective ability to influence legislation to change the bargaining terms.

Over time, governments' choices between these two policy approaches can polarize institutional evolution in one direction or the other. Social policy responds to further public demands, reconfiguring men's and women's power and options, resulting in further reallocations of work and constellations of power within households and labor markets, which then spawn further iterations.

COMPETITIVENESS AND WELFARE STATES

John Kenneth Galbraith asserts that the "new dialectic" in this era of free trade is between the haves and the have-nots: between those whose situations are improving and those whose real wages are falling; and between those with and those without jobs.[45] At least in the United States, pessimism concerning the effects of global pressures on governments' ability to buffer citizens appears to reinforce the assumption that labor force work warrants social insurance, while reproductive work does not.

As corporate tax revenues diminish or become negative, governments rely increasingly on personal income taxes. The working and middle classes—whose real incomes have fallen while those of the wealthy have risen—bridle against these higher taxes, fostering an antitax climate and consequently less scope for social policy, as the middle class blames social policy for the economic pressures they are feeling.

In part to reduce the cost of social policy, the United States is in the process of converting AFDC from an entitlement program to one consisting of block grants to the 50 states to implement measures largely as they see fit. This devolution of responsibility for social programs can only facilitate the states' ability to compete with one another for corporate investment. Arthur Schlesinger notes that, in light of their competition for private investment, states have an incentive "to attract corporations and keep out the poor by cutting costs through low wages, minimal working conditions, minimal environmental protection, no unions and no benefits."[46]

As Samuel Bowles and Herbert Gintis neatly summarize:

> When economies are so thoroughly integrated in the world economic system that the supply of investment in any given economy is highly responsive to small differences in the expected profit rate, the effective range of choices may be reduced to a single set of policies, a global equivalent to Henry Ford's "you can have any color car you want, as long as it is black."[47]

Schlesinger fears the effect of states' "debasing competition" on the quality of U.S. civilization.

MICHIGAN'S SOCIAL POLICY

As described above, because of changes in the family and the labor force, the ability of national and local governments to finance social services is constrained just at a time when such spending is needed. Michigan provides an interesting case study of these trends. Since it is a tax jurisdiction heavily affected by international competition in the automobile industry, we would expect the crunch on social policy to be especially severe in Michigan. The vast majority of U.S. automobile production takes place in Michigan,[48] but the U.S. share of world auto output dropped from about half in the 1960s to around 19 percent in 1989.[49] Employment in this industry peaked in 1978, and by 1994 about 25 percent of automotive jobs in Michigan had disappeared.[50]

While total manufacturing jobs in Michigan fell from 1973 to 1994, service-sector employment more than doubled.[51] This meant a fall in average real income because, while the state's average manufacturing job pays $735 per week, the more plentiful service-sector jobs range from $218 per week in personal service to $695 per week in engineering and management services. Temporary employment firms are expanding the most rapidly, as companies seek to reduce overhead, for greater flexibility and lower costs.[52]

State government revenues in Michigan fell from the nation's second highest level per capita in the 1950s to below the national average in the early 1990s.[53] Only with the recent resurgence in the U.S. auto industry have these revenues risen rapidly. Since Republican John Engler was elected governor in 1990, Michigan's Single Business Tax has been steadily reduced, and the categories of business subject to it have been increasingly limited. State taxes have been cut 16 times in the last five years.[54] Property taxes also have been severely restricted.[55] Recent legislation cutting taxes permanently will amount to tax relief of $447 million annually by 1997. In-state firms creating 75 new jobs in a year will be exempt from business and income taxes on that additional payroll; out-of-state firms creating 150 new jobs will also be exempt.[56]

Due to the shift from a Democratic to a Republican governor, trends in Michigan's social policy are more pronounced than they might have been. This has had a qualitative effect on support to poor families. In response to a budget shortfall in 1991, the state eliminated its General Assistance program, affecting 82,000 individuals. At the same time, the Emergency Assistance Program was drastically reduced.[57] Funding for the Michigan Department of Social Services fell by more than 15 percent from 1991 to 1992. Homelessness among former GA recipients rose from 2 percent to 25 percent within six months after the program ended.

Between 1990 and 1994, the value of AFDC and Food Stamps fell by 14 percent, after inflation. Cuts in assistance to single parents began earlier, however, in line with the rest of the United States. While the maximum AFDC payment and Food Stamps allotment together brought the incomes of Michigan recipients to about 85 percent of the poverty line in 1985, the comparable figure in 1994 was about 70 percent.[58]

Michigan was one of the first states to implement work incentives in its AFDC program under the Jobs Opportunities and Basic Skills component of the Family Support Act of 1988. Known as the Michigan Opportunity and Skills Training (MOST) program, it encouraged grant recipients to enroll in education or training programs and provided childcare services to those who did so. Any who did not enroll in such programs or who were employed less than 20 hours per week were placed in jobs and required to pay back a portion of their grants, with a limited childcare deduction.[59] By January 1994, about 24 percent of AFDC cases had earned income. After adjusting for inflation, state AFDC costs per client declined more than 20 percent between 1990 and 1994.

In October 1994 Michigan began to phase in the Work First program, which focuses on immediate employment rather than education and training. It requires new AFDC recipients to be employed a minimum of 20 hours per week, with very few exceptions.[60] If clients do not comply with Work First rules within a year, their case is to be closed.[61] In short, Michigan has veered away from an initial attempt to invest in the human capital of single parents, and is instead integrating AFDC clients directly into the labor market.[62] Thus, young mothers with few marketable skills are being asked to supplement their child-rearing and household work with labor force work. The childcare assistance provided by Work First (and the workfare program in MOST) is inadequate.[63]

Michigan is one of several states that have sought to dissolve the connection between property taxes and public school funding in order to equalize spending among wealthy and poor districts. In doing so, however, Michigan has doubled its reliance on the sales tax, a problematic source of school finance due to its regressivity and the variability of revenues, which are directly affected by recessions. Rather than introduce a progressive tax on income and wealth to fund schools, the state has added a burden that will reduce the availability of funding for other services in recessions, when they are most needed.

The nonprofit sector is much relied upon in the United States to offer innovative responses to the population's changing needs and demands. Wilson notes that the rate of employment in Michigan nonprofit organizations rose rapidly from 1982 to 1992, increasing by 41 percent.[64] Yet, while employment of nonprofit social service providers averaged a 14.6 percent annual growth rate in the late 1980s, growth slowed to 5.1 percent from 1989 to 1990 and fell to "limited or no growth" from 1991 to 1992.[65]

Marsh's study of the Detroit metropolitan area shows a particularly troubling trend. Although nonprofit employment, and thus nonprofit social services, grew rapidly from 1982 to 1992, growth was low or negative in precisely those minor civil divisions with the highest unemployment and poverty rates. Impoverished areas such as Ecorse, Inkster, Hamtramck, Highland Park, and River Rouge had the lowest number of nonprofit social service employers.[66] Marsh explains this trend as follows:

> According to one school of thought, nonprofits offer quick and innovative responses to changing population needs and fill the gaps in service not provided by the government or for-profit firms. Nonprofit services, however, are based on specialized groups addressing special needs and demands. Gaps in services, discrimination, and highly uneven patterns of service provision can result. The United States' unique style of nonprofit and government service provision, coupled with fragmented local governance structures and increasing differences in the wealth and mobility of the population, may exacerbate the negative situation of millions of poor.[67]

One last Michigan statistic illustrates the underside of the new trend in social policy. Perhaps in anticipation of the intensification of poverty that social assistance reductions may bring about, between 1981 and 1993, Michigan doubled the proportion of its budget allotted to police and corrections.[68]

CONCLUSION

This chapter has sought to point out the need for additional research on institutions that mediate between a society's paid and unpaid spheres in a world defined by increasingly freer trade. Focusing on the United States, I have sketched the constraints under which social policy operates, and I have outlined the apparent trend toward reducing social assistance, particularly for poor women and children. A case study of Michigan has provided a glimpse of policy and political direction in a state with a history of massive job loss due to international competition. The state's social policy did indeed precede that of other states with regard to cutbacks in general and implementation of workfare and, subsequently, the Work First program.

The lack of economic theory about the unpaid sphere, which consists mainly of household provisioning, is due to economists' blind spots regarding the household: since household production is not marketed, it is not counted. Since it is not counted, it is not taken seriously as work. The dearth of theory illuminating household dynamics reflects another problem, however, one that, like the others, also takes the form of a vicious cycle. Since household work brings in no income, it confers less power on the person doing it than does labor force work, with its more liquid and, thus, portable reward. What, then, should remind those who have marketable skills and, thus, cash income from labor force work not to "sweep household work under the rug"?

A growing but still small number of economists have recognized the undervaluation of reproduction, the maldistribution of the costs of child rearing among men and women (including foregone earnings), and the effects of these costs on women's and children's household power, human capital, and other assets. These economists have come to recognize the need for government intervention precisely in the interface between paid and unpaid work. Another small group of economists has recognized the need for a set of institutions to regulate global markets in order to halt the growing redistribution of power from governments to corporations.

This chapter shows that there is a pressing need for joint work by these two groups to analyze governments' proposed cutbacks in social policy. Such work should be directed toward the question of whether and to what extent governments should absorb the costs of reproduction, helping to "even the playing field" between men and women. At the same time, if not prior to this, it is necessary to establish whether it is even possible for individual governments to regulate and tax their private sectors while "competing governments" do not. Is the contest among jurisdictions to attract employers a "race to the bottom," as many fear, and will this competition lead states and nations to play an ever smaller role in redistributing resources among individuals and businesses within their borders?

These questions must be addressed in any debate concerning the relative merits of different social policy regimes. Whether or not free trade raises GNP growth rates, the political economy of class, gender, and age will be affected both by social policy and by states' bargaining power vis-à-vis firms. Thus, for social policy to have a future in defining and correcting market failures, governments must move from a national outlook to a global one, as firms have done.

At the ground level, the cost of state and national failure to regulate financial markets and to stop overbidding are borne most directly by poor children and the children they will have. These youth of the future pay for society's decisions to stigmatize and underinsure caregiving work. As Michigan seems to anticipate, the alternative to such regulation is rising prison costs. These, along with increasingly hardened social outcasts, will ultimately make the bottom—but only the very bottom—of social policy too costly.[69]

NOTES

1. Due to the range and variety of countries' social service cutbacks, the political science debate over the decline of welfare states seems to have turned to the definition of "retrenchment." For a state-of-the-art political science discussion of retrenchment, see Paul Pierson, *Dismantling the Welfare State? Reagan, Thatcher, and the Politics of Retrenchment* (Cambridge and New York: Cambridge University Press, 1994).

2. *Rationality* is defined by economists as maximization of individual self-interest.

3. Daniel Howes and Katherine Yung, "Michigan Is Ready to Rumble," *Detroit News and Free Press*, 28 May 1995, 1A, 8A.

4. Many economists have detailed the effects of the International Monetary Fund (IMF) structural adjustment policies on the extensive unpaid spheres of less industrialized economies. For example, see Carmen Deere, Peggy Antrobus, Lynn Bolles, Edwin Melendez, Peter Phillips, Marcia Rivera, and Helen Safa, eds., "Impact of the Crisis on Poor Women and Their Families," in *In the Shadow of the Sun: Caribbean Development Alternatives and U.S. Policy* (Boulder, Colo.: Westview Press, 1990), chap. 3. An anthology on this topic that includes a discussion of industrial nations' cutbacks in social policy is found in Isabella Bakker, ed., *The Strategic Silence: Gender and Economic Policy* (London: Zed Books, 1994). Evidence to support the theory that increased market penetration marginalizes the reproductive sphere is found in Nancy Folbre, *Who Pays for the Kids: Gender and the Structures of Constraint* (New York and London: Routledge, 1994).

5. Reinicke notes that, up to now, the forces driving economic globalization have been micro- rather than macroeconomic. The internationalization of trade, finance, and production has been due to new developments in corporate and industrial organization, involving greater movement of (increasingly intangible) capital, including finance, technology, and knowledge. Reinicke refers to this type of globalization as "deep integra-

tion." See Wolfgang Reinicke, "Integrating the World Economy: Economics Is Not Enough," in Klaus Schwab, ed., *Overcoming Indifference: Ten Key Challenges in Today's Changing World* (New York: New York University Press, 1994), 224-28.

6. Portfolio capital movement has increased to exceed the volume of out-flows of foreign direct investment, and the volume of foreign exchange transactions has dwarfed both types of capital movements. The exodus of capital and accompanying sales of a country's currency result in a depreciation of that currency, which fuels inflation and may lead to further outflow of capital and currency sales.

7. Fiscal policy causes inflation and raises interest rates, which encourages capital inflow and thus raises the value of a country's currency. In an open economy with floating exchange rates, this reduces exports, counteracting the expansionary effect of the policy.

8. Samuel Bowles and Herbert Gintis, *Democracy and Capitalism: Property, Community, and the Contradictions of Modern Social Thought* (New York: Basic Books, 1986), 190.

9. See Jim Stanford, Christine Elwell, and Scott Sinclair, *Social Dumping under North American Free Trade* (Ottawa: Canadian Center for Policy Alternatives, October 1993), 1-11, 63-66.

10. See Peter Gumbel, "Europe Faces Pressure to Cut Social Spending," *Wall Street Journal*, 8 May 1995, 1.

11. Low birth and death rates in Europe present a problem to social security and health care systems.

12. See Gosta Esping-Anderson, *After the Golden Age: The Future of the Welfare State in the New Global Order*, Occasional Paper No. 7, World Summit for Social Development (Geneva: United Nations Research Institute for Social Development, November 1994).

13. Negotiations for a binding social charter would be more difficult among NAFTA states, since unit labor costs vary much more widely among the United States, Canada, and Mexico than among EU states. See Stanford, Elwell, and Sinclair, *Social Dumping*.

14. See Paul Krugman, "Competitiveness: A Dangerous Obsession," *Foreign Affairs* 73, no. 2 (March/April 1994): 29-44.; and John Kenneth Galbraith, "The New Dialectic," *American Prospect* 18 (summer 1994): 9-11.

15. See William Schweke, Carl Rist, and Brian Dabson, *Bidding for Business: Are Cities and States Selling Themselves Short?* (Washington, D.C.: Corporation for Enterprise Development, 1994).

16. See Robert Frank, *Microeconomics and Behavior*, 2d ed. (New York: McGraw Hill, 1994), 240-45.

17. H. Brinton Milward and Heidi Hosbach Newman, "State Incentive Packages and the Industrial Location Decision," *Economic Development Quarterly* 3, no. 3 (August 1989): 203-22.

18. See Peter Applebome, "States Raise Stakes in Fight for Jobs," *New York Times*, 4 October 1993, 3.

19. See Fred Bleakley, "U.N. Urges Curbs on Incentives to Woo Multinational Employees," *Wall Street Journal*, 14 April 1995, 2, 7.
20. Chuck Collins, "Aid to Dependent Corporations: Exposing Federal Handouts to the Wealthy," *Dollars and Sense* no. 199 (May-June 1995): 15-17, 40.
21. Schweke, Rist, and, Dabson., *Bidding for Business*, 8.
22. Collins, "Aid to Dependent Corporations," 15.
23. See Melvin L. Burstein and Arthur J. Rolnick, "Congress Should End the Economic War among the States," Federal Reserve Bank of Minneapolis 1994 Annual Report, *The Region* 9, no. 1 (1994): 3-20. According to Burstein and Rolnick, the optimal tax (the least distorting tax) is one that is uniformly applied to all businesses. In contrast to the competition among states for individual firms' investment projects, the authors assert that competition among states in their general provision of public goods, through taxing and spending policies, is efficient. Their reasoning, following Charles Tiebout's 1956 argument, is that residents of different states vote with their feet, moving to the state that provides them with the public services they are willing to pay for. This logic seems to contradict the general position of their paper; if states compete to reduce taxes to many or all corporations, rather than only to certain firms, states' ability to provide public goods will be yet more strongly constrained. The logic here is presumably that states will not be able to afford to do this "across the board" for all investment without severe cutbacks in provision of public goods. But if competition among states for individual firms' investment results in all states simply giving a portion of their tax revenue to local businesses, the same argument can be made concerning states' competition for one or all firms' investment.
24. See United Nations Conference on Trade and Development Secretariat, Commission on International Investment and Transnational Corporations, "Incentives and Foreign Direct Investment," Background Report, UN Conference on Trade and Development, 21st Session (Geneva: UNCTAD, 24 April 1995).
25. Burstein and Rolnick, "Congress Should End the Economic War," 11-16.
26. The economic definition of "market failure" is, briefly, provision of a monoptimal amount of a good or service bought and sold in private markets. The example of education is widely used to illustrate this concept, because most economists agree that the free market does not generate optimal outcomes in this sector. If individuals (or their parents) merely purchase their (or their children's) education, the sum of their effective demand (backed by purchasing power) will be lower than the socially optimal level of skills, training, and general knowledge. The production and exchange of education is said to generate positive "externalities"; governments, therefore, must tax residents of their jurisdiction and use these revenues to bring about higher levels of education of their population. Education is also regarded by many economists and others as a "merit

good," to which all individuals have a right. This is seen as a foundation for their participation in society and the formal economy, as education affects individual ability to make use of resources, markets, and institutions.

Less widely accepted within mainstream economics, however, is the reality that no universal, scientifically verifiable "correct" method exists to assess which markets fail and which succeed, nor the optimality of different sets of property rights within which markets should operate. For example, there is no (proposed or accepted) theory of the combination of sex education, civics, multiculturalism, school prayer, and patriotism in which young people should be trained.

27. The federal AFDC program is denounced as the cause of the rise in single motherhood over the last few decades, although most of the expansion in the rate of out-of-wedlock births has been among middle- and upper-class women, rather than among those assisted by AFDC. The increase in out-of-wedlock births is also driven by the reduction of births to married couples. In actuality, the value of AFDC and food stamps has fallen while single motherhood has risen. See Robert Moffitt, "Incentive Effects of the U.S. Welfare System: A Review," *Journal of Economic Literature* 8 (fall 1994): 1-61.

28. A "life cycle" approach is used in Robert Haveman and Barbara Wolfe, *Succeeding Generations: On the Effects of Investment in Children* (New York: Russell Sage Foundation, 1994).

29. Folbre, *Who Pays for the Kids*, 91-131.

30. This continues to be the case, despite the passage of the Family Support Act in 1988.

31. About 25 percent of women work part-time, while about 10 percent of men work part-time. See Joyce P. Jacobsen, *The Economics of Gender* (Cambridge, Mass.: Blackwell, 1994).

32. With this development, the problematic nature of the distinction between "productive" labor force work and "unproductive" household work (performed by "dependent" wives) has become more apparent.

33. Marian Wright Edelman, "Vanishing Dreams of America's Young Families," *Challenge* 35, no. 3 (May-June 1992), 14-15.

34. David Cutler and Lawrence Katz, "Untouched by the Rising Tide," *Brookings Review* 10, no. 1 (winter 1992): 41-45.

35. Edelman, "Vanishing Dreams," 14-17.

36. See Carnegie Task Force on Meeting the Needs of Young Children, excerpts from *Starting Points: Meeting the Needs of Our Youngest Children* (New York: Carnegie Corporation, 1994).

37. Only 3 percent of these young families with children were headed by teenagers. Edelman, "Vanishing Dreams," 13-14.

38. See Nancy Folbre, "The Unproductive Housewife: Her Evolution in Nineteenth-Century Economic Thought," *Signs: Journal of Women in Culture and Society* 16, no. 3 (1991): 463-84.

39. See Frances Fox Piven, "Ideology and the State: Women, Power, and the Welfare State," in *Women, the State, and Welfare,* Linda Gordon, ed. (Madison: University of Wisconsin Press, 1990), 250-64; and Arnlaug Leira, "The 'Woman-Friendly' Welfare State?: The Case of Norway and Sweden," in Jane Lewis, ed., *Women and Social Policies in Europe: Work, Family and the State* (Brookfield, Vt.: Edward Elgar, 1993): 49-71.
40. See Leira, "The 'Woman-Friendly' Welfare State?", 49-71.
41. Moffitt, "Incentive Effects."
42. Approximately 40 percent of people age 18-64 years whose income is below the poverty line (and who are not receiving AFDC or Medicaid) have no health insurance for all or part of the year; Edelman, "Vanishing Dreams," 13-19. About 15 percent of the general U.S. population is not covered by health insurance.
43. Rebecca Blank, "Policy Watch: Proposals for Time Limited Welfare," *Journal of Economic Perspectives* 8, no. 4 (fall 1994): 183-93.
44. The Family Support Act of 1988, in fact, included a mandate that all states provide training and placement programs for work-eligible recipients of AFDC. The federal government was to provide matching funds to states to subsidize childcare costs for AFDC recipients with young children. Since then, very few states have implemented such programs, in part because the 1990-91 recession limited their ability to provide corollary support services, such as job placement and childcare assistance. Various states have, however, imposed restrictions on the receipt of AFDC benefits, such as limits to the size of a grant. New Jersey, for example, denies increased assistance to any additional children born to a mother already receiving AFDC.
45. Galbraith, "The New Dialetic," 10.
46. Arthur Schlesinger, Jr., "In Defense of Government," *Wall Street Journal*, 7 June 1995, A14.
47. Bowles and Gintis, *Democracy and Capitalism*, 191.
48. From 1978 to 1994 the proportion of U.S. auto industry employment located in Michigan fell slightly but was roughly maintained, dropping from about 88 percent to around 83 percent.
49. Peter Dicken, *Global Shift* (New York: Guilford Press, 1992), 271.
50. The number of jobs dropped from about 416,000 to 294,000. See Howes and Yung, "Michigan Is Ready to Rumble," 8A.
51. Manufacturing jobs fell from 1,178,800 to 944,000 in this period. See Joel Smith, "Services Are State's Fastest Growing Job Sector," *Detroit News and Free Press*, Sunday, May 28, 1995, 9A.
52. Howes and Yung, "Michigan is Ready to Rumble," 8A.
53. Interview with Gerald Faverman, Faverman Group, East Lansing, Mich.
54. Howes and Yung, "Michigan is Ready to Rumble," 1A.
55. A study of the business tax structure of 21 states ranks Michigan as average, twelth among the states studied, ranked by average effective tax rates on investment for 12 industries. This ranking occurred prior to passage of Michigan's latest tax-relief legislation. See Michael Vlaisavljevich and

Stephen Pollock, "Comparative Analysis of the Relationship of North Carolina's Tax Structure to Economic Development," *State Tax Notes*, 20 February 1995, 785-98.

56. See Peter Luke, "Engler Tax-cut Plan Sails Through Legislature," *Ann Arbor News* (1 March 1995). Governor Engler explained that these incentives are necessary to compete with neighboring states with similar tax breaks.

57. Until 1991, Michigan was one of 21 states with a state-funded General Assistance (GA) Program. Only 8 of these states extended aid to individuals who were not handicapped or elderly. Michigan continues to provide cash assistance to families formerly on GA, under the State Family Assistance (SFA) Program, and to individuals certified disabled, under the State Disability Assistance (SDA) Program. With the elimination of GA, 4,577 cases were converted to the SDA program, and 7,924 were converted to the SFA program. Most of these families were converted to AFDC in the following year (Michigan Department of Social Services, Information Packet, May 1994, 23-24). The number of individuals receiving state-funded Emergency Assistance fell from 222,473 in 1991 to 62,327 in 1992.

58. A statistician at the Michigan Department of Social Services notes that "grant increases for public assistance recipients have not kept pace with inflation, with the rates paid to firms that receive government contracts to provide social services, or with Medicaid hospital and long-term care payment levels. While payment rates to Medicaid service providers, daycare workers, hospitals, and child foster care providers rose 76 percent, 199 percent, 57 percent and 42 percent, respectively, from 1984 to 1993, the grant to AFDC recipients increased only 12 percent. Inflation, measured by the Consumer Price Index, rose by 35 percent during this period. See Michigan Department of Social Services, Information Packet, May 1994, 3.

59. To encourage labor force work, the first $200 of their earnings and 20 percent of remaining earnings were not deducted from their AFDC grants. To offset childcare expenses for these clients, an additional $175 to $200 was disregarded.

60. As a MOST program, Work First offers childcare and other support services only until a recipient is employed for at least 20 hours per week, at which point the income disregard is the only daycare assistance granted. Job search is to be facilitated through job clubs and other job search activities, and only if this is unsuccessful will a reassessment be conducted to determine the potential benefit of additional training or skill building.

The main category of AFDC recipients not referred to Work First is parents under age 20 who have not completed high school. Refugees are also exempted. Federal waivers were obtained in order to eliminate other exemptions from participation and to impose sanctions, including a 25 percent reduction in families' AFDC and Food Stamps grants and the requirement that AFDC applicants participate in job search activities while their AFDC eligibility is being determined.

61.Local Michigan Department of Social Services office directors may make exceptions based on labor market conditions; Michigan League for Human Services, "Questions and Answers," 1-4.

62. Current participants in other MOST programs are to be referred to Work First when they complete the MOST program or when their employability plan is reviewed.

63. If the AFDC parent is employed for 20 hours per week, the monthly income disregard of $175-200 for childcare amounts to $2.50 or less per hour.

64. In 1992, 5.9 percent of the state's workforce was employed in nonprofit organizations, up from 4.4 percent in 1987. See Mark Wilson, "Nonprofit Michigan," in Mark Wilson, ed., *The State of Nonprofit Michigan* (East Lansing: Institute for Public Policy and Social Research, Michigan State University, 1995), 15-23.

65. Included in social services, the second-largest component of Michigan's nonprofit sector after education, are "individual and family services, job training, child daycare services, and residential care services." Employment in social services comprised 10.7 percent of the state's nonprofit work force in 1992; ibid., 17.

66. F.K. Marsh, "Services, Equity, and Needs: Nonprofit Services in Metropolitan Detroit," in *The State of Non-Profit Michigan*, Mark Wilson, ed., 39-57. According to Marsh, the available data are inadequate to show whether nonprofit organizations have closed or never exceeded their current low levels in high-poverty areas of metropolitan Detroit.

67. Ibid., 55.

68. This rose from 3.4 percent to 6.2 percent of state expenditures, based on the author's calculations, using the State of Michigan, Department of Management and Budget, *Annual Financial Report* for the fiscal years ending in 1981-93.

69. I would like to thank Jutta Allmendinger, Peter Dorman, Nancy Folbre, Barbara Hopkins, Robert Kleine, John Myles, Jennifer Olmsted, Kevin Quinn, Elmar Reiger, Ian Robinson, and Mark Wilson.

IV.
Changes in Work and the Workforce with NAFTA

The Effects of NAFTA on Mexico-United States Immigration

Robert Aponte

Among the key selling points of NAFTA was the notion that the economic benefits of the treaty would slow immigration from Mexico to the United States. Whatever the ultimate extent of NAFTA's economic consequences, it is argued here that the treaty will stimulate more migration than it will stem. This is because neither the quality nor the quantity of NAFTA-induced jobs on the Mexican side, the key ingredient in the migration suppression hypothesis, will be sufficient to deter many northern-bound labor migrants. In addition, the economic integration process itself will entail job losses in Mexico that will stimulate increased migration. On balance, therefore, outmigration will increase, rather than decrease.

Despite this prediction, it is also argued here that Michigan, while sure to remain among the states most actively involved in financial dealings with Mexico, is not likely to be among the major receivers of the enhanced migration streams. Most migrants are likely to enter via existing trajectories, and the best data available suggest that very little direct immigration from Mexico is currently steered toward Michigan. For example, the Mexican-origin population in the state grew at a very low rate during the 1980s, a decade of record Mexican immigration, and only a portion of this growth could have been due to migration. Indeed, in absolute terms, Michigan's Mexican-origin population grew faster in the 1970s than the 1980s, and it is likely that the portion of the growth due to migration came largely from other parts of the United States, rather than from Mexico.

NAFTA AND MIGRATION

The potential effects of NAFTA on migration, like its predicted effects on U.S. and Mexican employment, are the subject of considerable disagreement,[1] with a general tendency for the treaty's proponents to expect decreased migration and vice versa. The conventional view is that the treaty will stimulate *increased* migration in the *short* to intermediate run but *decreased* migration in the intermediate to *long* run (10-20 years).[2] An alternative view, implied or expressed to varying degrees by various authors, is that NAFTA is likely to stimulate migration well into the foreseeable future.[3] The position taken here elaborates the latter perspective.

In order to evaluate the viability of any of these views, one must first understand precisely how NAFTA is supposed to affect the current migratory pattern, particularly since the treaty has no provisions dealing with migration. First, it must be understood that the sustained migration waves are composed overwhelmingly of low-skilled laborers pursuing economic opportunities that are simply not available in Mexico, an impoverished country with rampant joblessness and correspondingly low wages.[4] Second, the treaty is expected to have a substantial effect on the mix of labor opportunities in both the United States and Mexico, but most especially the latter for a variety of reasons. Key among these is size: as the smallest economy, Mexico will be disproportionately affected by any given volume of additional business. Also, given its abundant pools of low-wage labor, Mexico's economy is expected to attract more foreign investment from the other NAFTA countries than vice versa, particularly for labor-intensive production. Thus, the essential ingredient in the migration-suppression viewpoint, as elaborated below, is Mexican job growth.

The mechanism by which this is supposed to work is fairly straightforward. The increased investment in Mexican production and the commensurate expansion in Mexican exports should create an abundance of jobs, which will absorb potential migrants. While some employment will also be lost as less competitive Mexican producers are undermined by heightened competition, the balance is expected to be substantial net employment growth.

The effects of NAFTA on United States employment, by contrast, are considered largely irrelevant to any potential shifts in migration for the following reasons. First, NAFTA is clearly not expected to net any low-skilled work on the U.S. side; thus, the treaty cannot induce more migration through any expansion of opportunities it may produce in the United States. At the same time, however, it also will not decrease U.S. opportunities for those moving north. Rather, compelling evidence supports the widely held assumption that demand in the United States for low-skilled workers, those willing to toil at menial and/or difficult tasks for exceptionally low wages (that is, immigrant labor), will continue to increase in the foreseeable future, with or without NAFTA.[5] Hence, if NAFTA is to stem the flow of migrants, it must produce a substantial expansion of opportunities on the Mexican side of the border![6]

In focusing on jobs in Mexico, the debate over migration departs sharply from the larger debate in the United States over the advisability of entering into NAFTA. Whereas the latter focused on whether NAFTA would hurt employment prospects for United States workers, largely assuming major job gains to Mexico, the migration debate focuses on the adequacy of job creation in Mexico, irrespective of job gains or losses in the United States. One implication of this difference is that relatively little work by U.S. scholars has examined the precise net employment effects NAFTA is likely to produce in Mexico. Nevertheless, it cannot be overemphasized that migration-suppression ultimately rests almost entirely on those effects. But, as is argued here, the earnings level of the new jobs also will matter; if they are much lower than wages in accessible U.S. jobs, many laborers will perceive little incentive to stay home. While the pro-NAFTA literature often implies that Mexican wages will rise significantly under the treaty, such projections are ambiguous and unconvincing.[7]

The view taken here is that NAFTA will fail to produce the jobs or wages suggested by proponents and that, for these and related reasons, the treaty will stimulate more migration than it will stem. First, the likelihood that *net* job growth will be at levels sufficiently high to deter migrants is remote or nil. Second, wage levels will *not* rise to anywhere near the levels necessary to be competitive with U.S. standards for decades (if ever), thereby providing little attraction to most potential migrants. Third, the process of labor migration itself will prove relatively impervious to the opportunities promised by NAFTA.

THE NAFTA JOBS DEBATE: THE MEXICAN SIDE

The most fundamental and preliminary question is: Will NAFTA foster enough net job growth in Mexico to affect migration? Most observers agree that Mexican manufacturing employment will rise substantially under NAFTA, while agricultural work will considerably diminish, but the net outcome remains in dispute. A point on which there is much agreement, however, is that millions of rural Mexicans will be displaced from agriculture in the foreseeable future as a result of NAFTA. Indeed, the potential devastation is so great that the schedules for easing competitive restrictions on key agricultural commodities are to be phased in gradually. The complete lowering of restrictions on imports of U.S. corn, for example, is to be phased in over a full 15 years!

The expected agricultural displacement is the main reason proponents concede that, in the short term, NAFTA will actually stimulate migration. Yet, after an initial upsurge from rural displacement, they believe that migration will substantially fall as potential migrants increasingly respond to the NAFTA-induced expansion in industrial opportunities.[8] It is clear, therefore, that any ultimate net gains to Mexican employment from NAFTA will necessarily result from a balance of both major gains (in manufacturing) and major losses (in agriculture).

The varying estimates on NAFTA-induced employment shifts in Mexico range from one pessimistic of net job losses up to 1.6 million by the year 2000,[9] to a loss of 30 percent of current manufacturing employment (without regard to rural displacement).[10] Studies finding positive net gains for Mexican employment, the predominant position among U.S. scholars, have yielded precious few estimates that specify the actual level of projected job growth. The notable exception, one of many studies based on economic simulations, suggests NAFTA will produce a net gain of about 690,000 jobs to Mexico between 1995 and 1997.[11]

The widespread view that Mexico will reap major benefits from NAFTA rests largely upon this and related simulation modeling studies. Indeed, most such work has concluded that, in keeping with the comparative advantage argument of standard trade theory, all three economies will benefit from liberalized trade, especially Mexico.[12] As Martin summarizes, "Mexico is the economic 'winner' in NAFTA, but all three countries will have bigger economies, more jobs, and higher wages," a generalized finding echoed by "most government, academic, and industry studies."[13] Based on such generalizations, such "experts" as Nora Lustig of the Brookings Institution confidently trumpet the good news that NAFTA will unquestionably produce "higher incomes in Mexico" with a "doubling" of the rate of growth in the nation's "overall economy" and "wages."[14]

It is also likely that these ideas have gained wide acceptance because the greatly feared NAFTA-induced United States employment declines are generally assumed to translate directly into Mexican jobs. Aside from the immense popularity of 1994 presidential candidate Ross Perot's quip that NAFTA would induce a "giant sucking sound" as U.S. jobs migrated south of the border, there is also a growing awareness of the *maquiladora* experience. Widespread publicity about that program,[15] whereby hundreds of United States firms relocated or created production facilities in Mexico, thereby displacing United States workers, almost certainly helped implant the expectation that NAFTA will extend the pattern.[16]

Despite widespread acceptance of this view, however, there is reason to doubt its accuracy and, especially, the findings of the simulations. First, the models rest upon numerous dubious assumptions about the real world. The most serious is that full employment regimes characterize the economies in question, an obvious and significant flaw; others include the assumption of free competition (many producers, none with major market share advantages) and balanced trade. All of the modeling techniques used in making NAFTA projections rest upon these or related assumptions.[17]

The problems with these kinds of models are concisely and expertly summarized by James Stanford.[18] In brief, they necessarily begin with a set of assumptions about how an economy works. These are then applied to a "starting point" set of real economic indicators, after which the model tells us what *should* transpire in the various output variables (employment, trade, and so on), given a change in input variables (such as lower tariffs). The problem is that the prediction is wholly dependent upon the theoretical structure of the model itself, or its underlying assumptions. Referring to the so-called computable general equilibrium (CGE) models, the most widely used, Stanford notes:

> CGE models are circular: if trade theory holds that free trade is mutually beneficial, then a quantitative simulation model based on that theoretical structure will automatically show that free trade is mutually beneficial . . . if the economy actually behaves in the manner supposed by the modeler, *and the model itself sheds no light on this question*, then a properly calibrated model may provide a rough empirical estimate of the effects of a policy change. But the validity of the model hangs entirely on . . . [whether the model accurately represents the real world] (emphasis added).[19]

Stanford goes on to note that the apparent consensus of pro-NAFTA modelers "reflects more a consensus of prior theoretical views than a consensus of quantitative evidence."[20]

Basing their views more on recent trends than on modeling techniques, some analysts have even argued that manufacturing employment will experience *net declines* or only minuscule growth in Mexico under NAFTA.[21] They reason, first, that much Mexican industrial production, outside the *maquiladoras*, is known to be highly inefficient and therefore *itself* vulnerable to competitive displacement. Second, there were a number of massive layoffs in the 1980s, particularly in steel and autowork.[22] While about 600,000 industrial jobs were generated from 1980 to 1992, a matching number were lost. In fact, from 1985 to 1990, nearly 90 percent of all industrial job growth was due to *maquiladora* expansion.[23] As of 1992, there were actually fewer workers employed in industry than in 1980.[24] Because this relative thinning of industrial workers occurred during a period when Mexico's economy was gradually being privatized and opened to foreign penetration, a process to be accelerated under NAFTA, these observers expect few industrial job additions from NAFTA, despite the hoopla to the contrary.

These potential demand-side insufficiencies are matched by three mammoth supply-side surpluses that further undermine the NAFTA promise. First, the Mexican labor force adds around one million people each year,[25] but no one has dared suggest that the treaty can produce employment of that magnitude. In addition, millions of Mexicans already are un- or underemployed; it is reasonable to expect that many of these also would have to be absorbed if NAFTA were to have a major effect on labor migration. Finally, hundreds of thousands of agricultural workers—some estimates run into the millions—

are expected to be displaced by NAFTA and related policy shifts in Mexico.[26] This combination of needs dwarfs the magnitude of opportunities promised by even the most optimistic NAFTA scenarios.

A still more compelling factor undercutting the migration-suppression hypothesis is wages. NAFTA adherents consistently argue or imply that the projected economic growth will ensure wage growth, that productivity differences are the key reason for the existing differentials, and that the newly induced growth will progressively eradicate each of these. The recent record belies all such claims, however.

The contention that productivity differences fully account for the Mexican-U.S. industrial wage gap is especially contradicted by a wide body of findings. Indeed, figures deriving from the U.S. Bureau of Labor Statistics show that Mexican industrial productivity rose by roughly 40 percent from 1980 to 1992, yet real wages dropped by a full 32 percent over the period.[27] Another popular argument of NAFTA proponents, reflecting real supply and demand factors rather than "productivity" measures, is that the sheer increase in demand for industrial labor under NAFTA will force up wages. This also is belied by the *maquiladora* experience. Employment in these plants exploded from about 130,000 in 1980 to more than 500,000 in 1992.[28] Yet real wages also dropped in this sector, Mexico's main growth sector, and average wages there are likely to be even lower than in other industrial jobs.[29]

A recent inspection of a *maquiladora* plant by an economist visiting with a congressional team underscored the issue. The group's unannounced stop at a Sanyo plant led to a candid interview with the manager, who was asked how the plant's productivity compared with that of its U.S. counterparts. He responded that, after approximately four years in operation, the plant's productivity matched U.S. standards by 100 percent. As explained by the economist, Jeff Faux:

> Next question: "What is the ratio of entry wages in your plant versus entry wages in the United States?" Without blinking an eye, he said, "One to ten." This was no theoretical economist making that statement. This is the guy who runs the plant in Tijuana and signs the checks.[30]

Similar accounts have been reported by Harley Shaiken,[31] who studied four major foreign-owned plants in 1991-92 chosen for their superior quality. Together, they employed more than 7,000. Despite rapid turnover (about 130 percent in one year in one of the plants) and substantial worker dissatisfaction with wages and conditions, the plants were described as on a par with high-tech production facilities in both the United States and Japan.

Shaiken's summary remarks are instructive:

> All four plants have sustained remarkably high quality and efficiency since they began. The Universal engine plant scored among the company's highest in North America for almost a decade, frequently besting a United States plant producing the same engine. The Universal assembly plant . . . turned out the second-highest-quality small car sold in the United States market, eclipsing all Japanese-built rivals but one . . . the transmission plant produced the highest quality manual transaxle in the company's global operations within a few years of being launched. And the Honshu Electronics *maquiladora* matches the quality of its United States counterpart so closely that warranty results are not separated.[32]

The substantial disjunction between the workers' earnings and their productivity was indirectly ascertained by managers. Typical commentary on the plant's problems offered by one of the interviewed managers made the point: "You've got only one problem in that plant and that's wages. We took the cream of the workforce, . . . and we gave them all this training, and we're just not paying them enough money." Another noted: "We know this is not enough money for someone to survive."[33] Worse, the managers freely admitted that the Mexican government's policies helped to suppress wages. "We even get help from the government making sure we don't settle too high because of the economic reforms and the fact that we're so visible," stated one official, after which he made the following reference to a concession recently granted by workers: "We suspect that one of the reasons . . . was the amount of pressure the government was putting on CTM [the union] to settle at a low level because of . . . [our] . . . visibility." Still another supervisor pointed out: "The labor ministry takes an active part in negotiations, especially in companies our size. And they steer the level of increases.[34]

In short, the wages paid to Mexican workers bear little resemblance to their productivity. Rather, the effect of catastrophic joblessness on worker bargaining power, the strictly enforced government policy of low wages, and the tight control exerted by the government over the few unions allowed to operate are the most widely held and believable reasons for the persistence of the rock-bottom Mexican pay scales.[35] Consistent with the scenario of widespread dissatisfaction over wages and conditions, turnover is rampant throughout much of the industrial sector, particularly among the *maquiladoras*, despite the paucity of alternatives. Turnover rates as high as 300 percent in *maquiladora* plants have been reported by George.[36] Shaiken also reported high turnover rates in the four plants he studied.[37] In the worst of them, turnover averaged at least 100 percent per year; poor wages and conditions were said to be the main causes.

The problems of *maquiladora* jobs, in combination with their proximity to the United States border, have actually been shown to *stimulate* border crossings, a process engendering the term *stepping-stone migration*.[38] As explained by Faux:

> There is the assertion that NAFTA will slow immigration. The same claim was made thirty years ago when the Maquila agreement with Mexico was made. The Maquiladora program actually increased immigration. It drew workers to the border areas (where most of Mexico's growth will continue to occur because of its close location to United States markets). Once there, workers got jobs at wages kept low as a result of collusion among an authoritarian government, captive labor unions, and business associations. Not being able to raise a family on the wages paid, workers soon quit, climbed the fences, and crossed the river to the United States.[39]

Martin,[40] a NAFTA proponent, provides an in-depth review of the decidedly mixed literature on this issue and cautions against exaggerated interpretations of the extent of the stepping stone. Nevertheless, he concludes that while its scale is probably small at present, it apparently is growing and "could become a trampoline" that brings more Mexican workers to the United States.[41]

There is little reason to believe that NAFTA will provide more attractive wages or conditions to Mexican workers, especially since labor standards were deliberately left out of the accord.[42] Moreover, analytic studies of the prospects for wage convergence under NAFTA uniformly suggest that, if it comes, convergence could easily take many decades and will not necessarily consist, unilaterally, of upward movement on the Mexican side (upward convergence). Hufbauer and Schott,[43] the treaty's biggest boosters, expect that over three or four decades per capita income in Mexico could reach about half the U.S. level; this scenario assumes their rosy predictions of NAFTA's effects on Mexican income actually occur. More critical work on the potential for Mexican wages to rise to levels approaching U.S. standards has arrived at less optimistic conclusions.[44]

In summary, it has been argued that for NAFTA to produce a discernible effect on migration, the treaty must provide a substantial expansion in Mexican opportunities. This point is not really controversial and NAFTA proponents claim the treaty will produce just such an expansion. Their job creation projections are unrealistic, however, because they are based on dubious assumptions that, even if valid, fall far short of the mark. Furthermore, the expected rates of pay will parallel prevailing levels, but these are currently so low that they possess little holding power despite the paucity of alternatives. In the next section, support for the idea that NAFTA will not discernibly depress migration is provided by an entirely different set of items.

THE SOCIAL PROCESS OF MEXICAN-U.S. MIGRATION

A number of features associated with Mexican immigration to the United States, particularly undocumented migration, will strongly undercut the hypothesized deterrent effect of NAFTA. The more general characteristics of Mexican migration to the United States have been detailed in many treatises.[45] Our limited interest here is in two aspects that can be expected to mitigate the responsiveness of potential migrants to the emerging NAFTA opportunities. First, the movements are generated more by historical linkages to the host society than by mere socioeconomic differences between the two places. Hence, the presence or absence of opportunities (such as those NAFTA may provide) do not, by themselves, determine the pace of migration. Second, the mass movements are socially organized and collectively implemented, rather than representing a mere aggregation of individual enterprises. Hence, inducing potential migrants to stay home is not easily accomplished, particularly if the economic inducements are no more attractive than those in the communities currently targeted as destinations.

In general terms, rather than just occurring in response to existing differentials in opportunities, migrations tend to be triggered when the more developed society intrudes into the sending society in a variety of ways. As Alejandro Portes and Jozsef Borocz have noted, history is replete with examples "in which an absolute wage advantage in economically expanding areas has meant nothing to the population of more isolated regions; when their labor has been required, it has had to be coerced out of them."[46] Migrations require the establishment of ties—social, political, and economic—to facilitate the initial movement and set the stage for subsequent ones.

The initial exchanges usually set into motion both the push and pull factors leading to migration. For example, the traditional means of subsistence in the sending society are often replaced by the modern forms of production from the host society. These processes generally displace the peasantry, stimulating the "push" toward alternative available opportunities. The more common initiator of the major migration waves to the intrusive society, however, is the "pull" of labor recruitment.

Accordingly, labor recruitment by major agricultural concerns, railroad builders, steel mill operators, and so forth, all played a major role in initiating the early major flows from Mexico. A key facilitator during and after World War II was the U.S. government's Bracero Program, which permitted and regulated the use of Mexican agricultural "guestworkers" until the program was disbanded in the 1960s. Once the use of the workers became established, many factors came into being that facilitated the permanence or regularity of their presence.

A major example is agriculture. U.S. employers became dependent on immigrant farm labor as domestic workers became increasingly intolerant of the undesirable conditions (particularly seasonality) and meager wages. Employers therefore sought and developed ways (pressuring against strict immigration controls) to ensure the repeated use of such workers. Thus, a measure of permanence was created. In other instances, at least some members of the recruited work force remained in the area of employment after dismissal. Once a "critical mass" of the group accumulated, it became the U.S.-based bedrock of associational linkages, or social networks, spanning the two societies. In due course, these emerging networks attracted, channeled, and accommodated additional migrants.

The networks serve as "bridges" for sojourners from the sending to the host community by providing information, job contacts, and assistance, along with assorted other forms of inducements (such as stories about life and fortune in "El Norte") to potential migrants. It is across such forged linkages that the massive movements unfold, and the role played by the networks can be likened to that of the Underground Railroad in the pre-Civil War United States. Through network sponsorship, many incoming migrants find work within a few days of arrival; often jobs await them. The process becomes so regularized that it has been called a "culture of emigration."[47] Indeed, sending communities often dispatch half or more of their working-aged men on at least temporary forays north, and large numbers from one sending community will cluster in the same destination, effectively creating "satellite" settlements or "transnational" communities.

This helps explain why the settlement of the U.S. population of Mexican origin remains largely in its traditional patterning, mostly in the in the so-called big five southwestern states (California, Texas, North Mexico, Arizona, Colorado) and in the Chicago area. Since these were the areas of major recruitment effort in the United States, most of the social-network trajectories over which migrants travel lead to these general locations. This also helps explain why some communities in Mexico, the so-called traditional sending areas, export so many people, while other similarly impoverished areas export relatively few. The former are among those originally tapped by the major recruiters and, thus, are deeply imbedded in the web of migratory networks. Because the latter were "outside the loop," their potential migrants must expend more time, effort, and resources in order to launch similar forays. Of course, new linkages do form, but they are very slow to generate the volume of the mature networks.

These conditions affect the relative attractiveness of NAFTA-induced and other Mexican-based employment opportunities in a number of critical ways. Most important, they reduce the costs and uncertainties of heading north. Thus, in order for opportunities to deter migration, the returns to workers need to be far better than those already available. Moreover, a related and critical effect of these migration processes is that sending communities become dependent upon remittances from the migrants. An estimated $3.2 billion was sent home in 1990 alone.[48] Hence, the networks not only reduce the costs of migration but also induce a strong dose of *dependence* on Yankee-style wages. Accordingly, Rafael Alarcon reports that migration patterns failed to exhibit any discernible change in one traditional sending area he studied, despite substantial growth in manufacturing production there.[49]

In summary, the processes of migration undercut the attractiveness of NAFTA-style employment. This provides yet another reason to conclude that NAFTA cannot and will not succeed in appreciably reducing migration.

NAFTA, MEXICAN-U.S. MIGRATION, AND MICHIGAN COMMUNITIES

The state of Michigan currently ranks third among the fifty states in volume of business conducted with Mexico. There is little reason to expect a shift in that ranking, although the volume of business can be expected to increase with NAFTA. While it has been argued here that NAFTA will stimulate more migration than it will stem, Michigan is unlikely to be among the major receivers of the flow. This is because the best available evidence suggests that the state is not currently receiving many Mexican immigrants, and it is virtually certain that future migrants will mainly venture over established trajectories.

Many strands of evidence support this generalization. The most immediate concerns population growth. A recent analysis of the social and demographic characteristics of Latinos (Hispanics) in the Midwest shows that the Mexican-origin population of Michigan grew relatively slowly during the 1980s, a decade of record-breaking Mexican migration to the United States as a whole. This slow growth suggests little immigration. Moreover, between 1980 and 1990, the state's Mexican-origin population grew from about 112,000 to just over 138,000, or by slightly more than 26,000, in contrast to a growth of nearly 47,000 between 1970 and 1980.[50] Thus, it appears that Mexican migration to Michigan slowed rather than increased during the period of record Mexican immigration.

Indeed, there is good reason to believe that immigrants accounted for only a small amount of Michigan's total Mexican-origin population growth (73,000) over both decades. First, the relatively meager growth is likely to have stemmed from the balance between natural increase (excess of births over deaths) and net migration (more entries than exits), rather than mostly from arrivals from other areas. Thus, the total number of in-migrants cannot possibly match, much less exceed, the 73,000 figure, unless that statistic reflects substantial out-migration or major aberrations in typical mortality/fertility patterns, and there is no evidence to support either of these possibilities.

A second reason is that the portion of the growth attributable to new arrivals in Michigan may consist largely or solely of "internal" migrants (from other parts of the United States), rather than "immigrants" (from abroad/Mexico). This is supported by data about the state's Mexican-origin population from the 1990 Census. Although the state's 1990 Mexican-origin population is over twice its 1970 size, only about 10 percent of those enumerated in 1990 were actually born in Mexico. Hence, over the two decades, some combination of new births and migration from other states accounts for at least 80 percent of this population's growth.[51] Finally, extensive historical work on the evolution of the Mexican presence in the Midwest indicates that, after World War II, both agricultural and industrial employers of Mexican-origin workers primarily used Chicanos or Mexican Americans, rather than Mexicans.[52] Even migrant workers to the region, whose numbers have leveled off since the 1970s, tend to come from Texas rather than Mexico.

In view of the fact that nearly all of the predictable increase in Mexican-U.S. migration is likely to ensue along the current trajectories, and since these do not appear to lead to Michigan, the state is unlikely to gain many new Hispanic immigrants. Of course, new linkages do form, and a number of areas that previously had few Mexicans are now home to new communities. One example is New York City, where a sizable Mexican community has begun to flourish.[53] While the 1990 Census enumerated about 62,000 Mexicans in residence there, one researcher estimates the number to be closer to 96,000.[54] Moreover, within this group, large numbers hail from the same sending communities, and it appears that the "transnational communities" discussed earlier are now forming. Nevertheless, their growth was quite slow until very recently.[55] Therefore, while linkages between Michigan and Mexico could produce migration to the state, it will not happen rapidly.

CONCLUSION

It has been argued here that NAFTA will stimulate more migration than it will stem. Recent events noted below, which have wreaked havoc on the Mexican economy, ensure the basic thrust of the argument—namely, migration will increase, probably dramatically, regardless of whether Michigan receives many more immigrants. Moreover, the causes of the calamitous downturn in the Mexican economy are far more consistent with the critique advanced here than with the prescriptions of the treaty's proponents.

Rather than ushering in a period of political reform and social stability in Mexico, as promised by proponents, NAFTA's implementation triggered precisely the opposite. On the very day the treaty took effect, 1 January 1994, the world was stunned by news of the Chiapas rebellion, the first major antigovernment uprising in Mexico in decades. The "Zapatista" National Liberation Army cited many grievances, but chose to tie the uprising to the start of NAFTA, because, to them, it represented an extension of the kinds of "reforms" that were driving Mexico's workers and peasantry deeper and deeper into poverty and despair.[56]

The Chiapas uprising was followed by a number of prominent political assassinations.[57] While these incidents surely unnerved many potential investors, the single most important event undercutting the NAFTA promise has been the economic crisis unleashed by the severe devaluation of the Mexican peso. Its exchange value fell about 50 percent between December 1994 and March 1995, a devastating reduction in purchasing power.[58] The resulting crisis has been catastrophic in Mexico and has sent major shocks through the United States and other parts of Latin America. In Mexico, for example, inflation, interest rates, business and bank defaults, and layoffs have shot up, while tens of thousands (possibly hundreds of thousands) of United States workers also stand to lose their jobs.[59] The Clinton administration responded by masterminding a $50 billion dollar "bailout," to which the United States contributed $20 billion, but repair of the depressed state of the economy will, by all accounts, be years in the making and painful in the extreme.[60]

While few might have predicted the extent of the peso's fall, the overvaluation was hardly a secret. As noted by Marc Levinson in

Newsweek, "the problems that would lead to the peso's collapse were anything but secret."[61] The overvaluation was used during the Salinas presidency as a strategy to stimulate foreign investment. Levinson notes that both the World Bank and the United States Treasury favored devaluation by as much as 30 percent, although *this was not made public.* In addition, Moody's and Standard & Poor's both labeled investing in Mexico as high risk. Levinson quotes a University of California professor's candid assessment that "anyone who conducted business in Mexico or traveled in Mexico . . . knew the peso was overvalued."[62] Similarly realistic accounts of weaknesses in the Mexican economy can be found in the work of NAFTA opponents, particularly those focused on Mexican issues.[63]

In much of the key literature supporting NAFTA, however, almost no mention is made of these problems. For example, in the two major works by the treaty's most celebrated boosters, Hufbauer and Schott,[64] not a single reference to the potential perils of the peso's overvaluation can be found. Indeed, the authors advance the fantastic claim that NAFTA would lead to a *real increase* in the peso exchange rate of nearly 30 percent! Likewise, not a word is devoted to the grave social costs of Mexico's economic liberalization strategy, of which NAFTA is part and parcel, let alone the potential for social unrest that such a strategy undoubtedly entailed.

Despite the oversights of NAFTA proponents, one thing is certain: the Mexican economic crisis will increase migration. On the basis of interviews with Mexican workers and United States immigration experts, the *Wall Street Journal* published a story detailing the consensus that migration will increase, perhaps by as much as 25 percent, from traditional sending areas.[65] Moreover, even before the crisis unfolded, the failure of NAFTA to produce a rate of job growth sufficient to dampen migration was evident. As Anderson and others have noted, during the first six months of 1994, the entire (formal) Mexican economy expanded by only around 84,000 jobs—far, far fewer than the treaty's promoters implied or promised.[66] Furthermore, the displacements from agricultural production tied to NAFTA will add even more pressure to migrate.

The conclusion, therefore, is that NAFTA can only lead to more, not less, migration. Due to the nature of migration processes, however, relatively few migrants should find their way to areas in the United States not currently receiving Mexican immigrants. For this reason, Michigan is unlikely to see an increase, despite possible growth in trade or capital exchanges with Mexico. Given the current crisis, however, even the potential upsurge in business with Mexico may be in jeopardy for some time to come.[67]

NOTES

1. Rafael Alarcon, "Labor Migration from Mexico and Free Trade: Lessons from a Transnational Community," working paper, Chicano/Latino Policy Project, University of California, Berkeley, 1994; Peter Andreas, "The Making of Amerexico: (Mis)Handling Illegal Immigration," *World Policy Journal* 11, no. 2 (1994): 45-56; Norman A. Bailey, "The Economic Effects of *Not* Passing the NAFTA," in *Assessments of the North American Free Trade Agreement*, A.H. Moss Jr., ed. (New Brunswick, N.J.: Transaction Publishers, 1993), 1-18; Wayne A. Cornelius and Philip L. Martin, "The Uncertain Connection: Free Trade and Rural Mexican Migration to the United States," *International Migration Review* 27, no. 3 (1993): 484-512; Jeff Faux, "The NAFTA Illusion," *Challenge* 36, no. 4 (July/August 1993): 4-9; Raul Hinojosa Ojeda and Sherman Robinson, "Labor Issues in a North American Free Trade Area," in *North American Free Trade: Assessing the Impact*, Nora Lustig, B. P. Bosworth and R. Z. Lawrence, eds. (Washington, D.C.: Brookings Institution, 1992), 69-108; Philip Martin, *Trade and Migration: NAFTA and Agriculture* (Washington, D.C.: Institute for International Economics, 1993); and Sidney Weintraub, "NAFTA and Migration," *National Forum* 74, no. 3 (1994): 29-32.
2. Cornelius and Martin, "Uncertain Connection"; Gary C. Hufbauer and Jeffrey J. Schott, *North American Free Trade: Issues and Recommendations* (Washington, D.C.: Institute for International Economics, 1992); Martin, *Trade and Migration*; and Weintraub, "NAFTA and Migration."
3. Alarcon, "Labor Migration"; Andreas, "Amerexico"; Hinojosa Ojeda and Robinson, "Labor Issues"; and Timothy Koechlin and Mehrene Larudee, "The High Cost of NAFTA," *Challenge* 35, no. 5 (September/October 1992): 19-26.
4. Andreas, "Amerexico"; Richard S. Belous and Jonathan Lemco, "The NAFTA Development Model of Combining High and Low Wage Areas: An Introduction," in *NAFTA as a Model of Development: The Benefits and Costs of Merging High and Low Wage Areas*, R. S. Belous and J. Lemco, eds. (Washington, D.C.: National Planning Association, 1993), 1-17; Martin, *Trade and Migration*; Alexander Monto, *The Roots of Labor Migration* (Westport, Conn.: Praeger, 1994); and Thomas Muller and Thomas J. Espenshade, *The Fourth Wave: California's Newest Immigrants* (Washington, D.C.: Urban Institute, 1985).

5. Francisco Alba, "Migrant Labor Supply and Demand in Mexico and the United States: A Global Perspective," in *U.S.-Mexico Relations: Labor Market Interdependence*, J. A. Bustamante, C. W. Reynolds, R. A. Hinojosa Ojeda, eds. (Stanford, Calif.: Stanford University Press, 1992), 243-56; Hinojosa Ojeda and Robinson, "Labor Issues"; Martin, *Trade and Migration*; Philip Martin,"Immigration and Agriculture: An Endless Debate," *International Affairs* 74, no. 3 (1994): 23-28; and Thomas Muller, "The Demand for Hispanic Workers in Urban Areas of the United States," in *U.S.-Mexico Relations: Labor Market Interdependence*, J. A. Bustamante, C. W. Reynolds, R. A. Hinojosa Ojeda, eds. (Stanford, Calif.: Stanford University Press, 1992), 353-71.

6. Demand for immigrant labor in the United States will continue indefinitely in both agriculture and urban settings. On agriculture, see Martin, *Trade and Migration* and "Immigration and Agriculture"; and Richard Mines, Beatriz Boccalandro, and Susan Gabbard, "The Latinization of U.S. Farm Labor," *Report on the Americas* 26, no.1 (1992): 42-46. On demand for Hispanic workers and urban settings, see Muller and Espanshade, *Fourth Wave*; Michael J. Piore, *Birds of Passage: Migrant Labor and Industrial Societies* (New York: Cambidge University Press,1979); Saskia Sassan, "Why Immigration?" *Report on the Americas* 26, no.1 (1992): 14-19; Saskia Sassan and Robert C. Smith, "Post Industrial Growth and Economic Reorganization: Their Impact on Immigrant Employment," in *U.S.-Mexico Relations: Labor Market Interdependence*, J. A. Bustamante, C. W. Reynolds, R. A. Hinojosa Ojeda, eds. (Stanford, Calif.: Stanford University Press, 1992), 372-96.

In agricultural work, the seasonality, low wages, and increasingly distant locales (from native population concentrations) have led to lower proportions of native workers and more immigrants; see Martin, *Trade and Migration*; and Mines, Boccalandro, and Gabbard, "Latinization." In addition, the Bracero Program established links that facilitated immigration even after the program's demise, and the mere availability of cheaper labor influenced the structuring of the industry away from mechanization. According to Martin, "Agricultural engineers note that machines are available to harvest practically every fruit and vegetable grown in the United States, but that machines replace hand-pickers only when it is economically rational to make the switch—that is when the cost of machine harvesting is cheaper than the cost of hand harvesting" (*Trade and Migration*, 80). Finally, increased acreage devoted to growing, including vast areas under preparation for future harvesting, all foster increased demand for agriculturally based immigrant labor (Martin, "Immigration and Agriculture").

Demand for urban workers willing to take low-quality jobs will also increase because advanced economies cannot easily eradicate or make attractive low-level jobs (Piore, *Birds of Passage*; Sassan, "Why Immigration?"). Jobs that are highly unstable, have little social status (such as dog walkers or dishwashers), and, especially, entail *very low wages* and little upward mobility (such as household help), increasingly attract fewer domestic workers but still draw immigrants. Factors such as the rise of single-parent and dual-income households, for example, generate demand for some such workers (household help, child care), while in other cases, the mere presence of the cheaper workers is likely to influence demand, as with agriculture.

7. Nora Lustig, "NAFTA: Doing Well by Doing Good," *Brookings Review* 12, no. 1 (1994): 47; and Hufbauer and Schott, *North American Free Trade.*

8. Cornelius and Martin, "Uncertain Connection"; and Gary C. Hufbauer and Jeffrey J. Schott, *NAFTA: An Assessment* (Washington, D.C.: Institute for International Economics, 1993).

9. Koechlin and Larudee, "High Cost of NAFTA."

10. Alajandro Alvarez and Gabriel Mendoza, "Mexico: Neo-Liberal Disaster Zone," in *Crossing the Line: Canada and Free Trade with Mexico,* J. Sinclair, ed. (Vancouver: New Star Books, Ltd., 1992), 26-37.

11. Hufbauer and Schott, *North American Free Trade,* 52-57; they cite an obscure study that projected NAFTA would produce 1.5 million jobs in Mexico: KPMG Peat Marwick, "Analysis of Economic Effects of Free Trade Agreement between the United States and Mexico" (Washington, D.C.: U.S. Council of the Mexico-U.S. Business Committee, March 1991). The work is not widely available, and their description of the study does not make clear when the target would be reached or whether the estimate took into account the expected rural displacement of Mexican producers.

12. See reviews in Drucilla K. Brown, "The Impact of a North American Free Trade Area: Applied General Equilibrium Models," in *North American Free Trade: Assessing the Impact,* B. P. Bosworth and R. Z. Lawrence, eds. (Washington, D.C.: Brookings Institution, 1992), 26-68; Hinojosa Ojeda and Robinson, "Labor Issues"; Martin, *Trade and Migration*; and Sidney Weintraub, "Modeling the Industrial Effects of NAFTA," in *North American Free Trade: Assessing the Impact, Nora Lustig,* B. P. Bosworth and R. Z. Lawrence, eds. (Washington, D.C.: Brookings Institution, 1992), 109-43.

13. Martin, *Trade and Migration,* 38-39.

14. Lustig, "NAFTA," 47.

15. See, for example, Donald L. Barlett and James B. Steele, "America: What Went Wrong?" *Philadelphia Inquirer,* 20-28 October 1991; and *America: What Went Wrong?* (Kansas City, Mo.: Andrews and McMeel, 1992).

16. *Maquiladoras* are mostly foreign-owned (mainly by U.S. firms) or operated (Mexican-owned and U.S.-operated joint ventures) plants in Mexico, usually near the U.S. border, authorized by a special treaty. They primarily process or assemble imported products for reexport to the United States, capitalizing on workers' low wages and the favorable U.S. tariff treatment; see Hufbauer and Schott, *North American Free Trade.* By the 1990s, most U.S.-owned *maquiladoras* replaced or absorbed the expansion of similar production facilities in the United States, thereby discernibly shifting some U.S. employment south of the border; see Barlett and Steele, *America.*

17. See reviews in James M. Cypher, "The Ideology of Economic Science in the Selling of NAFTA: The Political Economy of Elite Decision-Making," *Review of Radical Political Economics* 25, no.4 (1993):146-64; Ray Marshall, "Internationalization: Implications for Workers," *Journal of International Affairs* 48, no.1 (1994): 59-94; and James Stanford, "Continental Economic Integration: Modeling the Impact on Labor," *Annals of the Academy of Political and Social Science* 526 (1993): 92-110.

18. Stanford, "Economic Integration."

19. Ibid., 100

20. Ibid.

21. Alvarez and Mendoza, Mexico; Teresa Rendon and Carlos Salas, "The Probable Impact of NAFTA on Non-Agricultural Employment in Mexico," *Review of Radical Political Economics* 25, no. 4 (1993): 109-19; and Janet M. Tanski, "Capital Concentration, Mexican Conglomerates and the Proposed North American Free Trade Agreement," *Review of Radical Political Economics* 25, no. 4 (1993): 72-90.

22. Alvarez and Mendoza, "Mexico."

23. Emilio Pradilla Cobo, "The Limits of the Mexican Maquiladora Industry," *Review of Radical Political Economics* 25, no. 4 (1993): 91-108.

24. David Barkin, "Salinastroika and Other Novel Ideas," from the *Progressive Economists Network*, 24 November 1992.

25. Hinojosa Ojeda and Robinson, "Labor Issues"; Martin, *Trade and Migration*; and Weintraub, "NAFTA and Migration."

26. Koechlin and Larudee, "High Cost of NAFTA"; and Martin, *Trade and Migration*.

27. Marshall, "Internationalization"; and Harley Shaiken, "Two Myths about Mexico," *New York Times*, 22 August 1993, E15.

28. Shaiken, "Two Myths."

29. Pradilla Cobo, "Maquiladora Industry"; Edward Y. George, "What Does the Future Hold for the Maquiladora Industry?" in *The Maquliadora Industry: Economic Solution or Problem?*, K. Fatemi, ed. (New York: Praeger, 1990), 219-33; and Martin, *Trade and Migration*.

30. Faux, "NAFTA Illusion," 6.

31. Harley Shaiken, "Advanced Manufacturing and Mexico: A New International Division of Labor?" *Latin American Research Review* 29, no.2 (1994): 39-71.

32. Shaiken, "Advanced Manufacturing and Mexico," 41.

33. Ibid., 58.

34. Ibid., 58-59.

35. Sarah Anderson, John Cavanagh, David Ranney, and Paul Schwalb, eds., *NAFTA's First Year: Lessons for the Hemisphere* (Washington, D.C.: Institute for Policy Studies, 1995); Alvarez and Mendoza, "Mexico"; Ernest F. Hollings, "Reform Mexico First," *Foreign Policy* 93 (winter 1993-94): 91-103; Marshall, "Internationalization"; and Shaiken, "Advanced Manufacturing and Mexico."

36. George, "What does the Future Hold."
37. Shaiken, "Advanced Manufacturing and Mexico."
38. Andreas, "Amerexico"; Martin, *Trade and Migration*; Faux, "NAFTA Illusion"; and Hollings, "Reform Mexico First."
39. Faux, "NAFTA Illusion," 6.
40. Martin, *Trade and Migration*.
41. Ibid., 126.
42. Labor and environmental issues (along with "import surge" issues) were left to the so-called side agreements. These did not entail the binding power of the regular treaty; rather, committees will oversee problem solving with minimal enforcement mechanisms. Moreover, disputes involving "labor organizations' right to strike, to bargain collectively, . . . (etc.)" could not be subject to any sanctions under this agreement; see Hufbauer and Schott, *NAFTA: An Assessment*, 181.
43. Hufbauer and Schott, *North American Free Trade*.
44. Alejandro Valle Baeza, "Mean Wage Differences between Canada, the United States and Mexico," *Review of Radical Political Economics* 25, no.4 (1993): 120-32; and Clark Reynolds, "The NAFTA and Wage Convergence: A Case of Winners and Losers," in *NAFTA as a Model of Development: The Benefits and Costs of Merging High and Low Wage Areas*, R. S. Belous and J. Lemco, eds. (Washington, DC: National Planning Association, 1992), 18-22.
45. Harley L. Browning and Nestor Rodriguez, "The Migration of Mexican Indocumentados as a Settlement Process: Implications for Work," in *Hispanics in the U.S. Economy*, G. J. Borjas and Marta Tienda, eds. (New York: Academic Press, 1985); Martin, *Trade and Migration*; Douglas S. Massey, "The Social Organization of Mexican Migration to the United States," *Annals of the American Academy of Political and Social Science* 487 (1986): 102-13; Douglas S. Massey, Rafael Alarcon, Jorge Durand, and Humberto Gonzales, *Return to Aztlan: The Social Process of International Migration from Western Mexico* (Berkeley: University of California Press, 1987); Monto, *Roots of Labor Migration*; Muller and Espenshade, *Fourth Wave*; Alejandro Portes, "Unauthorized Immigration and Immigration Reform: Present Trends and Prospects," in Sergio Diaz-Briquets and Sidney Weintraub, *Determinants of Emigration from Mexico, Central America, and the Caribbean* (Boulder, Colo.: Westview Press, 1991), 75-98; Alejandro Portes and Jozsef Borocz, "Contemporary Immigration: Theoretical Perspectives on Its Determinants and Models of Incorporation," *International Migration Review* 23, no. 3 (1989): 606-30; and Roger Waldinger, "The Integration of the New Immigrants," *Law and Contemporary Problems* 45, no. 2 (1982): 197-222.
46. Portes and Borocz, "Contemporary Immigration," 608.
47. Martin, *Trade and Migration*.
48. Fernando Lozano Ascencio, *Bringing It Back Home: Remittances to Mexico from Migrant Workers in the United States*, Monograph Series No. 37 (San

Diego, Calif.: Center for U.S.-Mexico Studies, University of California 1993).

49. Alarcon, "Labor Migration."

50. Robert Aponte and Marcelo Siles, Latinos in the Heartland: The Browning of the Midwest, Research Report No. 5, Julian Samora Research Institute, Michigan State University, 1994.

51. Ibid; U.S. Bureau of the Census, *1990 Census of Population*, Social and Economic Characteristics, Michigan, CP-2-24.

52. Dennis N. Valdes, *Al Norte: Agricultural Workers in the Great Lakes Region, 1917-1970* (Austin: University of Texas Press, 1991); and Zaragosa Vargas, *Proletarians of the North: A History of Mexican Industrial Workers in Detroit and the Midwest, 1917-1933* (Berkeley: University of California Press, 1993).

53. Sassan and Smith, "Post Industrial Growth"; and Robert Smith, "Mixteca in New York: New York in Mexteca," *Report on the Americas* 26, no. 1 (1992): 39-41.

54. Smith, "Mixteca."

55. Ibid.

56. Allan Nairn, "After NAFTA: Chiapas Uprising," *Multinational Monitor* 15, no. 1-2 (January/February 1994): 6-9.

57. Michael S. Serrill, "Real Life Soap Opera," *Time*, 20 March 1995, 56-57; and Russell Watson, "Blood Relations," *Newsweek*, 13 March 1995, 28-29.

58. Anthony DePalma, "Sweeping up the Rubble of the Peso: Dreams Dashed, Mexico Business Tries to Adjust," *New York Times*, 31 March 1995, C3.

59. Marc Levinson, "How it All Went South," *Newsweek*, 27 March 1995, 32-35; and Allen R. Myerson, "Strategies on Mexico Cast Aside: Peso's Fall Skews Trade Pact Hopes," *New York Times*, 14 February 1995, C1, 9.

60. Anthony DePalma, "U.S. Aid Plan Is Hardly a Cure-All: Mexico Likely to Face Recession, Debt Burden," *New York Times*, 23 February 1995, C3; Tim Golden, "Mexico's New Leader Finds Job Full of Painful Surprises," *New York Times*, 14 March 1995, A1, 7; and Levinson, "How It All Went South."

61. Levinson, "How It All Went South," 32, 35.

62. Ibid., 33

63. Cypher, "Ideology of Economic Science"; Faux, "NAFTA Illusion"; and Hollings, "Reform Mexico First."

64. Hufbauer and Schott, *North American Free Trade*; and *NAFTA: An Assessment*.

65. Frederick Rose and Dianne Solis, "Plunge of the Peso and Hard Times to Follow May Spur Surge of Mexican Immigration to U.S.," *Wall Street Journal*, 16 January 1995, A2.

66. Anderson et al., *NAFTA's First Year*.

67. The author gratefully acknowledges the helpful commentary of this volume's editors and reviewers on earlier versions of this essay; likewise for the commentary of David Arsen, Rosemary George, Cory Krupp, and, especially, Peter Dorman, although the usual disclaimers fully apply.

NAFTA, Collective Bargaining, and Employment Adjustments in the United States and Canada

Richard N. Block

The 1993 debate in the United States and Canada over the passage of NAFTA centered on jobs. Would the treaty encourage companies to shift production and jobs to Mexico, resulting in unemployment in the United States and Canada?[1] This fear was based on their large labor-cost differential relative to Mexico. In 1990, indices of hourly compensation cost in the three countries, with the United States indexed at 100, were 107 in Canada and 12 in Mexico.[2] In 1993, these figures were 100, 97, and 16, respectively. Expressed in U.S. dollars, average hourly compensation for manufacturing workers was $16.79 in the United States and $16.36 in Canada, but only $2.65 in Mexico.[3] In essence, there was concern about the United States and Canada entering a free trade arrangement with a country that seemed to be at a different stage of economic development, a concern that mirrored the debate in Europe around admitting the former Soviet bloc nations to the European Community.[4]

NAFTA's passage means the continuation of competitive pressures on U.S. and Canadian firms and workers. Put differently, the accord is the continuation of a trend toward free trade that firms in both countries have had to face over the past two decades. The key issue is not whether competitively driven adjustments in the employment relations system of firms will occur in the United States and Canada, but, rather, the process by which these adjustments will occur.[5] That is the topic of this chapter, which first will discuss the two major adjustment models: unilateral and negotiated through collective bargaining. The heart of the chapter then will explore the framework for negotiated adjustment in the United States and Canada, pointing out that collective bargaining is a more integral part of employment relations in Canada than in the United States, making negotiated adjustment far more likely in the former than in the latter. After a brief discussion of examples of negotiated adjustment structures in Canada, the implications for Michigan will be examined before the chapter ends with a short summary and conclusions.

RESPONSES TO COMPETITION IN THE UNITED STATES AND CANADA

Although the employment effects of NAFTA can only be estimated, it seems quite certain that Canadian and U.S. firms will face heightened competition from Mexican imports and that some will contemplate establishing facilities south of the border. The imports may affect both workers and shareholders, since total revenues of the firm may decline. The relocation burden falls primarily on workers, to the extent that production in a firm's Mexican facility replaces production in its U.S. and Canadian facilities. If shareholders are interested primarily in maximizing return on equity and share price, the locus of production is a matter of indifference to them.

Heightened competition likely will elicit a range of responses from firms, and the focus here is not on which firms will succeed or fail, but on the internal processes organizations will use to make adjustments and the implications of different types of processes. In particular, there are two broad categories of procedures at the shop-floor level for responding to competition—unilateral and negotiated. In a unilateral response, management makes whatever adjustments it deems necessary. In a negotiated response, management must involve employee representatives in the decision. Each of these procedures is examined in more detail in the following.

UNILATERAL ADJUSTMENTS BY MANAGEMENT

The classic situation in capitalist democracies is unilateral adjustments made by management. The corporation is a collectivity of shareholders whose primary interest is to maximize the share price and rate of return on investment. The firm is managed for the benefit of the shareholders, who govern the firm by electing a Board of Directors, who in turn appoint management. The legal obligation of the managers is to operate the firm so as to maximize the financial rate of return for the shareholders.[6] Management is the ultimate decision maker.

This model strongly favors the interests of firm management, but raises concerns about the effect of competitive adjustments on the other stakeholders. In some instances, management may perceive the interests of the shareholders as coinciding with those of the other stakeholders, but this is not always the case. What is clear from this model is that the needs of the shareholders, the owners of the firm, will be addressed.

NEGOTIATED ADJUSTMENTS

The second model of management response is negotiated adjustment. Although managers may have primary responsibility for formulating a response to competition, they must consult with employee representatives. While management *may* consult with other stakeholders, such as customers and the community, it *must* consult with its employees.

Such a model is operative when there is formal employee representation. Unlike in Germany, for example, where the law mandates such representation, in the United States and Canada there is workplace representation only if the employees have chosen a labor organization (usually a union) to represent them for collective bargaining purposes. In that case, the employer is obligated to negotiate with the union.

COMPARING THE TWO MODELS

It is clear that the basic difference in these two models of adjustment is the decision-making process. In the unilateral model decisions are made solely by management, while in the negotiated model, there is some level of consultation with employee representatives, usually the union. An organization whose institutional role is to represent workers is far more likely to consider their interests than is management acting alone in its legal capacity as the representative of the shareholders. Although it is possible for management to view the adjustment as an opportunity for workers and the shareholders to gain, it is equally possible for management to view the shareholder interests as being best served if the adjustment cuts labor costs through reducing employment and wage rates.

Based on the foregoing, one would conclude, other things being equal, that negotiated responses are more likely to be attentive to workers' interests than are unilateral adjustments. Moreover, to the extent that workers live in the community, their interests are likely to coincide with those of the surrounding community.

Yet it is also true that negotiation and consultation may be viewed by management as costly, hampering their ability to make the necessary changes with appropriate speed. Moreover, managers may believe that negotiation and the attendant sharing of information may result in proprietary information being released. In general, management views unencumbered decision making as in the best interests of the adjustment process of the firm.

More broadly, however, the fundamental question raised by the choice of decision-making models is who shall participate in the adjustment process. This question is important because participation defines whose interests will be represented. It is reasonable to believe that adjustments, to the extent that they involve changes in established patterns of work and employment, are likely to involve costs to some and benefits to others. If only management and the shareholders participate, they are most likely to receive the benefits. If employees participate, the benefits are more likely to be shared.

COLLECTIVE BARGAINING AND NEGOTIATED ADJUSTMENT: THE FRAMEWORK IN CANADA AND THE UNITED STATES

As the foregoing discussion indicates, negotiated adjustments to competitive pressures, including those resulting from NAFTA, are likely to address a wider range of concerns than unilateral responses to these competitive pressures. Because collective bargaining and unionization are the principal vehicles for negotiated responses, the bulk of this section analyzes the systems of collective bargaining in the United States and Canada.

OVERVIEW

It is well accepted that unionism and collective bargaining are far more prevalent in Canada than in the United States. In the mid-1950s, the unionization rate in both countries was approximately 35 percent, and through the 1990s, the Canadian rate remained at about that level, while the U.S. rate declined by roughly half.[7] This difference has been attributed to several factors, such as a more statist culture in Canada than in the United States and a three-party Canadian governmental system that gives unions political power disproportionate to their actual voting numbers.[8]

Whatever the intrinsic causes, comparative research over the last decade has demonstrated that Canadian labor laws are far more supportive of the institution of collective bargaining than are U.S. labor laws.[9] Although the two have labor laws that are outwardly quite similar, and the Canadian systems used the United States as a model, the two have diverged over the past fifty years.

GENERAL CHARACTERISTICS OF CANADIAN AND U.S. LABOR LAW SYSTEMS

The industrial relations legal structures in the United States and Canada are broadly similar. They are majoritarian, workplace-based systems under which representation is provided by independent trade unions only when the majority of the employees in a bargaining unit select the union to represent them. Negotiations then take place at the workplace level.

In the United States, an election is conducted in a bargaining unit if a union can demonstrate a showing of "substantial interest."[10] The union will be certified to represent the employees for collective bargaining if a majority of those workers vote for representation. The employer then is obligated to bargain in good faith with the union. The National Labor Relations Act (NLRA) is administered by the National Labor Relations Board (NLRB), a specialized administrative agency with authority to certify unions and remedy unfair labor practices.

The Canadian Constitution gives responsibility for most labor relations to provinces, with the federal government having jurisdiction only over the territories and certain industrial sectors that generally cross provincial boundaries.[11] The provinces have developed what

George Adams describes as a common core of legal principles governing industrial relations,[12] and for the most part, these are similar to the NLRA principles. Thus, each province provides a procedure by which a determination on majority status can be made, a certification process, and a requirement to bargain in good faith. Each jurisdiction except Quebec has a labor relations board that administers the provincial statute by making certification decisions and addressing unfair labor practice charges.[13] Unlike the NLRB, not all provincial labor boards in Canada use elections as the primary evidence that employees want a union.[14] Other proof includes signed membership cards, evidence of a financial commitment, and a match between employees and union eligibility requirements.[15]

The similarities between the United States and Canada are not surprising, since union political pressure for adoption of labor legislation began in the late 1930s in both countries. Although Canadian legislation at that time relied on criminal prosecution for enforcement, the growth in the labor movement simultaneous with World War II resulted in increased governmental involvement in labor relations to ensure industrial peace for the war effort. In 1944 a conference of labor ministers developed a set of principles incorporated into the federal Industrial Relations Disputes Investigation Act of 1948. It applied only within the federal jurisdiction, but by the early 1950s all the provinces had adopted laws consistent with its principles.[16]

Thus, the United States and Canada initially had industrial relations legal systems that were broadly similar, but differences developed after the 1950s. The Canadian system has at least three attributes that distinguish it from the U.S. system: normal maintenance of the system; a wider scope of informal activities and greater independence of the system; and tripartitism.

Normal Maintenance of the System

In the United States, the NLRA has rarely been amended. Enacted in 1935, it underwent major revisions in 1947, and minor amendments were made in 1959 and 1974. There has been no change to the basic rights protected under the law or to its basic remedial structure since 1947.

In contrast, the Canadian provinces are continually amending their industrial relations statutes. For example, the Alberta statute, enacted in 1947, was modified 13 times between 1950 and 1988.[17]

The Ontario Labor Relations Act, passed in 1950, was altered on 21 occasions from 1954 to 1995.[18] All of the provinces demonstrate a similar pattern.[19]

Although the various amendments are not of equal importance, this continual process demonstrates a vibrant industrial relations legal system in Canada, in which both parties are able to have their interests represented and in which the laws generally do not tilt too far in the direction of either side for too long a period. In essence, Canada has developed "normal maintenance" of the system, and this is not true of the United States.

One explanation is that the parliamentary system in Canada, in which the two major political parties form alliances with the labor-backed New Democratic Party (NDP; until 1991 the Cooperative Commonwealth Federation, or CCF) in order to form a government,[20] makes changes in labor legislation far more likely there than in the United States. But this does not detract from the fact that normal maintenance of the Canadian system enables the amendment of labor laws as needed.

Scope of Activities and Independence of the System

In the United States, the role of the NLRB (as well as other federal and state governmental agencies, such as the Federal Mediation and Conciliation Service) is generally quite passive during collective bargaining. The NLRB is only involved if a refusal to bargain or other unfair labor practice charge is filed, and then only to determine whether an unfair labor practice was committed. The Federal Mediation and Conciliation Service or state mediation agencies generally become involved only if invited.

Governments in Canada, however, usually play an active role in monitoring the bargaining process. Governmental mediation prior to a party engaging in a legal strike or lockout is required in the federal jurisdiction,[21] and in New Brunswick, Newfoundland, Nova Scotia, Prince Edward Island, and Ontario.[22] In all jurisdictions, one party may initiate the mediation process simply by requesting it, and the other party must cooperate. The appropriate governmental agency may initiate the process in British Columbia, Quebec, and Saskatchewan.[23] In some provinces, the Minister of Labor may appoint a conciliation board prior to a legal strike being called.[24] In British Columbia, Manitoba, Newfoundland, Ontario, Quebec,

Saskatchewan, and the federal jurisdiction there is a provision for first-agreement arbitration by the government, generally upon the application of either party.[25]

These mechanisms involve the government in the bargaining process to a much greater extent than in the United States. They help assure that employer power is not used to undermine the collective bargaining relationship and the existence of unions. Government intervention also can help assure that union power is not used to harm smaller employers severely.

In addition to the wider scope of government activities, labor relations boards in Canada are subject only to limited judicial oversight, resulting in far greater finality for their decisions than is the case in the United States. Canadian statutes generally restrict judicial review to disputes over a board's jurisdiction in a case or a claim that the party was denied "natural justice" (due process).[26] A court cannot overturn a board decision based on its view that the board misinterpreted the law.

The greater finality of labor board decisions in Canada is illustrated by the low appeal rate. The percentage of cases closed with a court decision averaged approximately 7.1 percent for Ontario from 1980 to 1992, 5.2 percent for British Columbia from 1988 to 1991, and 6.4 percent for the federal jurisdiction between 1980 and 1991. In contrast, for the period 1908-92, approximately 33 percent of all NLRB compliance orders were closed with a U.S. court decision.[27]

Deference to the labor boards means that the Canadian system is likely to be administered by appointed industrial relations experts, as opposed to judges, which is less true in the United States. Compared to the United States, the Canadian system is much more self-determinative and there is much less scope in Canada for challenging the board decisions. The result is that the parties are forced to address issues through industrial relations processes based on negotiations, as opposed to legal processes based on rights determined through an adversary proceeding.

Tripartitism

Several of the Canadian labor boards are structured differently from the NLRB, which is composed of political appointees with five-year terms. Seven Canadian provinces have tripartite boards consisting of representatives of labor and management, as well as neutral parties.[28]

The function of the NLRB is to administer the NLRA and protect the rights of employees, unions, and employers. It is designed to be a fair, impartial arbiter of the cases that come before it.[29] Under the legislation enacted between 1935 and 1947, the NLRB generally protected the rights of unions. With the Taft-Hartley changes in 1947, however, the board's role became essentially neutral and the NLRB now fundamentally serves as a detached adjudicative body.

In contrast, seven tripartite labor boards in Canada are composed of members chosen for their understanding of industrial relations and their ability to bring the perspective of their constituencies to any case. Tripartitism ensures that each party to a case comes before a board with members sympathetic to and familiar with its day-to-day concerns. This also enhances the chance that the result will be accepted, as the losing party knows that its point of view received a fair hearing. Another feature is that the possibility of compromise in the practical resolution of problems is increased.[30] As Adams notes, "the tripartite regulatory approach in Canada permitted the manning of the dispute resolution machinery, at least in part, by labor and management representatives and in this way created a commitment in the parties of interest to the workability of the system."[31]

The key word in this comment by Adams is "system." In other words, the tripartite board does more than simply protect rights. By including representatives of both parties, it is an institution with some interest in maintaining the overall system of industrial relations. The NLRB, as an adjudicator of the respective parties' rights, has no such system maintenance obligation.

DOCTRINAL ISSUES: THE DUTY TO BARGAIN IN THE UNITED STATES AND CANADA

While industrial relations structures facilitate negotiated adjustments, doctrinal issues also play an important role. To the extent that legal doctrine permits employers to make decisions on adjustments without consulting the union, there will be fewer negotiated adjustments. If legal doctrine requires negotiation, there will be more negotiated adjustments. There are vast differences in the manner in which the United States and Canada address the issue.

Bargaining Scope in the United States

Labor law doctrine in the United States has created a distinction between mandatory and permissive subjects of bargaining. Mandatory subjects are those involving terms or conditions of employment. An employer must negotiate about such issues with a union representing its employees. Permissive subjects do not affect terms or conditions of employment, and neither party has the obligation to bargain over these.[32]

Adjustments generally require decisions about what products will be produced, the production processes, and the locus of production. Thus, adjusting to competition may require changing a product mix, developing lower-cost processes, or consolidating work at one location. Such decisions often have profound effects on employees' interests in job security, promotion, wages, and so forth.

Generally, the employer has an interest in making these decisions unilaterally, without union negotiations. Unions generally wish to negotiate on these matters in order to protect the interests of members. Given these conflicting interests, resolution of the matter may come down to whether the law obligates the employer to negotiate with the union over decisions regarding the direction of the business.

Three types of adjustment options usually are considered: (1) facility closure; (2) relocation of work; and (3) changes in product mix and processes with no change in physical location. In *Textile Workers Union v. Darlington Manufacturing Company*,[33] the Supreme Court ruled that an employer has the absolute right to close a business, basing its decision on the view that the NLRA does not compel any person to be an employer. The ruling also states that an employer has broad authority to close part of its business, if this is not done for antiunion reasons.

Clearly, then, an employer in the United States may partially close operations, if this is done for business purposes. Such a decision need not be discussed with the union. Yet, a legitimate question arises as to when a partial closing is actually a work relocation. Is the employer truly eliminating the function performed at the facility to be closed, or is the function being shifted to another facility? Is the employer obligated to negotiate with the union over adjustments taking the form of a work relocation that also affect terms and conditions of employment? Three decisions, two by the Supreme Court and one by the NLRB, are relevant.

In 1964, in *Fibreboard Paper Products Corp.* v. *NLRB*,[34] the Court ruled that the employer was required to negotiate with the union regarding a decision to subcontract work done by its maintenance employees. The Court's decision was based on its finding that there was no change in the nature of the business, and the decision was based solely on labor costs, which is precisely the type of issue amenable to bargaining.

In 1981, in *First National Maintenance Corporation* v. *NLRB*,[35] the U.S. Supreme Court ruled that the employer need not negotiate with employees over termination of a maintenance contract with a nursing home because the decision was based solely on the size of the fee paid by the nursing home. That is, the matter had nothing to do with labor costs.

The basic lesson of these two cases is that the greater the importance of labor costs in the decision, the more likely it is that the employer has an obligation to bargain. Thus, subcontracting decisions based primarily on labor cost considerations and involving merely the substitution of one set of employees for another are subject to negotiations. A decision based on matters other than labor costs is not negotiable.[36]

How are such distinctions to be made? In *Dubuque Packing Co.*, decided in 1991,[37] the NLRB clarified the work relocation issue. First, it affirmed that the decision to close a facility for economic reasons was not a mandatory bargaining subject if the closure was not accompanied by a relocation of the work. Put differently, an employer need not negotiate with a union over a decision to eliminate part of its business. This is viewed as a basic change in the nature of business and not subject to union negotiation.

Making the distinction between a decision of *whether* to produce (a partial closing) and of *where* to produce, the NLRB said the latter is a relocation of work. Thus, a closing associated with shifting work is a relocation and is not associated with a basic change in the nature of the business. Unless the employer can demonstrate strong evidence to the contrary, relocation is considered to be a mandatory bargaining subject. In *Dubuque Packing*, the NLRB discussed the situations in which an employer could avoid a bargaining obligation: (1) work at the new location varies significantly from work at the old location; (2) work at the new location is part of a basic change in the nature of the business, such as a new production process; (3) labor costs are not a factor in the decision, so negotiation could not have changed the decision; and (4) labor costs are a factor, but union concessions could not have been sufficient to change the decision.

Changes in production techniques and processes unaccompanied by a relocation normally are addressed through the provisions of and procedures in an existing collective bargaining agreement. Such changes may involve job reassignments, retraining, new rates of pay, and so forth.

Bargaining Scope in Canada

Canada has never established a distinction between mandatory and permissive subjects of bargaining, although the parties may not negotiate over unlawful matters and may not insist on items that would change the structure of bargaining (for example, from multi-employer to single employer). In contrast to Canada, Adams has observed that, in the United States,

> subcontracting and plant-closing decisions have had a stormy history in terms of [the mandatory-permissive] classification. . . . The broader ambit of collective bargaining in Canada implicitly rejects the concept of a field of employer interest which cannot be encroached upon by joint deliberation. Collective bargaining arose in response to unilateral employer power and a limited scope to the bargaining duty is seen as inconsistent with this history.[38]

BARGAINING SCOPE SUMMARY

The foregoing discussion indicates a much higher status for collective bargaining in Canada than in the United States. This implies that the Canadian system is a much more widespread, institutionalized structure, in which all issues can be negotiated. In the United States, whether or not an adjustment must be negotiated may be the subject of litigation, and the mandatory-permissive distinction may create a barrier to innovation if it is used by one party to eliminate issues from the table, or if it is used as the basis of litigation that, in itself, can frustrate bargaining.[39] These differences can be expected to result in a larger percentage of negotiated responses to competition in Canada than in the United States.

NEGOTIATED ADJUSTMENTS: CANADIAN EXAMPLES

The greater integration of collective bargaining and employee representation into the Canadian economy has resulted in structures for adjustment that involve government, employers, and unions. For example, at the federal level, the Canadian Labor Market and Productivity Centre (CLMPC) is jointly managed by labor and business. It undertakes a major survey of training needs and practices and sponsors a labor-management joint task force on economic restructuring. The Canadian Labor Force Development Board is another joint endeavor providing advice to the federal government on training policy.[40]

The federal and provincial governments have created labor-management sectoral councils focused on human resource issues. For example, the Canadian Steel Trade and Employment Congress (CSTEC) provides jointly administered training and worker redeployment with the federal government's support.[41]

An example at the provincial level is Quebec, where government participates in tripartite industry-level meetings and generally has been active in encouraging labor and management to cooperate. Specifically, the province has worked with labor and management to develop a "social contract" to guarantee labor peace, such as the 1991 Sammi-Atlas Steel Company six-year pact associated with a C$105 million loan from the provincial government. Similar arrangements were established in 1994, both with and without government help.[42]

These structures were created not because of NAFTA, but because of a recognition that industrial restructuring for competitive purposes is a long-term process. Seen in this light, NAFTA is not a special situation; it is simply one more source of competition that must be addressed. The creation of these structures acknowledges that any adjustment to competition in Canada must involve both employers and employees and must recognize that a strong union movement is a legitimate actor with a right to a "seat at the table" when such decisions are made.

Comparable national, state, or industrial structures do not exist in the United States, with its lower level of unionization, and their absence is significant. Although some U.S. companies and unions have worked together to adjust to competition, the prevailing view is that these decisions are solely the province of management, unless there is a legal obligation to negotiate. In essence, while Canada seems to view adjustment issues as affecting shareholders and employees, the U.S. view seems to include only shareholders.

NEGOTIATED ADJUSTEMENT PROCESSES: IMPLICATIONS FOR MICHIGAN

Because collective bargaining coverage is far greater in Canada than in the United States, Canada is more likely to have negotiated adjustments that take into account the multiple interests of employees and employers. In both countries, firms with unionized employees are far more likely to have adjustments carried out through negotiation than through unilateral employer actions. Where collective bargaining exists, the needs of both parties are likely to be addressed.

Michigan is one of the most highly unionized states in the country. According to 1988 data, its 28.3 percent unionization rate was well above the national average of 18.8 percent (at that time) and ranked Michigan third, behind only Hawaii and New York.[43] Thus, one would expect Michigan to have more negotiated adjustments than other states, and the importance of such accords can be understood by examining the 1993 agreement between General Motors and the United Auto Workers. It provides for the company and the union to work together at the local and national level to improve organizational effectiveness, including appropriate plant investments, nonlabor cost savings and efficiencies, and work standards that make full use of employees. Recognizing the interest of employees in job security, the agreement provides for redeployment of those whose jobs are eliminated because of process improvement. There are also provisions for area hire, which permits workers laid off at one plant to transfer to another.[44]

Not all accords are as comprehensive as the GM-UAW pact, but the point is that a negotiated approach to economic adjustment can protect the interests of both the employer and employees. The state's interests also are protected, for collective bargaining has the little-noticed but important benefit of internalizing the costs of the adjustment. That is, in the absence of a negotiated agreement, employees laid off by a unilateral company response will immediately enter the unemployment rolls, essentially shifting the cost of the adjustment to the public. Internalizing those costs increases the probability that they will be borne by parties who will benefit most if the adjustment succeeds—the company and the union. Put differently, GM and the UAW have effectively created a private social safety net for the employees covered by the agreement, funded by themselves.

SUMMARY AND CONCLUSION

The purpose of this chapter was to lay out the policy situation associated with unilateral and negotiated adjustment. The basic argument is that negotiated processes are more likely to address the interests of all stakeholders and reduce the social costs of adjustments, as compared to unilateral decisions by employers. It also was pointed out that the more broadly based system of collective bargaining in Canada will result in a broader range of negotiated adjustments than in the United States. As a highly unionized state, Michigan, however, is more likely to have negotiated structures than are less unionized states, resulting in lower social costs for adjustments than otherwise would be the case.

The general message is that while collective bargaining and unionization may be seen as hampering the right of management to make necessary changes, they equally may be seen as vehicles for addressing the interests of multiple firm stakeholders in adapting to competition. To the extent that the United States makes a policy choice to restrain unionization and collective bargaining, the result will be greater weight given to the interests of firm management and shareholders in making adjustments to competition and less weight given to the interest of employees and other shareholders.

NOTES

1. For a press account, see, for example, "NAFTA and Jobs: In a Numbers War No One Can Count," *New York Times*, 14 November 1993, 4-1.
2. Patricia Capdevielle, "International Comparisons of Compensation Costs," *Monthly Labor Review* 114 (August 1991): 34-38.
3. "International Comparisons of Manufacturing Hourly Compensation Costs, 1993," *News: United States Department of Labor, Bureau of Labor Statistics*, USDL-94-261, 24 May 1994.

4. See, for example, Flora Lewis, "Bringing in the East," *Foreign Affairs* 69 (fall 1990): 15-22; and Craig Whitney, "European Union to Open Talks on Expanding East," *New York Times*, 11 December 1994, 28.

5. For the purpose of this chapter, an adjustment in the employment relations system is defined as any change in employment levels or terms or conditions of employment undertaken to permit a firm to compete more effectively in the market. Such adjustments may include layoffs, early retirement incentives, wage changes, work rule changes, and changes in staffing patterns.

6. For discussions of this view of management, see, for example, Betty Bock, Harvey J. Goldschmid, Ira M. Millstein, and F. M. Scherer, eds., *The Impact of the Modern Corporation* (New York: Columbia University Press, 1984); and William H. Shaw and Vincent Barry, *Moral Issues in Business*, 6th ed. (Belmont, Calif.: Wadsworth Publishing Co., 1995), especially 199-257.

7. See, for example, Leo Troy, *Trade Union Membership, 1897-1962* (New York: National Bureau of Economic Research, 1965); Gary N. Chaison and Joseph B. Rose, "The Macrodeterminants of Union Growth and Decline," in *The State of the Unions*, Industrial Relations Research Association Series, George B. Strauss, Daniel G. Gallagher, and Jack Fiorito, eds. (Madison, Wis.: Industrial Relations Research Association, 1991), 3-47; Richard P. Chaykowski and Anil Verma, "Adjustment and Restructuring in Canadian Industrial Relations: Challenges to the Traditional System," in *Industrial Relations in Canadian Industry*, Richard P. Chaykowski and Anil Verma, eds. (Toronto: Holt, Rinehart and Winston of Canada, Ltd., 1992), 1-38; and "UNWA Members in 1995," USDOL News Release, 96-41, 9 February 1996

8. See, for example, Seymour Martin Lipset, *Continental Divide: The Values and Institutions of the United States and Canada* (Toronto and Washington, D.C.: Howe Institute and National Planning Association, 1989); and Peter G. Bruce, "Political Parties and Labor Legislation in Canada and the U.S.," *Industrial Relations* 28, no. 2 (spring 1989): 115-41.

9. See, for example, Richard N. Block, "Reforming U.S. Labor Law and Collective Bargaining: Some Proposals Based on the Canadian System," in *Restoring the Promise of American Labor Law*, Sheldon Friedman, Richard Hurd, Ronald Oswald, and Ronald Seeber, eds. (Ithaca, N.Y.: ILR Press, 1994), 250-59.

10. This chapter will focus on the U.S. system under the jurisdiction of the National Labor Relations Act. Railroads and airlines are covered by the Railway Labor Act, which has its own election process. Public employees below the federal level are covered by state law, many of which have election systems modeled after the NLRA.

11. The following sectors are under the federal jurisdiction: air transportation; banking; broadcasting and communications; crown corporations (for example, Canada Post); flour, feed mills, and grain elevators; longshoring; railways (interprovincial and international); road transport (interprovincial and international); shipping and navigation; and others. See Canada Labour Relations Board, *Annual Report, 1990-91* (Ottawa: CLRB, 1991), 4.

12. George W. Adams, *Canadian Labour Law*, 2d ed. (Aurora, Ont.: Canada Law Book, 1993-95), 2-87 - 2-95.
13. Ibid., 2-2 - 2-87.
14. Although an election is necessary for a union to be certified as the collective bargaining representative of a unit of employees, the NLRB may direct an employer to bargain if it finds that the employer's unfair labor practices are so serious as to make an election impossible, and if the union can provide evidence that it has majority status. See *NLRB* v. *Gissel Packing Co.*, 395 U.S. 575 (1969).
15. Adams, *Canadian Labour Law*, 2d ed., 7-50 - 7-80.
16. Ibid., 2-87 - 2-95.
17. Ibid., 2-8 - 2-16.
18. Ibid., 2-54 - 2-64.2.
19. Ibid., 2-1 - 2-95.
20. Bruce, "Political Parties," 127-35.
21. Certain industries viewed as having a direct effect on interprovincial commerce are covered by federal labor law in Canada and regulated by the Canada Labor Relations Board (CLRB); see note 11 above. These jurisdictional distinctions are based on an interpretation of the Constitution Act of 1867, which gives broad powers to the provinces. For a more detailed discussion, see Adams, *Canadian Labour Law*, 1-8; and A.W.R. Carrothers, E.E. Palmer, and W.B. Raynor, *Collective Bargaining Law in Canada*, 2d ed. (Toronto and Vancouver: Butterworths, 1986), 129-41.
22. Adams, *Canadian Labour Law*, 2d ed., 11-48.
23. Ibid., 11-49.
24. Ibid.
25. Ibid., 10-134 - 10-140. In a system of first-agreement arbitration, the governing authority may require a company and a union to submit differences over negotiating a first agreement to final and binding arbitration. The assumption is that difficulties in negotiating the first agreement are due to the inexperience of the parties. First-agreement arbitration allows the parties to enter into a first agreement without the threat of a strike and to become familiar with each other and with collective bargaining.
26. Adams, *Canadian Labour Law*, 2d ed., 4-1 - 4-52.
27. See Block, "Reforming U.S. Labor Law"; and Richard N. Block and Myron Roomkin, "Observations on Legalism in Industrial Relations in the United States," a paper delivered at the 47th Annual Meeting of the Industrial Relations Research Association, Washington, D.C., 6-8 January 1995.
28. The seven provinces with tripartite boards are British Columbia, Manitoba, New Brunswick, Newfoundland, Nova Scotia, Ontario, and Saskatchewan. Quebec has a system of labor courts. See Adams, *Canadian Labour Law*, 2d ed., 5-11 - 5-14.
29. Although the board was and is supposed to be neutral as between unions and employers, creating a board of political appointees also means that decisions in NLRA cases generally follow any changes in the political con-

sensus on labor-management relations. In general, Democratic appointees are considered to be more protective of union interests, and Republican appointees are considered to be more protective of the interests of employers and individuals.

30. For a brief discussion of this tripartitism, see Noah Meltz, "Unionism in Canada, U.S: On Parallel Treadmills," *Forum for Applied Research and Public Policy* 15 (winter 1989): 46-52.

31. George W. Adams, *Canadian Labor Law* (Aurora, Ont.: Canada Law Book, 1985), 219.

32. *NLRB* v. *Wooster Division of Borg Warner*, 356 U.S. 342, (1958).

33. 380 U.S. 263 (1965).

34. 379 U.S. 203 (1964).

35. 452 U.S. 666 (1981).

36. See Patrick Hardin, editor-in-chief, *The Developing Labor Law*, 3d ed. (Washington, D.C.: BNA, 1992-94), 903-12.

37. 303 N.L.R.B. No. 66, enf. 143 LRRM 3001 (C.A.D.C., 1993).

38. Adams, *Canadian Labour Law*, 2d ed., 10-97.

39. See, for example, Richard N. Block and Benjamin W. Wolkinson, "Impediments to Innovative Employee Relations Arrangements," in *Investing in People: A Strategy to Address America's Workforce Crisis* (Washington, D.C.: U.S. Department of Labor, Commission on Workforce Quality and Labor Market Efficiency, September 1989), 2003-56.

40. Richard P. Chaykowski and Anil Verma, "Innovation in Industrial Relations: Challenges to Organizations and Public Policy," in *Stabilization, Growth and Distribution: Linkages in the Knowledge Era*, Thomas J. Courchene, ed., The Bell Canada Papers on Economic and Public Policy, vol. 2 (Kingston, Ont.: John Deutsch Institute, Queen's University, 1994), 395.

41. See, for example, Chaykowski and Verma, "Innovation," 395; Canadian Steel Trade and Employment Congress, *Skills Training Program, 1993* (Ottawa: CSTEC).

42. Jean Guy Bergeron and Reynold Bourque, "Union-Management Cooperation in Quebec: New Developments and Perspectives," a paper presented at the Fourth Bargaining Group Conference, University of Toronto, 14-15 October 1994. See also Morley Gunderson and Andrew Sharpe, "Lessons from the Canadian Experience with Sectoral Councils," paper presented at the Conference on the Emergence of Sectoral Councils in Canada, Montreal, Quebec, 12-13 January 1996

43. Michael A. Curme, Barry T. Hirsch, and David Macpherson, "Union Membership and Contract Coverage in the United States, 1983-88," *Industrial and Labor Relations Review* 44 (October 1990): 5-33.

44. *Agreement Between General Motors Corporation and the UAW*, 24 October 1993, 163-71, 199-219, 225-27, 267-73.

The Effect of Free Trade on Contingent Work in Michigan

Karen Roberts, Doug Hyatt, and Peter Dorman

The public debate over the passage of NAFTA was acrimonious in the United States primarily because of concerns over employment and the quality of working conditions. The basic fear was that U.S. jobs would be lost to Mexico, where wages are lower and enforcement of labor standards is perceived as more lax. A further concern was that as competition increased within the trade region, pressures to harmonize labor standards and other forms of worker protection would generally lower the quality of work in both the United States and Canada. In other words, it was feared that NAFTA would bring not only a loss of jobs, but also a loss of "good" jobs. This concern was especially great in Michigan, with its comparatively high concentration of high-wage manufacturing jobs.

Fears of job loss from NAFTA can best be understood through the lens of institutional labor economics. From this perspective, the workplace is divided into two sorts of work arrangements, core and periphery.[1] The primary attributes of core employment are that it is full-time, expected to be permanent, and implies a long-term relationship between the employer and the worker. Peripheral employment does not imply a long-term relationship because it arises to meet a transitory need for labor.[2] The fear was that NAFTA would cost core jobs and only add jobs at the periphery.

One prerequisite for a stable employment relationship—core jobs—is stability in the product market.[3] Stable product demand provides for some degree of predictability in production technologies and, therefore, predictability in how many and what sort of employees are required. This then gives employers the opportunity to offer stable employment and, in the better firms, training and the potential for upward mobility. Variability and uncertainty in the product market erode employer ability to offer a stable, permanent work arrangement. The presence of a peripheral work force allows the employer to share some of the product market uncertainty with workers by using workers only to the extent required by product demand in the current period. While this description is phrased in terms of goods production, the logic also applies to many service industries.

As trade barriers drop, opportunities for new product markets expand, but uncertainty increases as a result of greater competition. Examples in Michigan of sectors that simultaneously face new opportunities but potential competition from Mexican producers are auto suppliers, furniture, and agriculture. It might be expected that employers would respond to the added uncertainty by increased use of part-time and temporary workers, while reducing the size of the core, full-time work force. After Canada, Mexico is Michigan's second-largest export market. Thus, implementation of NAFTA raises legitimate concerns about the potential for certain structural shifts in Michigan's labor market.[4] The rising use of contingent workers raises several issues for Michigan policy makers. The first is the potential erosion of income security for the state's population as core jobs are transformed into contingent work. The second is the question of how to assure continued statutory labor standards protection for the Michigan workforce. The third is potential revenue loss as employers shift to contingent work arrangements to avoid certain payroll taxes. The fourth is the possible increase in demand for publicly provided health and welfare services that employers offer privately to core employees, but not to contingent workers.

This chapter begins with the premise that producers in all three NAFTA countries face similar pressures in goods and services markets. All three trade globally, and together they have created a common market for goods and services that will reduce consumer prices but will also enhance competition among producers in the three countries. Each partner entered the agreement with different labor laws and standards for working conditions, as well as different propensities to use contingent workers.[5] This chapter provides an overview of contingent work, reviews the state of contingent work in each nation, and discusses some of the implications for Michigan. Summary comments conclude the chapter.

OVERVIEW OF PERIPHERAL WORK

Because contingent work arrangements, also referred to as the casualization of work or peripheral work, take so many forms, they are difficult to define and are more often understood by what they are not—full-time, permanent employment with a single employer. The most common forms of contingent work arrangements in developed countries such as the United States and Canada include part-time jobs, temporary employment, contract employment, leased employees, self-employment, work in the business services sector, and home-based employment.[6] Leasing, temporary employment, and subcontracting may be done through a broker, such as a temporary help firm, or on a direct-hire basis.[7] With the exception of part-time workers permanently employed by a single employer and the self-employed, who may have a permanent commitment to their own business, the common characteristic of contingent work is the lack of permanent attachment between the employer and the worker, the low level of job security, and the absence of nonwage benefits.[8]

Contingent work arrangements exist for a variety of reasons. From the worker's perspective, the advantage is that the hours are often better suited for balancing family or school and work.[9] From the employer's perspective, temporary or leased workers may also be used to fill in for sick or vacationing core employees. Another reason is that employers may require a particular skill only temporarily. Also, some employers use contingent work as a screening mechanism to identify prospective permanent employees.[10] However, the chief advantage to employers is flexibility, the use and pay of employees only on an as-needed basis without the high fixed costs associated with permanent employment. Direct costs for contingent workers tend to be lower, both because their hourly wages are usually lower and because nonwage benefits often are not offered.[11]

Contingent work arrangements are on the rise in Europe, Japan, and North America.[12] Multiple explanations are given, but nearly all rest on employer need for more flexibility. Free trade in product markets, propelled forward by agreements such as NAFTA, means that employers want more latitude in deploying workers.[13] While free trade allows the sale of goods and services in international markets, unencumbered by tariffs or other barriers, it also means that foreign producers have easier access to domestic markets, thus increasing competition among producers within the trading bloc. Competition in a global economy introduces uncertainties along multiple dimensions for producers: what, how, and where to produce and what technologies to use.[14] Obtaining good information about and gaining even partial control over an international product market is more difficult than for a relatively protected domestic market.

The core/periphery dichotomy in the Mexican labor market is between the formal and informal sectors, rather than between permanent and contingent work.[15] The data are poor, but suggest that the difference between the formal and informal sectors corresponds to that between permanent and contingent work in several ways. First, employment in the formal sector tends to be comparatively stable and represents a long-term attachment to a single employer. This sector is governed by labor standards legislation and a high level of mandatory employer-paid benefits. Jobs in the informal sector tend to pay lower wages and are not protected by the safety net specified by Mexican labor law. Unlike contingent work arrangements in the United States and Canada, which are largely legal, in Mexico these are quite common but illegal. The absence of good labor market data for Mexico, however, makes it difficult to determine whether informal employment is growing in ways comparable to the increased use of contingent work in the United States and Canada.

CONTINGENT WORK IN THE UNITED STATES

It is generally acknowledged that contingent work is on the rise in the United States, but there is less consensus on exactly what constitutes this category. Contingent work arrangements can be divided into two broad types, part-time and temporary, within which are subcategories. The clearest delineation within the part-time work force is between those who are voluntarily part-time versus those who work part-time for economic reasons. Temporary work encompasses a wider variety of arrangements, including on-call employment, limited duration direct hires, intermittent employment, leased employment, and consultants.[16]

The nature of contingent work is such that it is not always directly measurable. Despite this, there is consensus that all forms are growing and account for a disproportionate share of new job growth in the United States.[17] According to the General Accounting Office (GAO) in 1988, 25 percent of the workforce was made up of part-time, temporary, contract, or other nontraditional workers. Another estimate suggests that approximately one-half of the new jobs generated during 1993 were contingent.[18] For certain types of contingent work, specifically part-time employment and jobs in the temporary employment industry (SIC 7362), data are collected regularly by the Bureau of Labor Statistics (BLS). For most of the other types, only estimates based on special surveys or imputations are available.[19]

Table 1 provides information about the size of the U.S. part-time workforce, the most easily observable component of contingent work, from 1970 through 1992. Part-time employment has nearly doubled, now accounting for about 20 percent of the labor force; one out of five of these would prefer full-time employment and is working part-time for economic reasons. The BLS defines involuntary part-time (or part-time for economic reasons) as those working fewer hours due to slack work, inability to find a full-time job, or other reasons (which usually apply only to people typically working full-time, but who are part-time during the survey week).[20] Part-time workers continue to be predominately female, and slightly more than 80 percent of them are voluntarily part time, compared to about 90 percent two decades ago.

The most likely explanation for the increase is the shift away from manufacturing and toward trade and services.[21] While the percentage of part-time workers in any given industry has remained stable, the employment share of sectors that most heavily use part-time workers, especially services, has grown substantially. Between 1970 and 1991, total employment in services (nongoods producing) increased from 60.2 percent to 73.5 percent of the U.S. total. Although that sector's proportion of part-time employment dropped slightly, from 26.2 percent in 1979 to 23.6 percent in 1992,[22] the sector's overall job rise meant a net gain in part-time employment.

Part-time workers earn less per hour than comparable full-time employees and are less likely to be covered by employer benefit plans. In 1993, the average part-time worker had a median wage of $5.55, compared to $8.89 for full-time workers.[23] This gap narrows but does not disappear after controlling for education, age, industry, occupa-

Table 1.
Part-time Employment in the United States, 1970-92.

Year	Total (000s)	Total Part-time (000s)	% Part-time	Voluntary Part-time	Part-time for Economic Reasons	% Female Part-time	% Female Voluntary Part-time	% Male Voluntary Part-time
1970	66,753	11,925	17.86	90.68%	9.31%	65.06	91.94	88.34
1971	66,973	12,393	18.50	88.92%	11.08%	64.76	90.44	86.15
1972	69,214	12,939	18.69	88.86%	11.14%	65.04	90.14	86.47
1973	71,803	13,262	18.47	89.86%	10.14%	66.02	91.03	87.57
1974	73,093	13,701	18.74	88.85%	11.15%	66.09	90.19	86.20
1975	71,586	14,260	19.92	85.91%	14.08%	65.86	87.58	82.71
1976	73,964	14,788	19.99	85.75%	14.25%	66.26	87.63	82.04
1977	76,625	15,391	20.09	85.79%	14.21%	66.36	87.34	82.73
1978	80;193	15,855	19.77	86.72%	13.28%	67.22	87.81	84.49
1979	82,654	16,171	19.56	87.00%	13.00%	67.96	87.93	85.00
1980	82,562	16,740	20.28	85.27%	14.73%	67.32	86.77	82.23
1981	83,243	17,154	20.61	83.19%	16.81%	68.00	84.95	79.47
1982	81,421	18,106	22.24	78.64%	21.36%	67.22	81.33	73.15
1983	82,322	18,511	22.49	76.56%	23.44%	66.81	79.41	70.83
1984	86,544	18,462	21.33	78.17%	21.83%	67.39	80.66	73.01
1985	88,534	18,615	21.03	79.31%	20.69%	67.62	81.66	74.42
1986	90,529	19,069	21.06	79.82%	20.18%	67.45	82.13	75.04
1987	92,957	19,483	20.96	81.03%	18.97%	67.36	83.28	76.40
1988	95,214	19,754	20.75	82.56%	17.44%	67.32	84.89	77.74
1989	97,369	19,973	20.51	84.16%	15.84%	67.81	86.21	79.84
1990	97,994	19,920	20.33	83.82%	16.18%	67.61	85.98	79.32
1991	96,575	20,302	21.02	81.02%	18.98%	67.21	83.97	74.97
1992	97,026	20,572	21.20	78.81%	21.19%	66.42	81.84	72.83

Source: Bureau of Labor Statistics, *Employment and Earnings*, various years

tion, and gender.[24] Comparing hourly wage rates understates the differential, however, because part-time workers are significantly less likely to receive nonwage benefits.[25] For example, 21 percent are not covered by employer health insurance plans, compared to 16 percent of full-time workers, although 23.3 percent of involuntary and 41.6 percent of voluntary part-time workers are covered by dependent or spouse plans. Thirty-one percent of voluntary and 24.7 percent of involuntary part-time workers are covered by employer pension plans.[26] In addition, many states exclude part-time workers from unemployment insurance coverage.[27]

Temporary employment is the fastest growing segment of contingent work and includes any type of arrangement that is expected to be temporary by both the employer and employee.[28] Between 1979 and 1988, the number of temporary workers increased by 164 percent, compared to a 16 percent increase in the total civilian workforce.[29] Included are employment in the temporary help industry, as well as individual arrangements made between employers and workers.[30] Data on the temporary help industry are regularly collected by the BLS, but information on the other forms of temporary work is collected more sporadically, usually in the form of a special survey.[31]

As firms divide their workforce into core and periphery, the use of temporary employees becomes cyclically sensitive, declining in an economic downturn and rising when the economy picks up. According to one estimate, the number of temporary and leased employees hired through temporary employment agencies was 1.3 million during 1990, fell to 1.2 million during the 1991 recession, and then rose to 1.6 million in April 1993.[32] Table 2 shows the number and percentage of workers in temporary help supply services (SIC 7362) from 1982 to 1992. Except for the dip in 1991, both the number and share of this part of the labor force has risen steadily.

Traditionally, temporary workers serve three markets—offices, industry and health care—with the office market, primarily clerical occupations, accounting for approximately half of the temporary worker occupations.[33] There is anecdotal evidence, however, that this pattern is changing, with an increase in the use of temporary technical and professional workers.[34]

There are few systematically collected data for other sorts of temporary work arrangements outside the temporary help industries, but there are indications that growth is substantial in leasing and self-employment. According to the National Staff Leasing Association, more than one million workers were leased during 1993, about half through approximately 200 to 300 leasing companies, an increase from approximately 100,000 workers in 1980.[35] According to BLS statistics, self-employment as a share of total U.S. employment grew from 7.4 percent in 1988 to 8.3 percent in 1991, then dropped to 8 percent in 1992. The growth estimate for 1980-90 is 25 percent, although there is significant variation across industries. Self-employment grew at an estimated 150 percent in finance, insurance, and real

Table 2.
Employment in the U.S. Temporary Help Supply Services Sector, 1982-92.

	# SIC 7362	% SIC 7363
1982	417	.47%
1983	488.1	.54%
1984	642.5	.68%
1985	732.0	.75%
1986	836.5	.84%
1987	988.9	.97%
1988	1,125.9	1.07%
1989	1,215.8	1.13%
1990	1,288.2	1.18%
1991	1,268.4	1.17%
1992	1,426.5	1.31%

Source: Bureau of Labor Statistics, *Employment and Earnings*, various years.

estate, 113 percent in construction, and 89 percent in services over the same period.[36]

The federal government is becoming concerned about the increase in contingent work, because more employers are either hiring or converting existing employees into contingent workers in order to avoid certain payroll taxes, resulting in a loss of federal tax revenues and placing an unfair tax burden on employers who comply with the law. Anticipated revenue loss due to misclassification of employees for 1996-2004 is estimated at $34 billion.[37] Also, the reduction in employer-paid benefits and income security associated with core employment is forcing more people to public sources, adding to government expenditures.[38]

The recent debate over health care drew attention to the practice of employers classifying their workers as independent contractors rather than as employees. The fear is that as employers face what they perceive to be a growing payroll tax burden, they will attempt to reclassify their workers to shift the cost of health care and other benefits to the employees and the government. The misclassification problem appears to be greater in some industries than in others. The IRS uses a 20-factor test to determine whether a worker is an independent contractor or an employee. Even if a worker satisfies enough of these criteria, according to current law, employers have three "safe harbors" allowing them to treat employees as independent contractors: (1) judicial precedent, (2) a past IRS audit that did not result in a reclassification of employees, and (3) reliance on long-standing industry practices.[39]

Deliberate misclassification traditionally has been concentrated in certain industries and in smaller firms. In 1984, according to the U.S. Treasury Department, approximately 19 percent of employers in construction and in finance, insurance, and real estate misclassified at least some of their employees as independent contractors. The figure is about 16 percent for agriculture, manufacturing, and services. Trade and government employers (9.6 percent) are least likely to misclassify their work force. Small employers are the worst offenders. According to one estimate, firms with 100 or fewer employees account for 40 percent of the workforce but 90 percent of misclassified employees.[40] The savings can be substantial, since employers can avoid Social Security, unemployment, and workers' compensation taxes and do not have to offer health insurance or pension plan coverage to independent contractors. One estimate for the construction industry is a savings of 25 percent of hourly labor costs,[41] and a further incentive is the low likelihood of being caught.

Anecdotal evidence suggests that the practice of converting full-time employees to "consultants" is becoming more common among larger employers.[42] This not only eliminates benefit costs, but also allows use of these workers on an at-will basis. What is not clear is the extent to which this practice will continue to grow. Close examination shows that contingent workers are not necessarily cost-effective, since they are not as productive as core employees in all jobs, particularly those that require training beyond a few months.[43]

CONTINGENT WORK IN CANADA

The formal definition of contingent work in Canada is both as well and as poorly developed as in the United States. Canadian contingent work is generally construed to include seasonal or part-year full-time jobs, part-time jobs, self-employment if the individual is the only employee, and temporary help. Fortunately, the definition is sufficiently similar across the two countries to make data comparisons at least broadly consistent.

Policy makers in Canada and the United States share concerns about the emerging contingent work force. As aptly expressed by Harvey Krahn:

> Non-standard jobs typically provide less job security, lower pay and fewer fringe benefits. To the extent that non-standard employment is replacing full-time, year-round, permanent work, the financial security of some Canadians may be decreasing. Non-standard jobs are concentrated within particular segments of the labor market, and are more likely to be held by specific population subgroups, so their impact is unequally distributed.
>
> Contingent work provides employers a more flexible workforce and a simpler way to adjust to the ebbs and flows of product demand. In addition, it may afford workers with alternative work scheduling options that accommodate their preferences for time devoted to the labor market.
>
> It would be inaccurate to suggest, however, that contingent work is an option to which all of the workers observed in contingent work situations self-select. While some individuals embrace contingent work, others are compelled to become self-employed, or to work part-time, because full-time, full year,"employee-status" employment is unavailable.[44]

Krahn notes that contingent work arrangements were uncommon in the 1950s, but have increased since the early 1970s. From 1980 to 1988, they accounted for almost half of the new jobs created. Providing detail on the nature and extent of contingent work at a particular time is precarious because the picture can change depending on the period chosen. This issue aside, Table 3 provides data on the nature of contingent employment in Canada in 1989 (when the labor market was in better shape than during much of the time since). The data on different components are disaggregated by gender, age, and industry.

Of the 12.5 million people employed in 1989, about 35 percent fell into one of the contingent categories. About 2.5 million, (45 percent) of female employment was contingent, while 1.9 million males (28 percent) were so employed. Younger workers, age 15-24, were over-represented in contingent jobs.

Table 3.
Contingent Employment by Category in Canada 1989 (employment numbers are in 1000s).

	Part-Time Employment	Part-Year Employment	Own- Employment	Temporary Employment	Contingent Employment	Total Employment
Men	505	510	531	391	1,937	6,933
15-24	352	164	57	151	724	1,151
25-54	117	279	397	192	985	5,045
55-64	36	67	77	48	228	736
Women	1,400	368	327	408	2,503	5,535
15-24	437	103	31	136	707	1,091
25-54	852	248	261	253	1,614	3,987
55-64	111	—	35	—	146	457
Industry						
Agriculture	—	34	124	—	158	278
Natural resource-based	97	—	28	125	818	
Manufacturing	71	103	39	73	286	1,779
Construction	35	107	81	69	292	626
Distributive services	89	88	86	50	313	1,326
Business services	135	48	123	52	358	1,337
Education/health/ welfare	484	127	77	184	872	2,050
Public administration	74	66	—	90	230	1,124
Retail trade	515	68	117	88	788	1,628
Other cons. services	424	122	152	136	834	1,337
TOTAL	1,905[a]	878	858	799	4,440	12,468

[a] This figure is slightly different from the total employment reported in table 2 due to the use of different surveys to derive the data in the two tables and due to data revisions since the data in this table were published.

Source: Adapted from Harvey Krahn, "Non-Standard Work Arrangements," *Perspectives on Labour and Income* 6 (Autumn 1991): 3.

Note: "—" indicates fewer than 25,000 individuals in the entry and therefore not reported by Statistics Canada.

Table 3 also reveals that 15 percent of working Canadians were employed part time (fewer than 30 hours per week). Around 7 percent worked part of the year (fewer than ten months annually in their main job). Another 7 percent were self-employed with no employees (own-account). Finally, 6 percent held temporary employment (a specific end date).

The most complete data and analysis on contingent work in Canada has focused on part-time employment, defined as fewer than 30 hours per week. From 1975 to 1993, the number of such jobs increased by 1.8 percent annually. The compound annual growth rate of full-time jobs over that period was 1.2 percent, compared with 4.5 percent for part-time jobs.[45]

Table 4 shows Canadian employment from 1980-93 broken down by full- and part-time jobs. The part-time figures are further disaggregated into voluntary and involuntary. Voluntary refers to workers who have chosen this option because of family or personal responsibilities, school attendance, illness or disability, or no desire for full-time employment. Involuntary refers to those who indicated they would prefer full-time work but were unable to find it. Canadians employed part time rose to just over 17 percent of all workers in 1993, from about 13 percent in 1980. Of these, 35.5 percent are involuntary, compared to 17.6 percent in 1980. The data also show that, as in the United States, the proportion of involuntary part-time workers appears to be positively related to economic cycles.

CASUAL LABOR IN MEXICO

The dynamics of the Mexican labor market differ from those in the United States and Canada, although the extent is difficult to assess confidently because of a very different market structure and lack of good labor market information. Until recently, reliable data about the Mexican labor market were scarce, particularly for the low-wage, low-productivity sectors. In the late 1980s this condition began to be rectified, and credible statistics are now available for 1988 onward. While this is a positive development, long-term comparisons with U.S. and Canadian labor markets are not possible.

The concept of casualization, or contingent work, as it is understood in developed countries is more complicated in a developing

Table 4.

Full-Time and Part-Time Employment in Canada, 1980-93 (in thousands).

Year	Total Employment	Total Part-Time Employment	Involuntary Part-Time
1980	10,708	1,392	245
1981	11,001	1,486	268
1982	10,618	1,528	379
1983	10,675	1,639	467
1984	10,932	1,668	502
1985	11,221	1,737	509
1986	11,531	1,789	506
1987	11,861	1,804	479
1988	12,245	1,882	446
1989	12,486	1,888	420
1990	12,572	1,932	432
1991	12,340	2,023	561
1992	12,240	2,058	669
1993	12,383	2,143	760

Source: Nathalie Noreau, "Involuntary Part-Timers," *Perspectives on Labour and Income* 6, no. 3 (Autumn 1994): 25-30.

country such as Mexico. As in the United States and Canada, peripheral employment is most meaningful in relation to the benchmark provided by core employment. This benchmark in all three NAFTA countries encompasses work that is full-time, permanent, and governed by various procedural safeguards attached to the contractual status of employment. The process of casualization suggests various departures from this benchmark: short or irregular hours, temporary employment, work outside the employer's usual place of business, and employment outside the normal jurisdiction of labor law, that is, independent or third-party contracts.

A fundamental distinction between peripheral work in Mexico and that in the United States and Canada is that arrangements departing from this benchmark are illegal in Mexico. Hence, data collection on the nature of casualization, including hours at work, pay, and employment status at the work place, is hampered. Protective labor market legislation in Mexico offers guarantees that are quite generous by North American standards: double and in some cases triple pay for overtime, paid vacations of up to 14 working days, arbitration of disputes, and mandatory profit sharing.[46] Not surprisingly, many employers evade these requirements by securing labor services from the informal sector. The 1992 Microenterprise Survey conducted by the Instituto Nacional de Estadistica, Geografia, e Informatica (INEGI) revealed that fewer than one-fourth of all employees in its small business sample were covered by explicit individual or collectively bargained contracts, and barely one-tenth were registered for social insurance.[47] Moreover, at the end of the 1980s, approximately half of all Mexican workers were paid wages below the legally stipulated minimum.[48]

Two other aspects of the Mexican economy contribute to its labor market organization. First, like most developing countries, Mexico has far more people who want paid employment in the formal sector than there are jobs available. Second, Mexico provides no social safety net for this surplus labor population. There is no unemployment insurance or other form of income maintenance, so workers who fail to find jobs in the formal sector must accept marginal employment or create their own sources of income. These factors combine to produce a large informal labor market sector.[49]

Estimating the size of the informal sector depends in part on how it is defined. Clara Jusidman de Bialostozky, in a survey of relevant research, describes three general approaches to characterizing the informal sector. The "productive rationality" view perceives diverse employment needs as stemming from uneven development within an economy. The "illegality" perspective sees informality as a product of the state's overregulation and/or underenforcement. The "market rationality" view maintains that oligopolistic firms exploit vulnerable labor through subcontracting and other mechanisms to externalize their costs. Regardless of which perspective best explains the presence of an informal sector in Mexico, the important point for U.S. and Canadian workers is that it is large. In one recent overview, Teresa Rendon and Carlos Salas combined the different approaches and estimated that up to one-third of urban workers in Mexico were in the informal sector at the end of the 1980s.

Although data on the informal sector are difficult to obtain, evidence suggests that informal employment is associated with low wages.[50] For example, the 1992 INEGI sample indicated that half the workers in the microenterprise sector received subminimum wages (Mexico has three "zones" covering different sectors of the economy, each with a different minimum wage rate). In addition, the study noted a strong negative correlation between reported pay and indicators of informal employment: the correlation between wages and the percentage of workers with only a verbal and temporary arrangement with their employers is -.51 across nine reported two-digit manufacturing industries, statistically significant at the 10 percent level.

Because of the sharp discrepancy in employment quality between the informal and formal or modern sectors, there is a long queue for jobs in the latter. This, in fact, constitutes the primary form of labor market segmentation in Mexico, in contrast to the more incremental forms typically found in the United States and Canada. This is a fundamental distinction between the two types of economies, and it has profound implications for the effect of NAFTA on all three countries.

One concern articulated during the NAFTA debate was that trade liberalization is likely to erode at least some of the safeguards embedded in the Canadian and U.S. industrial relations systems. This is likely for Mexico as well. The principal labor market divisions in Mexico, unlike in its northern neighbors, are between the formal and informal sectors, not the permanent and contingent sectors. The net effect of NAFTA on the Mexican labor market depends on whether free trade generally improves the quality of employment by speeding the transformation of peripheral employment into core employment relationships (with perhaps less generous legally mandated protections for workers in the formal sector) or further erodes the quality of work in both sectors.

Even without NAFTA, there would be enormous pressure to reform Mexican labor law. In part, this is because its generosity to modern-sector workers is widely perceived to be at odds with the need for more rapid employment growth to absorb the growing surplus labor population. In addition, these guarantees are under attack because they are seen as sustaining a highly unequal income distribution. Finally, the general trend toward deregulation in Mexico has called into question all forms of state intervention, including the extensive regulation of the labor market.

NAFTA is likely to intensify these pressures. Its signing was predicated on, among other things, a Mexican commitment to deregulation, particularly in areas of foreign investment, elevating that policy approach from domestic status to a treaty commitment. In addition, NAFTA exposes domestic producers to competition from which they have previously been protected. Cut off from traditional subsidies, many of these Mexican firms are ill-prepared to compete and will no longer be able to afford their previous level of wage and employment guarantees, regardless of changes in the regulatory environment.

Free trade is likely to exert another influence on labor standards by reducing the importance of the domestic consumer market. One political pressure that favors protective labor legislation is that economic growth requires a healthy consumer market. As is true for the other two partners, NAFTA reduces the importance of the consumer market in Mexico for long-term national economic growth. The U.S. market alone is twenty times the size of Mexico's. Under liberalized trade, an export orientation is inevitable, which will tend to reduce the political support for measures designed to bolster domestic wages and effective demand.

Two fundamental changes to Mexican labor law are anticipated that will intensify the degree of competition within Mexican labor markets. Although the timing is uncertain, analysts expect that Mexico will at some point dismantle its system of arbitration and institute employment-at-will. The objective is to make Mexico more attractive to foreign firms that wish to shift locations, products, and contractors.[51] To accomplish this, it is expected that Mexico will end the system of state-supported, state-dominated unionism.[52] This is in response both to the demands of employers, who would prefer no representation, and to the U.S. and Canadian labor movements, who strongly oppose Mexico's restrictions on independent union organizing. What sort of collective bargaining environment will emerge in Mexico after these reforms is open to question. The policy choice in Mexico, much like that in the United States and Canada, is how to introduce the desired flexibility while protecting and in fact improving the quality of work.

IMPLICATIONS FOR MICHIGAN

The creation of a hemispheric consumer market puts producers in all three countries in competition with one another. As mentioned, one producer response to product market competition is to rely more heavily on the contingent work force. It would be an oversimplification to say that in the United States the distinction between core and contingent work is essentially the same as between good and bad jobs. Contingent work arrangements do meet the needs of some employees.[53] For example, there is evidence that the lower wages paid to part-time female workers may be offset by the benefit of being able to work less than full-time.[54] Yet, systematically lower pay, absence of benefits, lack of job security, and exclusion from most of the major labor standards protection argue against the explanation that the rise of contingent work is a worker-driven phenomenon.

Table 5 shows total, part-time, and personnel services industry employment for Michigan from 1988 through 1994. While part-time work declined in Michigan, the involuntary share of that employment increased by more than 17 percent. Employment in the personnel services industry increased by 65 percent. The decrease in part-time work is probably the result of Michigan's relatively heavy concentration in manufacturing, as compared to the national average. Yet, the rise in involuntary part-time and personnel services employment indicates that the state is following the national trend toward greater reliance on contingent work. For example, one temporary services firm employs 15,000 temporary workers in the Lansing area.

Table 5.
Employment in Michigan, 1988-94 (in thousands).

	Total Employment	Employment Part-time	Part-time Economic Reasons	Personnel Services Industry
1988	4232	899	210	54.2
1989	4267	837	188	55.7
1990	4234	834	210	55.9
1991	4125	841	249	54.3
1992	4205	847	265	66.6
1993	4373	845	246	79.7
1994	—	—	—	89.7

Source: U.S. Bureau of Labor Statistics, unpublished data.

NAFTA has been in effect almost a year, and so far there have been dividends for Michigan. During the past five years, Michigan exports to Mexico rose by $500 million and have become increasingly diverse: transportation equipment, which accounted for 76 percent of those exports five years ago, dropped to 50 percent by 1991. Other Michigan industries benefiting from free trade with Mexico are pharmaceuticals and office furniture industries.[55] This growth in export activity cannot be expected to last, however. The recent peso devaluation severely diminishes, in the short term, the Mexican market for consumer products. Although a devalued peso translates into lower production costs, the general economic uncertainty has curtailed foreign investment. The positive employment effects in the auto industry in Michigan attributed to NAFTA have been based on consumer demand in Mexico for cars, and a devalued peso and rising interest rates will seriously dint that demand.

The second caveat for Michigan workers is that despite any short-term net job gains for the United States, there will be fundamental industrial restructuring over time as producers adapt to a free trade environment. One possible result is eventual job loss in U.S. industries that initially experience gains. One feature of NAFTA likely to contribute to eventual job loss in Michigan is domestic content rules, which determine how much of a product must be made in a particular place to qualify it as point of origin. Leaving aside the ambiguities of measuring domestic content, the UAW has argued that the NAFTA rules favor border producers and that, over time, auto workers and employees in auto supply firms outside the border areas will face a net job loss.[56] Certainly that was one interpretation given to the relatively recent GM decision to shift production from Ypsilanti, Michigan to Arlington, Texas.

In acknowledgment of the concerns about NAFTA's potential deleterious effects on U.S. and Canadian workers, the North American Agreement on Labor Cooperation, referred to as the labor side agreement, was finalized in September 1993.[57] Its underlying assumption was that economic growth generated by free trade will result in higher wages and improved quality of work life for all three partners. Its broad objectives were to improve working conditions and living standards in the three countries, while respecting each jurisdiction's sovereignty to set its own labor standards and enforce its own laws. The agreement explicitly lists areas such as the right to organize and bargain collectively, minimum labor standards, and rights to safe workplaces. An important point about the labor side agreement is that it was designed to protect the political sovereignty of the three nations, not the economic status quo. This means that there are no implied protections against market-driven harmonization pressures on existing labor standards or job quality. It is important for Michigan policy makers to recognize that such protections of the workforce cannot be expected to be guaranteed at the federal level.

An additional important point about the labor side agreement is that neither the use of contingent workers and the protection of their rights nor labor standards in the informal sector are on the list of covered activities (Article 11) and the definition of relevant labor law (Article 49). This omission is significant for Michigan because contingent workers are often not covered by existing labor standards laws and are excluded from collective bargaining units, providing a significant loophole in any efforts to regulate working conditions for a growing portion of the state's workforce, as shown in table 5.

CONTINGENT WORK: STATUTORY AND COLLECTIVE BARGAINING PROTECTION

Typically, worker protection against the downside of market competition comes from two sources: collective bargaining agreements and government legislation. Contingent workers are a thorny issue for labor unions. Contractually, unions can take one of two contradictory directions: they can try to limit employer use of contingent work or they can organize contingent workers and explicitly structure their conditions of work within the collective bargaining agreement.[58] The first option is difficult because employers resist infringement on what they perceive as their managerial prerogative to schedule work and frequently argue they need the flexibility that comes with using labor on some basis other than full-time and permanent.

Thus far, the second option also has been difficult.[59] Unions in both the United States and Canada have not generally embraced part-time workers; when they have, it has been difficult to organize them. The issue for the labor relations boards in the United States and Canada is the extent to which contingent workers can be seen as sharing a community of interest with the core employees.[60] In the

United States, case law rules are evolving from National Labor Relations Board decisions defining community of interest. The definition varies with the type of worker (part-time, temporary, leased, and so on). Labor relations boards across Canada have not included full- and part-time workers in the same bargaining unit, with the rationale that they represent separate communities of interest. Unions traditionally have been concerned that bargaining power might be undermined by combined units.

Assuming a community of interest can be established, unions can seek to bargain for better wages and benefits and incorporate provisions for establishing seniority rights and employment security among the contingent work portion of the bargaining unit. Alternatively, they can encompass part-time or other intermittent work arrangements to create flexible scheduling options for the entire membership.[61] These provisions are difficult to operationalize for several reasons. First, of course, management prefers to retain the ability to use labor on an as-needed basis. This creates tensions within the bargaining unit between full- and part-time members. Second, it is difficult to structure work arrangements that protect the flexibility that workers would like while also not being exploitative. Language covering contingent work arrangements is beginning to appear in isolated contracts, but is far from universal.

On the legislative front, as of this writing, there is no pending or proposed legislation in Michigan that would explicitly extend existing labor standards protection to contingent workers. At the federal level, however, both the House and Senate have drafted legislation to address problems associated with contingent work, although only the House bill has been introduced (H.R. 2188). Both bills are designed to extend the protection afforded core employees to contingent workers. In addition, both require employers to offer whatever benefits they provide to regular employees to contingent workers, and both amend the Internal Revenue Code to tighten the definition of employee as distinct from independent contractor. The thrust of this legislation is to eliminate the pro rata cost advantage to employers of using contingent workers. The draft of the Senate bill, entitled the Contingent Workforce Equity Act, is somewhat broader than the House bill, The Part-time and Temporary Workers Protection Act of 1993.[62]

A primary motivation behind this legislation is a concern that the economic safety nets employers provide to regular employees and deny to contingent workers will have to be provided by the government.[63] As discussed above, contingent workers are far less likely to receive the nonwage compensation available to core workers, such as medical insurance, pension plan coverage, or disability insurance. Denying contingent workers access to these benefits puts pressure on Medicaid and the Social Security system.

A second reason for the federal legislation is that as long as there is a financial advantage to employers to classify their workers as contingent, there will be some degree of deliberate misclassification. One estimate suggests a loss of $3.3 billion in revenue for the federal government in 1996 in the form of failure to contribute to the unemployment insurance system, Social Security, and Medicaid.[64] While comparable estimates have not been done for the states, misclassification has the potential to affect them similarly, such as in the state portion of unemployment insurance. Currently, there is an initiative at the federal level to transfer many of its health and welfare responsibilities to the states. To the extent that this transfer actually occurs, increased pressure on publicly provided services coupled with revenue loss from misclassification will make contingent work a public policy issue for Michigan.

CONCLUSION

Free trade will sustain the heightened competition among producers in North America. Market competition implies greater economic uncertainties for the individual producer. Contingent work arrangements provide the flexibility employers seek in an environment of uncertainty. An increasing number of Michigan workers are employed under such an arrangement, and free trade will accelerate that trend. The policy challenges this poses are how to address the reduced income levels and job security of the Michigan workforce, the associated pressures on publicly provided services, and a diminished revenue base with which to provide those services. To the extent that Michigan unions can successfully integrate contingent workers into collective bargaining agreements, the potential problems will be alleviated, at least for the portion of the workforce covered by those agreements. Yet, a comprehensive union response to the challenge of contingent work has been slow to develop. In the absence of federal legislation, a Michigan public policy response needs to be considered.[65]

NOTES

1. Richard Belous, *The Contingent Economy* (Washington, D.C.: National Planning Association, 1989); and Peter Doeringer and Michael Piore, *Internal Labor Markets and Manpower Analysis* (Lexington, Mass.: D.C. Heath & Co., 1971).
2. Anne E. Polivka and Thomas Nardone, "On the Definition of 'Contingent Work,'" *Monthly Labor Review* 112 (December 1989): 9-16.
3. Michael Piore and Charles Sabel, *The Second Industrial Divide* (New York: Basic Books, 1984).
4. Michigan Department of Commerce, "What the North American Free Trade Agreement Means to Michigan" (Lansing: Lansing Office of Policy and Legislative Affairs, nd.).
5. Anil Verma and Mark Thompson, "Managerial Strategies in Canada and the U.S. in the 1980s," *Proceedings of the Annual Meeting of the Industrial Relations Research Association* (Madison, Wisc.: Industrial Relations Research Association, 1988), 257-71.
6. Delores Crockett, Testimony before the Subcommittee on Labor of the Committee on Labor and Human Resources, U.S. Senate, 103d Cong., 1st sess.15 June 1993.
7. Francoise Carre, "Temporary Employment in the Eighties," in Virginia duRivage, ed., *New Policies for the Part-Time and Contingent Workforce* (New York: M.E. Sharpe, Inc. 1992), 45-87; and U.S. General Accounting Office, "Workers at Risk: Increased Numbers in Contingent Employment Lack Insurance, Other Benefits," Report to the Chairman, Subcommittee on Employment and Housing, Committee on Government Operations, House of Representatives, GAO/HRD-91-56, March.
8. Polly Callaghan and Heidi Hartmann, *Contingent Work: A Chart Book on Part-Time and Temporary Employment* (Washington, D.C.: Economic Policy Institute, 1991); and Polivka and Nardone, "'Contingent Work,'" 9-16.
9. Howard Hayghe and Suzanne Bianchi, "Married Mothers' Work Patterns: The Job-Family Compromise," *Monthly Labor Review* 117, no. 6 (June 1994): 24-30.
10. Katherine Abraham, "Restructuring the Employment Relationship: The Growth of Market-Mediated Work Arrangements," in *New Developments in the Labor Market*, Katherine Abraham and Robert McKersie, eds. (Cambridge, Mass.: M.I.T. Press, 1990), 85-119.
11. Callaghan and Hartmann, *Contingent Work*.
12. OECD, *Employment Outlook*, Paris, July 1993; Tixiano Treu, "Labour Flexibility in Europe," *Industrial Labour Review* 131, no. 4-5 (1992): 497-

512; U.S. G.A.O., 1991; and Gijsbert Van Liemt, "Economic Globalization: Labour options and Business Strategies in High Labour Cost Countries," *Industrial Labour Review* 131, no. 4-5 (1992): 453-70.

13. Callaghan and Hartmann, *Contingent Work.*
14. Piore and Sabel, *The Second Industrial Divide.*
15. Clara Jusidman de Bialostozky, *The Informal Sector in Mexico*, Occasional Paper, no 1., Secretaria del Trabajo y Prevision Social de Mexico, U.S. Department of Labor, 1992.
16. Belous, *The Contingent Economy.*
17. Ibid.; Chris Tilly, *Short Hours, Short Shrift: Causes and Consequences of Part-time Work* (Washington, D.C.: Economic Policy Institute, 1992).; and Richard L. Worsnop, "Part-time Work," *Editorial Research Reports*, 1, no. 22 (1987): 290-98.
18. Harold Metzenbaum, Opening statement before the Subcommittee on Labor of the Committee on Labor and Human Resources, U.S. Senate, 103rd Cong., 1st sess., 15 June 1993.
19. Abraham, "Restructuring"; and Richard Belous, "How Human Resource Systems Adjust to the Shift Toward Contingent Workers," *Monthly Labor Review* 112, no. 3 (1989): 7-12.
20. Sar Levitan and Elizabeth Conway. "Part-time Employment: Living on Half Rations," (Washington, D.C.: Center for Social Policy Studies, Georgetown University, 1988).
21. Tilly, *Short Hours.*
22. U.S. Department of Labor, *Employment and Earnings*, (Washington, D.C.: Bureau of Labor Statistics, various years).
23. Bureau of National Affairs, "International Labor Organization Adopts Protections to Assist Part-time workers," *Daily Labor Reporter* 122 (28 June 1994): A-2.
24. See Rebecca Blank, "Part-time and Temporary Work," in *Investing in People*, vol. 2 (Washington, D.C.: U.S. Dept. of Labor, 1989); and Bureau of National Affairs, "As Part-time Employment Expand, Employer Flexibility Grows, Pay Lags," *Daily Labor Reporter* 102 (31 May 1994): C1-C2.
25. Blank, "Part-time and Temporary Work"; Tilly, *Short Hours*; and U.S. G.A.O.
26. Bureau of National Affairs, "Part-time Employment Expands," C1-C2.
27. Service Employees International Union (SEIU), *Part-time, Temporary, and Contracted Work: Coping with the Growing "Contingent" Workforce* (Washington, D.C.: SEIU Research Department, 1993).
28. Belous, "How Human Resources . . ."; and Callaghan and Hartmann, *Contingent Work.*
29. U.S. G.A.O.
30. Carre, "Temporary Employment in the Eighties."
31. Abraham, "Restructuring"; and Harry B. Williams, "What Temporary Workers Earn: Findings from New BLS Survey," *Monthly Labor Review* 112, no. 3 (March 1989): 3-12.

32. Eileen Appelbaum, Testimony before the Subcommittee on Labor of the Committee on Labor and Human Resources, U.S. Senate, 103rd Cong., 1st sess., 15 June 1993.

33. Max Carey and Kim Hazelbaker, "Employment Growth in the Temporary Help Industry," *Monthly Labor Review* 109, no. 4 (April 1986): 37-44; and Williams, "What Temporary Workers Earn."

34. Americans for Democratic Action, Inc. "Shift from Full-time Employment Breeds Insecurity—Lower Living Standards," Statement to the Subcommittee on Labor of the Committee on Labor and Human Resources, U.S. Senate, 103rd Cong., 1st sess., 15 June 1993; and Jimmie Ruth Daughtrey, Testimony before the Subcommittee on Labor of the Committee on Labor and Human Resources, U.S. Senate, 103rd Cong., 1st sess., 15 June 1993.

35. Delores Crockett, Testimony before the Subcommittee on Labor of the Committee on Labor and Human Resources, U.S. Senate, 103rd Cong., 1st sess., 15 June 1993.

36. Coopers and Lybrand, *Projection of the Loss in Federal Tax Revenues due to Misclassification of Workers*, prepared for Coalition for Fair Worker Classification, June 1994.

37. Ibid.

38. U.S. GAO.

39. Coopers and Lybrand, *Projection of the Loss*.

40. Ibid.

41. Michael D. Hobbs, Testimony before the Subcommittee on Labor of the Committee on Labor and Human Resources, U.S. Senate, 103rd Cong., 1st sess., 15 June 1993.

42. Richard Delaney, Testimony before the Subcommittee on Labor of the Committee on Labor and Human Resources, U.S. Senate, 103rd Cong., 1st sess., 15 June 1993; and Daughtrey, Testimony.

43. Stanley Nollen, "Exploding the Myth: Is Contingent Labor Cost-Effective?", entered as testimony by Helen Axel before the Subcommittee on Labor of the Committee on Labor and Human Resources, U.S. Senate, 103rd Cong., 1st sess., 15 June 1993.

44. Harvey Krahn, "Non-Standard Work Arrangements." *Perspectives on Labour and Income* 6, no. 3 (autumn 1991): 35.

45. Henry Pold, "Jobs! Jobs! Jobs!" *Perspectives on Labour and Income* 6, no. 3 (autumn 1994): 14-17.

46. Secretatia del Trabajo y Prevision Social de Mexico/U.S. Department of Labor, *A Comparison of Labor Law in the United States and Mexico: An Overview* (Washington, D.C: Goverment Printing Office, 1992).

47. Instituto Nacional de Estadistica, Geografia e Informatica, *Encuesta Nacional de Micronegocios, 1992* (Mexico: STPS, 1994).

48. Teresa Rendon and Carlos Salas, *Caracteristicas y Dimensio del Sector Informal en Mexico* (Mexico: UNAM/STPS, 1992).

49. In economic terms, this can be understood as relatively small capital stock contributing to low marginal product of labor and therefore wage rates.
50. Jusidman de Bialostozky, *The Informal Sector in Mexico*.
51. STPS/USDOL, *A Comparison of Labor Law*.
52. Rendon and Salas, *Caracteristicas y Dimensio*.
53. Appelbaum, Testimony; and Tilly, *Short Hours*.
54. Blank, "Part-time and Temporary Work."
55. Douglas Busbey, "An Introduction to NAFTA," presented to the Human Resource Management Association of Mid-Michigan, Lansing, Mich., 24 February 1994.
56. Ibid.
57. U.S. Department of Labor, *North American Agreement on Labor Cooperation*, NAFTA Supplemental Agreements (Washington, D.C.: U.S. Government Printing Office, 1993).
58. SEIU, see note 27 above.
59. Kate Bronfenbrenner, "Unions and the Contingent Work Force," *Interface* 17, no. 4 (fall 1988): 1-4.
60. SEIU, see note 27 above.
61. Ibid.
62. Coopers and Lybrand, *Projection of the Loss*; and U.S. G.A.O..
63. Details of the Senate bill include the following.

Title I of the bill amends labor standards legislation to explicitly extend protection to contingent workers. It would amend:

o The **Fair Labor Standards Act of 1938**, by both increasing the minimum wage rate and prohibiting employers and labor organizations from discriminating on the basis of employment status

o The **Revised Statutes**, so that part-time and temporary workers are offered the full protection of the Civil Rights Act of 1964, the Age Discrimination in Employment Act of 1967, and the Americans with Disabilities Act of 1990.

o The **National Labor Relations Act**, by adding that employees shall not be excluded from a collective bargaining unit on the basis of employment status.

o The **Occupational Safety and Health Act**, to offer full rights to a safe workplace, as is the case for full-time employees.

o The **Worker Adjustment and Retraining Notification Act**, by defining an employer as any enterprise employing 100 or more employees and by striking exclusions of part-time employees that are currently in that statute.

Title II addresses employee benefits offered to contingent workers. Specifically, it amends:

o The **Family and Medical Leave Act** and the **Employee Retirement Income Security Act of 1974**, by reducing the minimum number of hours of employment required prior to coverage.

The Bill also requires employers to prorate the employer-provided premiums under group health plans for employees who regularly works fewer than 30 hours per week.

Finally, *Title II* amends certain requirements associated with unemployment insurance.

Title III addresses the question of misclassification of employees as independent contractors by amending the **Internal Revenue Code of 1986.**

64. Coopers and Lybrand, *Projection of the Loss.*
65. The authors would like to thank Mark Phillips for his extraordinary research assistance.

From Diversity to Diversimilarity: Shifting Paradigms to Match Global and National Realities

Joseph Ofori-Dankwa

The emerging global village, increasing global and national competition, forecasts of greater numbers of women and ethnic minorities entering the U.S. workforce, and the identification of potential competitive advantages associated with these trends have led to intensive corporate and institutional efforts at diversity management. The more adaptable and flexible organizations are shifting their focus from government-monitored, mandatory affirmative action programs to self-monitored, voluntary initiatives affirming diversity.[1] Organizations in Michigan such as General Motors, Ford Motor Co., and Dow Chemical have launched intensive efforts of this kind. The strategies and policies put in place by institutions, organizations, and various levels of government dealing with a diverse workforce are referred to as diversity management.

The framework used most often in diversity management is the diversity paradigm, which emphasizes valuing and appreciating individuals' differences, whereas little or no emphasis is placed on appreciating their commonalities. This perspective has replaced the assimilation paradigm, which stressed conformity to the values of the dominant white male culture by people from other backgrounds.

Although the diversity paradigm is useful, three emerging national and international trends strongly suggest that to gain and maintain the competitive edge in the marketplace, another framework is more appropriate. The diversimilarity paradigm advocates valuing and appreciating both the similarities and differences among individuals and communities.

The three important trends mentioned above are the growing number of minorities and women in the workforce, the decline in the number of international companies locating in the United States and heightened local competition to attract them, and the increasing number of U.S. companies entering the global and regional (Canadian and Mexican) markets. States, communities, and organizations that can quickly and effectively develop and implement policies in response to these trends are likely to gain competitive advantage. This chapter argues that these trends cannot be adequately managed within the context of the diversity paradigm, which has limitations that must be recognized and addressed. Policy makers and managers in Michigan should begin to devise strategies based on the diversimilarity paradigm, because it better addresses these three important trends and will lead to more effective diversity management. Steps toward that end are suggested in the latter part of this chapter.

THE DIVERSITY PARADIGM: ADVANTAGES AND LIMITATIONS

In 1987 the Hudson report identified demographic changes that organizations and institutions will have to face by the year 2000.[2] It projected more women and minorities in the labor force, particularly the latter, who will constitute the largest proportion of new entrants. At the same time, other researchers have pointed out the competitive advantages to be gained by an organization's effective management of diversity. Roosevelt Thomas argues that this makes good business sense and illustrates the point with the examples of Dow Corning and Avon, whose successful recruitment of minority employees has enabled the companies to tap into the minority market.[3] Taylor Cox and Stacy Blake identify a number of competitive advantages that can be gained: (1) lower costs associated with integrating a diverse workforce, (2) ability to attract the best personnel, (3) an edge in international and community markets due to cultural insights and sensitivity, (4) greater creativity and problem-solving ability, and (5) more flexibility in adopting to changes in the environment.[4]

The diversity management at G.E. Silicones is a good example. During the 1980s, the company was characterized by traditional white male values. But in 1989, several women and minorities started an informal networking system to discuss work environment, coworker attitudes, and the apparent shortage of promotional opportunities for them. When their concerns were made known to management, G.E. Silicones moved to initiate a diversity program. Top management gave its full commitment to a volunteer steering committee that formed teams to examine such issues as family leave, minority recruiting, mentoring, and professional and personal development for employees. As a result, the company collaborated with local organizations to form a community child care facility, an employee wellness program and center, a stronger minority recruitment effort on college campuses, and an on-site support group for minorities and women. In addition, diversity training for employees was instituted, and the performance review of managers included a criterion to evaluate their success in diversifying the workforce.[5] Another example is Pacific Gas and Electric, which put 110 employees through an intensive program to become certified diversity awareness trainers so that they, in turn, could train other employees.[6]

As noted earlier, most organizations use the diversity paradigm to guide policy and develop training programs. The primary focus of that paradigm is on valuing and appreciating individual differences, not the similarities among people from diverse cultural backgrounds. Peggy Stuart points out that "as an appreciation of diversity has led to an appreciation of the individual—the new diversity—companies now want to use this uniqueness to enhance the effectiveness of training."[7]

Although the paradigm can lead to greater workforce diversity and creativity, it also can generate conflict and backlash in the workplace. For example, a diversity training session in a small midwestern manufacturing company focused on differences between whites and minorities. Expressions of resentment and anger by the minority employees led to outrage among the whites, a sense of vulnerability among the minorities, and a worsening of work relations.[8]

These attitudes are by no means isolated to training sessions and may permeate the whole workplace. An article in *Newsweek* points to the "rage" of minority professionals who feel that no matter how hard they work and regardless of their accomplishments, members of the majority population see their elevated position as due to "quotas" and "handouts."[9] In the *New Republic*, Heather MacDonald describes fears in the majority population that they are losing hiring opportunities, jobs, promotions, and benefits because of "preferential treatment" for minorities.[10]

Paradoxically, because the diversity paradigm focuses on differences, it may hamper an appreciation of diversity by reinforcing the very stereotypes it seeks to alter. An emphasis on diversity clouds the fact that sometimes perceived differences are only skin deep. These limitations and the questionable effectiveness of the diversity paradigm in dealing with the three trends described earlier, argue for a shift to the diversimilarity framework. This approach views the appreciation of some commonalities and similarities as necessary to an appreciation of diversity and differences.

THE NEED FOR A PARADIGM SHIFT

The principles of diversimilarity have been presented in more detail elsewhere and may be summarized as follows.[11]

- There is adversity and creativity in diversity.
- There is conformity and compatibility in similarity.
- There are diversities within diversities.
- There are similarities across diversities.
- Effective diversity management entails effective management of diversimilarity.

The diversimilarity approach argues that people from diverse cultural and national backgrounds have important differences that need to be identified, valued, and appreciated, but the same is true of their similarities. This search for common ground means that we must begin the process of similation, or the search for commonalities across diversities. In contrast, assimilation takes as reference point the standards and ideals of the dominant culture and attempts to make people from minority cultures conform to these. Assimilation attempts to negate, suppress, and modify existing minority values, whereas similation attempts to identify common strands, themes, and values among individuals of different races, religions, genders, nationalities, and sexual preferences. The relation of these concepts to the three important emerging trends and the rationale for a paradigm shift from diversity to diversimilarity are explored below.

TREND ONE: CHANGING COMPOSITION OF THE WORKFORCE

It is projected that 47 percent of the workforce will be female by the year 2000, compared to 41 percent in 1976 and 45 percent in 1988. Also, by the turn of the century, African, Asian, and Hispanic Americans are projected, respectively, to represent, 12 percent, 4 percent, and 10 percent of the workforce,[12] as compared to 11 percent, 3 percent, and 7 percent in 1988. From 79 percent in 1988, the proportion of white Americans in the workforce is projected to drop to 74 percent by the year 2000.

Between 1989 and 2000, 25 million people will join the labor force, 85 percent of whom will be minorities.[13] It is also estimated that between 1988 and 2000, the average annual percentage change in workforce representation will increase by 4 percent for Hispanic Americans, 3.6 percent for Asian Americans and others, 1.9 percent for African Americans, and 1.1 percent for whites.[14] Much of this change will be due to net immigration to the United States, which accounted for 39 percent of population growth from 1980 to 1990. In 1990, 67.8 percent of immigrants were from Latin America and the Caribbean, compared to 25.8 percent from Europe and Canada; Mexico alone accounted for 21.6 percent.[15]

Michigan is also experiencing an increase in minorities entering the workforce. According to the 1990 Census, minorities comprised 14 percent of the state's labor force, compared to 13 percent in 1980. In 1980, whites constituted 84.9 percent of Michigan workers, versus 83.4 percent in 1990.

Clearly, this trend must be taken into account by employers. It is argued here that businesses have four competitive and strategic reasons for shifting from the diversity paradigm to the diversimilarity paradigm.

First, since the diversity paradigm stresses differences, it can produce a backlash in both the minority and in the majority populations. An overemphasis of differences and a deemphasis of similarities tends to divide workers and creates the basis for racial and gender tensions and conflict.[16]

Second, the diversity approach does not take into account important similarities in qualifications, values, goals, and aspirations among people from different cultural backgrounds. Third, the diversity paradigm excludes an important cultural issue. Geert Hofstede identifies the individualism-collectivism continuum as an important dimension of cultures.[17] A whole body of literature tends to confirm the results of the study by Taylor Cox and his associates, which points to the fact that minority populations seem to have a more cooperative and team-oriented approach than Anglo populations, who tend to have a more individualistic approach.[18] Carol Tavris suggests that women and men have several things in common, as well as several differences.[19] The concept of diversimilarity better reflects both of these situations.

Fourth, most recent immigrants to the United States are from Latin America and the Caribbean, where societies are more collectivist in nature.[20] The diversity paradigm is biased toward individualism, whereas diversimilarity takes a collectivist orientation into account.

TREND TWO: DECLINING FOREIGN INVESTMENT IN THE UNITED STATES

In the 1980s there was a huge amount of foreign investment in the United States. Employment by foreign-owned companies rose by 19 percent from 1987 to 1988 and by 16 percent from 1988 to 1989. Nonbank U.S affiliates of foreign-owned companies had 4.4 million employees in 1989, half of them in the manufacturing sector.[21] In 1990, more than 80 percent of U.S. manufacturing employment, shipments, and value added originated in firms based in seven countries—Canada, France, Germany, Japan, The Netherlands, Switzerland, and the United Kingdom.[22] The largest foreign-owned establishments are British (23 percent), Canadian (15 percent), and Japanese (13 percent).

Foreign direct investment (FDI) in the United States decreased during the 1990s.[23] For example, net FDI in U.S. plants, equipment, and other capital assets dropped from $11.5 billion in 1991 to $2.4 billion in 1992.[24] The primary reasons are economic downturns in the major investing countries and greater competition from locations in China, Asia, Africa, Latin America, and elsewhere.

International investors play an important role in local economies. They inject capital and technology and create jobs. BMW, for example, will invest about $300 million and employ about 2,000 people in South Carolina. Associated investments by BMW suppliers, airport expansion, and other multiplier effects are estimated by the state at $1 billion over the next 20 years, which may create 10,000 jobs.[25] In 1985, Toyota opened a car assembly plant in Georgetown, Kentucky, that now employs 4,000 workers.[26] The average size of plants due to FDI tends to be much larger than that of U.S.-owned establishments.[27] In addition, FDI operations tend to be in higher wage industries and tend to pay higher hourly wages than U.S. companies.

In 1990, the estimated number of manufacturing employees in Japanese-owned facilities was 200,000, and the 1995 figure is likely to be significantly higher.[28] During the 1980s, for example, six automobile assembly plants were built by Japanese corporations in Ohio, Tennessee, Michigan, Illinois, Kentucky, and Indiana for a total investment of more than $7 billion.[29]

In 1990 Michigan ranked eleventh and tenth, respectively, in terms of the number of FDI establishments (396) and employees (70,914) in the United States.[30] The state accounts for 3 percent of FDI manufacturing plants in the United States. The Michigan Department of Commerce has been spearheading efforts to attract and retain international business, and in 1990 the state ranked fifth nationally in the number of Japanese-owned manufacturing facilities.[31]

FDI is an important asset for any community. A survey by Japan External Trade Organization (JETRO) pointed out that foreign-owned firms "are reinvesting more of their profits locally and are doing more research and development in the United States, as well as forming better contacts with local suppliers."[32] A study reported in *Business Week* indicates that foreign-owned or affiliated plants in the United States use more up-to-date technology and continue to invest more money in new machinery and equipment than do U.S factories.[33]

Given all of these benefits, different states have made substantial efforts to attract and retain FDI. The highly competitive nature of the plant location process has increased because of changes in the global marketplace, a few of which are highlighted here. A major event was the replacement of the Soviet empire with more capitalistic, free-market economies. Several countries, such as Poland and Hungary, are emerging quickly from the command economy structure, and this will increase the competition for plant locations worldwide. The competition is not limited to the former Soviet satellites and Russia. The gradual transition of China into a free-market economy represents even more competition. In Africa, several countries have undertaken structural adjustments under the auspices of the IMF and the World Bank with the aim of developing a market orientation. In South Africa, the relatively smooth transition from the apartheid regime to democracy has made the country very attractive to FDI.

In the United States, various localities offer different features and financial incentives to make themselves attractive to foreign investors. South Carolina, for example, has a large nonunionized workforce, average wages substantially lower than in most states, and a "combination of big city culture and small-town feel." [34] Given the increasing state and international competition for plant location, Michigan must develop policies and strategies that make it stand out. One potential incentive is a workforce that understands diversimilarity, that appreciates and values differences as well as commonalities among people. The 1990 JETRO survey of Japanese-owned manufacturing facilities in the United States revealed differences in customs and philosophies between Japanese and Americans and labor-management issues were the problems most cited by respondents.[35] Foreign-owned companies go to great lengths to try to blend the different cultures. In the Toyota plant in Georgetown, Kentucky, for example, the goal is "to create a new management philosophy that combines the best of Japanese style and the best of American management style." [36] If Michigan prepares its workforce and communities for this cultural blending, then the state is likely to be more attractive to foreign investors. The diversimilarity approach readily lends itself to that process.

In the past, it seemed that U.S. interests were best served by U.S. corporations, even if these were located overseas. A current debate among policy makers, including U.S. Secretary of Labor Robert Reich, suggests that foreign-owned companies in the United States may serve U.S. economic interests just as well.[37] This shift in thinking has been used to explain why Brother, a Japanese-owned manufacturer of electric typewriters with plants in Tennessee, was recently cleared of dumping complaints lodged by Smith Corona, which has plants in Singapore and Indonesia.[38]

In summary, FDI yields major dividends to states through job creation and the introduction of new technologies. Yet, the trend is toward less FDI in the United States and heightened competition for these investments worldwide. As this trend becomes more pronounced, Michigan will need to develop new and innovative strategies to attract international investment. A recent study comparing the techniques used in Ontario and Michigan found that the Canadians are much more entrepreneurial and innovative.[39] Teaching diversimilarity skills to the Michigan workforce will be a helpful strategy in the competition for foreign investment.

TREND THREE: THE FOREIGN RELOCATION OF U.S. COMPANIES

Several Michigan corporations representing different industries are in the forefront of the regional and global thrust of U.S. business. Regionally, the U.S., Canadian, and Mexican economies have been gradually merging over the last decades. NAFTA appears to have accelerated that process.[40] It reflects the global trend toward regional economic blocs evident in Europe, Asia, Africa, and Latin America.[41]

At the regional level, labor relations in Canada and Mexico differ substantially from those in the United States, which are guided primarily by the diversity paradigm and a management philosophy of union avoidance.[42] Although there are differences, labor relations in Canada appear to have some important similarities to those in Mexico. In neither country do employers practice union avoidance, and union power tends to be protected by both governments.[43] The diversity paradigm, with its concomitant high levels of labor-management conflict, therefore may be an inappropriate framework for effective operation of U.S. business in Canada and Mexico.

Among the Michigan companies with foreign pressure, automobile manufacturers are the most obvious. Investments by the Big Three in Asia over the next few years are projected to exceed $2 billion.[44] Car sales in Asia (excluding Japan) are estimated to be in excess of three million units.[45] Chrysler is expanding its sales network by linking up with about 30 Daihatsu dealerships in Japan.[46] The automakers are also planning to enter or expand operations in Latin America, Europe, and Africa.[47] In the pharmaceutical industry, Upjohn has continued its global thrust, most recently through a joint venture in China worth $30 million.

Whirlpool, a Michigan-based manufacturer and distributor of household appliances, has plants in 11 countries and distributes its products in 120 countries. Whirlpool CEO David Whitman, in an interview reported in the *Harvard Business Review*, points out that several corporations have global strategies that in reality are only flag planting. He also believes that three critical areas of diversimilarity have to be effectively managed to ensure a successful globalization strategy.[48] The first is technological diversimilarity. Whitman argues that despite varying regional and geographical preferences, many of the technological and manufacturing processes involved are similar. The various Whirlpool facilities, therefore, share the best technological and manufacturing processes the corporation can devise. (Dow's current process of internal global benchmarking across divisions in different countries can be seen as an another example of the technological diversimilarity management process.[49])

Second, Whitman suggests that there must be proper management of vision diversimilarity. Despite the different cultural milieus in which the Whirlpool operations are located, it is critical that each unit share the same vision and have the same mission.

Third, diversimilarity in corporate values must be managed. According to Whitman, despite cultural differences throughout the world, successful globalization is based on a clearly articulated and defined set of organizational values and core culture.[50] A strong corporate culture is needed to ensure clarity of vision and effective communication of the corporate mission.[51]

Whitman says that "top managers often incorrectly assume that since consumers differ from location to location, their businesses can't operate effectively as a unified entity. As a result, they see their industry as a mosaic of specialized businesses, each with its own unique constraints and its own finite opportunities." [52] He illustrates the usefulness of the diversimilarity paradigm when he notes: "And in the process, it became clear to us that the basics of managing our business and its process and product technologies were the same in Europe, North America, Asia, and Latin America. We were already good at what we did. What we needed was to enter the appliance markets in other parts of the world and learn how to satisfy different kinds of customers." [53]

The success of the global strategy used by McDonald's resides, in part in a strong emphasis on common architectural design (the golden arches), common food, and common high service quality, with slight modifications to suit local tastes and preferences. Based on my travels to different nations, I believe a major factor in the company's success is its worldwide consistency in design, food quality, and service. Kellogg's strategy for introducing cereals into the Asian market is going to be based on diversimilarity principles.

As organizations increasingly go global, there is a clear need for a strong organizational culture, with clarity of vision and focus. Indeed, paradoxically, the more decentralized an organization's operations become, the greater is the need to manage diversimilarity in vision, technology, and values. Furthermore, from a regional perspective, labor relations in Canada and Mexico do not readily lend themselves to the diversity paradigm that shapes most labor relations in the United States. U.S. corporations entering the regional and global marketplace will be well served by a better understanding of the diversimilarity framework.

ENGINEERING A PARADIGM SHIFT

What are the implications for Michigan of the three major trends and their management through the diversimilarity paradigm? Clearly, businesses, institutions, and policy makers should begin to move away from the diversity framework, but a paradigm shift can be a difficult process. Adopting the diversimilarity approach is further compounded by the fact that the assimilation perspective still prevails in some organizations. Nevertheless, it is important that strategies and policies be developed to facilitate the shift to diversimilarity. Three steps are recommended here: increase community awareness, change educational curricula, and alter the assumptions underlying training programs to "manage work force diversity." The following brief discussion of each lays the groundwork for further exploration.

INCREASING COMMUNITY AWARENESS

Organizations and policy makers in Michigan can play an important role in generating discussion about diversimilarity. Such agencies as the Office of Equity in the Michigan Department of Education can sponsor conferences and workshops to heighten awareness of recognizing and valuing both commonalities and differences among people and communities, as well as the potential advantages of this perspective. The discussions also can identify the policy options and strategies such a paradigmatic shift will entail.

CURRICULAR CHANGES

The educational system plays a major role in shaping the attitudes of young people and in preparing them for productive work and responsible citizenship. A first step would be to include the diversimilarity concept in school curricula, as proposed by Johnnella Butler and John Walter.[54] Butler notes: "It does not stop at adding and celebrating diversity. It demands that we do something with these experiences, this diversity, in order ultimately to understand the whole. It demands that we add, delete, decenter, re-vision and reorganize in order to transform our curricula to reflect a kind of unity, a wholeness that is all inclusive in its content, methodology, and pedagogy."[55] She points out that two basic problems are the "lack of a sense of human commonality and communality" and a "distorted and limited treatment of gender difference and similarities."[56] A truly transformative curriculum requires an academic atmosphere that "corrects distortions and exclusions, and allows for syncretism and an interaction among differences and sameness so that we see all of ourselves as vibrant parts of the past, present, and future of the many dimensions of this nation."[57]

Institutions of higher learning should undertake pioneering work in curriculum transformation, such as that being done at the University of Washington. The next step should be to sponsor pilot studies to implement the changes in schools. The final step should be to use that experience to make any necessary adjustments and then undertake full-scale implementation of the curricular changes.

CHANGE DIVERSITY MANAGEMENT TRAINING

A clear distinction needs to be made between the diversity paradigm and diversity management. The effective management of a diverse work force is the goal, and the diversity paradigm is only one approach for achieving that end. In the 1940s and 1950s, diversity management was based on the assimilation paradigm, following in the 1960s by the increasing use of the diversity framework. As suggested here, a shift to the diversimilarity approach is now needed, to incorporate the important aspect of commonalities and similarities among individuals.

Training programs in diversity management should recognize and emphasize the dual and complementary notions of diversity and similarities. This will mean developing employee workshops and seminars that lead to sensitivity in both respects, as well as helping companies plan and implement a diversimilarity management program.

CONCLUSIONS

Given the inadequacy of the diversity paradigm for effectively addressing three emerging national and global trends, the concept of diversimilarity offers a unique way to manage workforce diversity and to respond to those trends. To accomplish the paradigm shift, policy makers should develop strategies for increasing community awareness of diversimilarity, changing educational curricula, and altering the assumptions that underlie current efforts to manage workforce diversity. This is a challenge not only for policy makers, but also for top management in the public and private sector, a challenge Michigan must meet in order to remain competitive in the face of global economic developments.

NOTES

1. Roosevelt Thomas, *Beyond Race and Gender: Unleashing the Power of Your Total Workforce by Managing Diversity* (New York: Amacom, 1991).
2. William Johnston and Arnold Packer, *Workforce 2000: Work and Workers for the 21st Century* (Indianapolis: Hudson Institute, 1987).
3. Thomas, *Beyond Race and Gender*
4. Taylor Cox and Stacy Blake, "Managing Cultural Diversity: Implications for Organizational Competitiveness," *Academy of Management Executive* 5 no. 3 (1991): 45-56.
5. Vicki Clark, "Employees Drive Diversity Efforts at GE Silicones," *Personnel Journal* 72 (May 1993): 148-53.
6. Ronita B. Johnson and Julie O'Mara, "Shedding New Light on Diversity Training," *Training and Development* 46 (May 1992): 45-52.
7. Peggy Stuart, "New Directions in Training Individuals," *Personnel Journal* 71 (September 1992): 86-94.
8. See Shari Caudron, "Training Can Damage Diversity Efforts," *Personnel Journal* 72 (April 1993): 51-55. See also H. B. Karp and Nancy Sutton,

"Where Diversity Training Goes Wrong," *Training* 30, no. 7 (July 1993): 30-34. For further discussion on backlash associated with the diversity paradigm, see Michael Mobley and Tamara Payne, "Backlash! The Challenge to Diversity Training," *Training & Development* 46 (December 1992): 45-52; Ellis Cose, "Rage of the Privileged," *Newsweek*, 15 November 1993, 56-63; Heather MacDonald, "The Diversity Industry," *The New Republic* 209 (5 July 1993): 22-25; Chris Chen, "The Diversity Paradox," *Personnel Journal* 71 (January 1992): 32-36; and Jack Falvey, "Diversity Divides," *Sales & Marketing Management* 145 (May 1993): 16-17.

9. Cose, "Rage."

10. MacDonald, "Diversity Industry."

11. For more detailed discussion on the diversimilarity principles, see Joseph Ofori-Dankwa and Connie Sysak, "Shifting Paradigms: From Diversity to Diversimilarity Training," Paper presented at the Second World Conference on Management, International Federation of Scholarly Associations of Management, Dallas, Texas, 17-19 August 1994.

12. Howard Fullerton, "New Labor Force Projections, Spanning 1988 to 2000," *Monthly Labor Review* 112 (November 1989): 3-12.

13. Charlene Marmer Solomon, "The Corporate Response to Workforce Diversity," *Personnel Journal* 68 (August 1989): 43-53.

14. Ronald Kutscher, "New B.L.S. Projections: Findings and Implications," *Monthly Labor Review* 114 (November 1991): 3-12.

15. Ruben Rumbaut, "Immigrant America: A Contemporary Portrait, Windows on Our Global Future," Contemporary Issues Symposium, Michigan State University, East Lansing, 22 October 1993.

16. For discussions on backlash associated with the diversity paradigm, see note 8 above.

17. Geert Hofstede, *Culture's Consequences: International Differences in Work Related Values* (Beverly Hills, Calif.: Sage, 1984).

18. Taylor Cox, Sharon Lobel, and Poppy Lauretta McLeod, "Effects of Ethnic Group Cultural Differences on Cooperative and Competitive Behavior on a Group Task", *Academy of Management Journal* 34, no. 4 (1991): 827-47.

19. Carol Tavris, *The Mismeasure of Woman* (New York: Simon & Schuster, 1992), 287-301.

20. Ruben Rumbaut, "Immigrant America"; and Jan Larson, "A Yen for the U.S.A.," *American Demographics* 14 (March 1992): 44-47.

21. Steve Bezirganian, "U.S. Affiliates of Foreign Companies: Operations in 1989," *Survey of Current Business* 71 (July 1991): 72-93.

22. Ned Howenstine and William Zeile, "Characteristics of Foreign-owned U.S. Manufacturing Establishments," *Survey of Current Business* 74 (January 1994): 34-59.

23. Larson, "A Yen," 46.

24. Gustavs Lombo, "The Deal Flow Dries Up," *Forbes Magazine* 153 (19 July 1993): 174-80.

25. Sally Solo, "Why Foreigners Flock To South Carolina," *Fortune*, 2 November 1992, 48.
26. Larson, "A Yen," 44.
27. Howenstine and Zeile, "Characteristics," 34.
28. Japan External Trade Organization, "Japanese Manufacturers Employing More, Buying More in U.S.," *JETRO Monitor* 10 (March 1990): 1-2.
29. Robert Perrucci, *Japanese Auto Transplants in the Heartland* (Hawthorne, N.Y.: Aldine de Gruyter, 1994).
30. Howenstine and Zeile, "Characteristics," 41.
31. JETRO, "Japanese Manufacturers," 2.
32. Ibid.
33. Fluer Templeton, "Why U.S. Companies are Losing Ground in Their Own Background," *Business Week* 10 February 1992, 124.
34. Solo, "Why Foreigners Flock," 48.
35. JETRO, "Japanese Manufacturers," 2.
36. Larson, "A Yen," 47.
37. Susuma Awanohara, "Borderless Firms," *Far Eastern Economic Review* 155 (9 January 1992): 43.
38. Ibid.
39. Laura Reese, "Local Economic Development Practices across the Northern Border," *Urban Affairs Quarterly* 28, no. 4 (June 1993): 571-92.
40. Jaime Serra. Puche, "The North American Free Trade Agreement: A Source of Competitiveness," *Vital Speeches of the Day* 59 (15 April 1993): 395-98; David Dilts, William Walker, and Constanza Hagmann, "The Impact of the North American Free Trade Agreement on Public Sector Collective Bargaining," *Journal of Collective Negotiation* 23, no. 1 (1994): 91-96.
41. Richard Belous and Rebecca Hartley, "The Growth of Regional Trading Blocs in the Global Economy" (Washington, D.C.: National Planning Association, 1990).
42. Joseph Ofori-Dankwa, "Murray and Reshef Revisited: Toward a Typology/Theory of Paradigms of National Trade Union Movements," *Academy of Management Review* 18, no. 2 (1993): 269-92.
43. Michael Ballot, *Labor-Management Relations in a Changing Environment* (New York: Wiley Publishers, 1992), 133-35.
44. Sally Goll and Douglas Lavin, "Detroit Pushes Pedal to the Floor in Asia" *Wall Street Journal*, 21 June 1994, sec. A, p. 19 (col. 1).
45. Ibid.
46. "Chrysler plans links to Daihatsu dealers for Japan expansion," *Wall Street Journal*, 29 July 1994, sec. A, p. 4 (col. 3); and "Japan outlets for Chrysler," *New York Times*, 1 August 1994, sec. D, p. 4 (col. 3).
47. Robert Simison, "Chrysler to expand its sales efforts in Latin America," *Wall Street Journal*, 6 September 1994, p. 6 (col. 5).
48. Regina Maruca, "The Right Way to Go Global: An Interview with Whirlpool C.E.O. David Whitman," *Harvard Business Review* 72 (March-April 1994): 135-45.

49. Andrew Stern, "Technology Transfer, Dow Chemical," *Financial World*, 162 (28 September 1993): 54.

50. Maruca, "The Right Way," 141.

51. Charlene Solomon, "HR in the Global Age: Transplanting Corporate Cultures Globally," *Personnel Journal* 72 (October 1993): 75-88.

52. Maruca, "The Right Way," 137.

53. Ibid.

54. Johnnella Butler and John Walter, eds., *Transforming the Curriculum, Ethnic Studies and Women's Studies* (New York: State University of New York Press, 1991).

55. Johnnella Butler, "The Difficult Dialogue of Curriculum Transformation: Ethnic Studies and Women's Studies," in *Transforming the Curriculum*, Butler and Walter, eds., 10.

56. Ibid.

57. Ibid., 12.

Appendices

Appendix 1

Panel Discussion: NAFTA on the Shop Floor in Canada

This appendix is an edited transcript of the panel discussion that took place at the November 1994 conference. Introductory remarks have been deleted. Panelist Richard Block's remarks formed the basis for chapter 11 of this volume and are not repeated here.

RICHARD CHAYKOWSKI

WORKPLACE CHANGES UNDER NAFTA

I feel that NAFTA is an almost unlimited area to explore. I would like to focus my comments on what has driven, and what I think will drive, workplace change under NAFTA, because clearly it is too soon to say that specific outcomes may or may not occur at the workplace level. Perhaps the more important issue is what will drive change at the organizational level. I'll begin by laying out a couple of assumptions under which my comments and observations operate. First, I'd like to say that I think that what occurs at the organizational level (and by that I mean the firm level as well as the union level) will be driven significantly by macroeconomic developments. Second, and I think this is extremely important, the changes at the organizational level will be shaped by public policy responses chosen by the Canadian, Mexican, and U.S. governments. Furthermore, I believe that all three countries have considerable scope with respect to the public policies that they choose to initiate.

There's a big "but" here, though. Coordinated responses in the public policy area are also very difficult to envisage. We are witnessing that in practice in Canada today, not only with regard to federal-provincial relations, but also with regard to the broader debate over social policy reform. From a Canadian perspective, I think that NAFTA is certainly, in the short run, a natural but somewhat marginal extension of a longer-term process of economic integration with the United States, which has progressed steadily since the 1970s. It is not some discrete shift in policy. Rather, it is a natural outgrowth of other trade developments that have built up over the decades.

However, I think NAFTA does represent a significant departure for Canada with respect to historic trade developments. First, it has the potential to open up important new socioeconomic opportunities with Mexico. That is a fundamentally different dimension for Canada to explore. Second, it explicitly affects workplace issues and standards, as well as labor relations, and that is somewhat new with regard to North American trade developments. In what follows I direct my comments toward the process of industrial relations and organizational change at the firm level and what I think is the scope for public policy to shape change in what I call the "NAFTA environment."

Two labor market outcomes that we must consider under a free-trade environment include the pressures to compete on the basis of low labor costs and the impact on the redistribution of income. Pressure to compete on the basis of low labor cost is not new, but it is extremely important because it affects three other key areas. First, it puts immense pressure on trade unions, and that occurs, obviously, at the bargaining table. Second, it puts pressure on workplace standards where workplace standards are often viewed as costly. Third, it puts pressure on the labor demand side of the market, with regard to the technical skills needed for upskilling, retraining, and so on, and potentially with regard to unemployment, created as industries restructure.

The impact on redistribution of income has not received a lot of attention. The impacts will be both direct (depending on which groups tend to benefit and which groups tend to lose in the labor market) and indirect (through their impacts on unions). For a country like Canada, which is still heavily unionized, there is a real argument that unions, by benefiting the less advantaged, have had a significant effect on the distribution of income; to the extent that freer trade affects labor unions, it certainly will affect the distribution of income in Canada.

So, what of labor relations? Across individual firms and unions in Canada, it is probably fair to say that change in labor relations and in human resource management practices has occurred largely in a somewhat static public policy environment. That is to say, Canada's public policy environment has remained fundamentally more reflective of the socioeconomic environment of the period between 1950 and 1980 than of the environment that emerged in the late 1980s and into the 1990s. In the 1950-80 period, public policies themselves assumed a context: steadily growing markets, the prevalence of regulated industries, efficiency gains based on standardized technologies, and a reliance on the economies of scale in production. But by the late 1980s, these conditions clearly no longer held in most industries. In the 1990s, labor relations change has been driven chiefly by competitive pressures.

What has been the nature of the change process in Canada? On the one hand, there has been tremendous pressure on unions. At the macro level, across industries, firms probably place greater value now on nonunion status. Overall, Canadian private sector union density has declined in several industries over the past decade. I attribute that, in part, to the pressure on labor unions at the macro level.

At the organizational level, the pressures and changes occurring in Canada are very similar to the changes that have been occurring in the United States. In collective bargaining, firms have sought lower wage settlements and moved to introduce flexible compensation systems. In the workplace, they have tried to introduce increased operating flexibilities and have engaged in pervasive workplace restructuring.

A consensus is emerging that long-run investments in human resources will be a key component of any strategy to move toward a "high performance workplace" in the new competitive economy, whether within NAFTA or in a broader context. Yet, there is very little objective evidence to suggest either that management has that committed increased financial resources to training and to skills development or that management has recognized a substantive role for unions in developing the "high performance workplace." In unionized environments, one prerequisite to achieving a more competitive, high-performance work system is likely to be the advancement of positive labor relations. This, in turn, could facilitate firm-level initiatives such as work reorganization or joint labor-management training and technology programs. These are all required in order to increase productivity. Firms and unions both recognize the need for such initiatives in order to ensure our competitive capability.

I have several broader observations regarding changes that have been occurring in Canada. First, pressures for change have progressively intensified as a result of federal policies related to the Canada-U.S. Free Trade Agreement (which had a major impact on Canada), to deregulation in key industries (which has been ongoing and will continue) and, in the future, to NAFTA. These factors together have dramatically increased competitive pressures. Second, labor relations and human resource management changes have been driven by management and unions at the organizational level. The responses appear to be highly individualized to date. Third, innovative changes have occurred, for the most part, within the context of the established labor relations framework. There has been little role, in my view, for proactive public policies in Canada.

As firms and unions adapt their labor relations practices to the emerging socioeconomic context, it is natural to expect considerable variations in the types of approaches undertaken. This begs the critical question of whether public policies can be proactive in order to encourage and sustain labor-management innovation. Under the current labor relations framework, the rapid pace and significant extent of change suggest that the individual parties may themselves be best suited to developing their own solutions. We have seen a broad spectrum of changes occurring in Canada, ranging from entrenchment or a drive to achieve nonunion status to what people view as very progressive responses (for example, at companies like Bell Canada), where they are moving toward joint approaches in the workplace, to the other extreme of employee ownership at major corporations like Algoma Steel. While employee ownership is, even by Canadian standards, something quite extraordinary, the fact remains that when it occurred, it was driven by the parties, and was not substantively fostered by public policies.

The set of legislative frameworks governing various aspects of industrial relations in Canada may require substantial modification before they can foster a transformation in industrial relations approaches. Importantly, while labor relations reforms in Ontario and British Columbia in the past decade have sometimes provided stronger legal support for traditional unionism and collective bargaining, their impact on transforming the conduct of labor relations and on changing the workplace was almost negligible. Rather, these types of legislative reforms have served only to heighten the debate in Canada (for example, in Ontario in 1995) over whether these previous public policy adjustments have, perhaps even marginally, created a competitive disadvantage by imposing costs on domestic unionized firms.

Where does this leave us? I can only raise several policy issues in response to these observations. First, does the current system of labor law in Canada favor the status quo in the industrial relations system? Perhaps yes. Or perhaps the current system of labor law will provide sufficient flexibility to encourage widespread innovation in industrial relations and in workplace practices—innovation that will enhance both workplace equity and the productivity needed to compete in a NAFTA environment. Is the current legal and legislative (policy) framework the one that is best suited to promoting these kinds of far-reaching innovations and approaches at the organizational level and fostering the changes in work systems that unions and firms have begun, if only slowly, to embrace? Given the already high level of economic integration between Canada and the United States, and the increasing integration of the Canadian, U.S., and Mexican economies, I would suggest that a broader issue concerns how we go about maintaining substantially different public policies in labor markets.

As North American economic integration unfolds under NAFTA, I think the economic pressures to harmonize policies will escalate, and consequently the costs of maintaining unique national policies (or, in our case, provincial policies) will also increase. In view of these costs, we must attach greater importance to identifying and prioritizing workplace economic objectives and workplace equity objectives in the "new economy." Current labor policies will naturally evolve. The legal and legislative system that guides the practice and shapes the substantive outcomes of industrial relations in the emerging economy must reflect the national policies that each country seeks to maintain.

GREGOR MURRY

CHALLENGES TO THE CANADIAN LABOR MOVEMENT UNDER NAFTA

I would like to preface my remarks with two qualifications. First, since I have no pretense of expertise on industrial relations in Mexico, or the United States, or Michigan, I am obliged to confine my observations largely to Canada, particularly Quebec, the largely French-speaking province in which I live. A second qualification is that discussing the impact of NAFTA on patterns of industrial relations poses a formidable difficulty. Most analysts agree it is virtually impossible to disentangle the effects of NAFTA from the other effects of internationalization, economic recession, economic recovery, and restructuring. NAFTA is not unique. Similar processes of trade liberalization are taking place elsewhere in the world. So what can be attributed to NAFTA as opposed to restructuring and globalization is very difficult to untangle as they are part of the same process. Therefore, I am obliged to depict a broader portrait of the process of adjustment in Canada and the reaction of unions to that.

My remarks will cover three general points. First, I will talk about the Canadian labor movement, then some of the changes that are affecting it, and, finally, what I see as the challenges for both union organizations and public policy makers. The question that I ultimately discuss is that of the relative autonomy of nations (or any geographical unit, such as provinces, states, or regions) to build their own economic institutions that define the social relationships that they want to prevail in the marketplace. This is why it is particularly important to look not just at the NAFTA countries when trying to understand the impact of globalization. We have to look at a broader range of countries and see how different national or regional economies, operating nationally and internationally, define institutions that allow them to trade and compete but still reflect the kinds of relationships that have been developed over their history. In some respects Richard Chaykowski raised similar questions about the cost of having distinctive economic institutions, but cost is not the only issue. Homogenization of institutions is not inevitable, but rather only one possible and rather improbable outcome of how we deal with the global economy.

PORTRAIT OF UNIONISM IN CANADA

The Canadian trade union movement might be characterized as fairly stable, highly decentralized, increasingly fragmented and under considerable challenge. While the labor movement has declined in many countries, the recent history of Canadian trade unionism is somewhat of an anomaly, especially when compared with the United States. It has not declined in absolute or relative terms, at least until very recently. In general, the Canadian labor movement is stable in two ways: in overall membership and in union density. It should be emphasized that among the group of seven big industrial countries (G7), only the German union movement has demonstrated a comparable stability in membership over the last decade. Union density has actually increased in Quebec. Over the last decade, in the industrialized nations only Sweden has demonstrated a similar increase.

The second characteristic of both the Canadian union movement and Canadian industrial relations is their high degree of decentralization and fragmentation. The norm, except in the public sector, is the negotiation of a single agreement, with a single employer, in a single work setting. This highly decentralized system allows considerable flexibility in terms of adjustment. This pattern of decentralization is further exacerbated by public policy fragmentation. This fragmentation can be understood as an outgrowth of the Canadian political system. The one-party rule of the British parliamentary system facilitates frequent changes. Also, Canadian legislatures do not have the filibuster rules and other tools that U.S. institutions have to slow down the pace of legislative change. As a result, we have frequent legislative adjustments. This is occurring in a context where there is more ideological diversity in the political approaches of Canadian unions than there used to be. The Canadian Labour Congress represents approximately 58 percent of union members—it used to represent 75 percent, a significant development toward greater union pluralism.

The Canadian labor movement is undoubtedly increasingly under challenge. First, the areas of employment in which labor unions have traditionally been strong are declining, and even within these, union density has been declining. While it is not clear that union density is declining in the private sector, it is certainly declining in manufacturing. It has increased in private services, but whether that increase in private services has yet offset the decrease in manufacturing remains to be seen. Certainly public-sector union density has increased and remains very high. The second challenge is that even where unionism has been strongest—in manufacturing—it is under considerable stresses and strains, as is indicated by the decline in manufacturing union density. Yet, several indicators point to a fairly innovative and adaptive union movement: continuing high levels of recruitment activity; considerable innovation in bargaining agenda and levels of bargaining; its recognition in various bipartite and tripartite forums concerned with economic adjustment; and a high public profile in a variety of issue-oriented campaigns and coalitions, notably on NAFTA.

A final point on the characteristics of the union movement in Canada concerns the issue of convergence or divergence between U.S. and Canadian union movements. This is a debate between some U.S. and Canadian scholars that I do not want to belabor here. Some point to divergence—notably, people like Richard Block. These scholars see distinctive features of the U.S. and Canadian systems that will direct their development in significantly different directions. Others point to convergence and argue that Canada is simply a case of retarded development; that we shall join U.S. patterns as international economic pressures come to bear more heavily on Canadian industrial relations. Neither of these explanations is entirely satisfactory. I will return to this point, but we need to try to place this discussion more decidedly in the context of the political economy and the history of worker representation in each country. There are elements of convergence; there are elements of divergence; and there's no inevitability. Rather, developments in the two labor movements are playing out differently in the two countries.

FACTORS OF CHANGE

Turning to my second area of concern, what then are the changes affecting the Canadian union movement? There are four sets of interrelated factors. The first one is the global economic environment, which is exerting considerable pressure for adjustment in Canadian industrial relations. Apart from the impact on the formal structures of industrial relations, such as the breaking down of coordinated bargaining and pattern bargaining, plus the increasing decentralization of bargaining, what is particularly important is the abandonment for most unions of the magic productivity formula that characterized the post-World War II period. We have lost the belief that growth in the fortunes of the firm means employment security. This shift poses particular problems for business unionism, because it challenges the assumption that economic growth invariably translates into wage and employment growth. Over the post-World War II period, union negotiators have concentrated on distributive and employment security issues. That is no longer enough.

A second set of changes affecting the Canadian labor movement is related to the organization of the firm, in particular the emergence of high-performance work organization models such as teamwork and a range of other innovations. Canadian firms have adapted them, and they are having a profound effect. These new organizational structures generate contradictory tendencies in internal labor markets: with the implementation of high-performance models comes the pronounced acceleration of various forms of contingent employment, subcontracting and the distancing, both contractually and physically, of workers within the firm. Different public policy demands flow out of these differing firm strategies: how they intend to use their workers, what contractual status is given to these workers, whether they intend to internalize or externalize these costs, and so on.

The third area of change is in regional and national labor markets, changing structural employment, on the one hand, and changing demographic composition of the labor force, on the other. These have profound implications for the labor movement and its ability to represent increasingly heterogeneous groups of workers. Because of the increasing polarization of fortunes within the labor market, the labor movement, with its inclusiveness ideology (it aspires to represent all groups of workers), is faced with internal contradictions. These have to be debated internally, as opposed to externally, between unions. This kind of division is in evidence both within labor centrals and within labor organizations.

Finally, the fourth area of change is in the patterns of state and social regulation. First, as an employer, the state has been slow to innovate and is just now implementing many of the changes already occurring in the private sector. This is particularly important because of the significant pressures on public spending in Canada. Over the coming years an important restructuring of social programs is likely to occur. With it will come much reorganization of work in order to achieve cost savings. This will have very important consequences for public sector unionism and will pose a lot of challenges for public sector unions who have been fairly timid to date and will have to become much more adventurous. There is also a fragmentation of the polity, demonstrated by the emergence of a variety of new interest groups or stakeholders. Unions are now in competition with other groups in the public policy forum and will have to justify their existence and develop new working relationships with these other groups. This is particularly evident in Ontario. There is an increasing recognition of the greater heterogeneity of legitimate interests in the polity; states are having problems dealing with this, and it poses challenges to labor movements as well.

None of these four areas of change is entirely driven by NAFTA, of course. Yet NAFTA appears to have considerable influence directly on the first two, economic environment and corporate strategies, and more indirectly on labor markets and state policy. Some would suggest that these common pressures lead to singular adjustments, that is, the convergence theory. That, as I have said already, is too simplistic. Although there are common pressures on industrial relations, in part from internationalization, we can by no means presume identical results. We need to look at these specific institutional configurations. Industrial relations institutions arise out of differing historical circumstances and existing arrangements are resistant to change. There is a lot of scope for comparative work, which we have hardly begun among the three NAFTA partners.

There is no single model. What is striking is the increasing heterogeneity in labor and product markets: high commitment versus highly contingent work organizations, leading edge versus trailing edge, product market strategies, varieties of business unionism versus varieties of social unionism. As researchers, we really do need to look at some of the tensions and pressures arising from these different strategies.

CHALLENGES FOR UNIONS AND PUBLIC POLICY

What are the challenges for unions and public policy? First, in terms of union organizing and recruitment, clearly economic restructuring challenges the representativeness of unions and, hence, their legitimacy. Canadian unions, like other union movements, are weakly implanted in the sectors of greatest growth. Unions appear to be responding on several fronts. There is evidence in Canada of significant new organizational activity on the ground, which translates into aggregate stability in terms of members, at least thus far. In addition, boundaries between organizational jurisdictions are breaking down, which has led to the creation of general unionism in place of industrial unionism. This is happening in unions like the steel union in Canada, which has maintained membership, and in jurisdictions like Quebec, where organization has increased in private sector services rather than in traditional manufacturing areas. Unions have also secured some changes in labor laws to facilitate access, but these are fairly limited. Perhaps more significantly, unions are beginning to argue for minimum standards for part-time workers and other nonunionized workers, a new strategy emerging in some jurisdictions. Unions used to be against this thing, but have come around to thinking that it is necessary and important and that they alone cannot play the protective role in the labor market, something that they previously aspired to do.

A second challenge is the need to make internal structural adjustments. To be brief, I will just say that unions are adapting their own structures considerably. They are making significant attempts to represent increasingly diverse groups of workers and to come to terms with what this entails, in an organizational sense.

A third adjustment is in bargaining structures and strategies: economic restructuring weighs heavily on both bargaining structure and the content of collective agreement. In terms of decentralization, there has been a movement away from pattern bargaining. There are now new forms of coordination, especially in private services. At the same time that we are moving away from coordination in manufacturing, we are constructing coordinating mechanisms within private sector services, where there is sometimes a common employer interest in taking wages out of competition because of the competitive nature of these private sector services. For example, in areas like subcontract cleaning in Quebec, there are wide-ranging coordinating mechanisms. This is beginning to occur in the retail sector also. There is also a need to create transnational linkages in bargaining; currently these are almost nonexistent. There are a few exceptions. For example, there is a trilateral informal agreement on organizing between communications workers' unions in Canada, Mexico and the United States. But it is difficult to assess the real importance of that type of agreement at this point.

There have been debates over the role of the union in the reorganization of work. Although some unions have taken different positions, there is a fair degree of homogeneity in union positions in practice, despite their public discourse. The scope for debate over the effect of the new production models is potentially quite large. One question is how diffused these models really are and how public policy relates to promoting this diffusion. A further question is how these policy decisions affect the rest of the labor force, for which implementation of these new production models seems a fairly distant reality. There are obviously significant pressures on work rules as employers seek greater flexibility in terms of both multiskilling and employment levels (functional and numerical flexibility). Thus, there is real adjustment taking place, which is perhaps not surprising in a small, open economy like that of Canada.

What is different is that union adjustments traditionally were reactive, but are becoming proactive. Canada is on the lead-in end of world downturns because we produce more natural resources than other things; so when manufacturing orders stop, the workers that get hit first are in the primary economic sectors. As a result, work rule adjustments traditionally have been reactive—mainly concerned with layoffs. Unions are becoming more proactive in their thinking about how to make adjustments in work rules. This is particularly evident in Quebec, where language and culture are additional factors and there has been more intensive consultation and concertation in the exposed international sectors than probably anywhere else in Canada. An area where there has been specific public policy change in Quebec is in legislation to allow longer agreements, which entail other kinds of problem-resolving mechanisms in order to foster these new types of production-model relationships. This was first seen in Quebec but is now spreading elsewhere.

Another new form of economic intervention is union participation in various economic restructuring mechanisms at a macro level, such as the Canadian Labour Market and Productivity Center. I should also mention the existence of the Quebec Solidarity Fund, a union venture capital fund based on retirement savings to make risk investments to secure jobs. This represents a new kind of labor strategy, because it is linked not just to the investment mix, but also to when and where investments are made. This should change the kinds of relationships currently in place. For example, there is a lot of economic education activity taking place around these investments, illustrating a shift in union thinking. There are also many kinds of new training institutions being set in place.

RETHINKING LABOR MARKET INSTITUTIONS

To conclude, there is immense scope for change in the way that we think about social relations at work. These trends pose significant challenges for the union movement in Canada in terms of adaptation and its further growth. If the changes in the nature of representation in the workplace are to be accomplished in an enduring way, they must be organized beyond the workplace at central, regional, macro, and transnational levels (in the sense that the linkages here are fairly important). Finally, the process of internationalization and adjustment currently taking place is not unique to North America—we need to look beyond our common borders to where changes are also not uniform. I refer to a recent commentary by a European observer, Richard Hyman, looking at seventeen nations across Europe over the last decade. He notes that changes in Western European industrial relations elude the most simplistic and popular generalizations. There is no simple trend toward convergence. There is space, he argues, for the persistence of national idiosyncracies; specific historical inheritances condition and pace the direction of institutional change. This presents a dual challenge.

Internationally, we need to think seriously and develop new forms of beneficial social control that might be placed on economic relations, such as transnational linkages and structures, both formal and informal, and parallel accords with real content—better yet, trade agreements with a significant social dimension. The criticism is that most trade agreements have a significant social effect, but address these effects in postscripts or parallel agreements. Forward thinking on the social dimensions of trade has been very limited and public policy makers do not seem to have thought about it a lot. It is the responsibility of the university sector, where this conference is taking place, to consider the social implications of trade because they are so critical for future development. We saw this in the European Community's social initiatives in the early 1990s. It is important to realize that liberalization does not appear to be a solution to unemployment. It is a solution to growth and productivity, to the creation of new wealth, but it does not resolve, in and of itself, the social problems related to economic structural adjustment. Both the Organization for Economic Cooperation and Development (OECD) and the European Union have begun to think about the social dimensions of the liberalization of trade and cross-border strategies for the promotion of employment.

The second challenge is the need to engage in institution building at the local level. This is why regions are important economic entities, be it Michigan, or Quebec, or California. We need to have the creation and the diffusion of new types of social relations in the workplace and beyond, and we have some examples of this in different places. In turn, this ultimately raises the question, and I believe it is a key question with regard to internationalization, of the scope and the capacity of small economies, be they countries or states or regions, to engage in economic institution building that reflects the particular dynamics of the social actors in their locality and the quality of economic and political democracy at work.

Appendix 2

NAFTA Timeline

COMPILED BY MANUEL CHAVEZ, VINCENT FRILLICI,
MARC TOMLINSON, AND SCOTT WHITEFORD.

1989

January 1: Canadian-U.S. Free Trade Agreement goes into effect ending virtually all trade barriers within ten years.

October 3: President Bush and President Carlos Salinas de Gortari sign broad economic agreement to enlarge trade and investment between the United States and Mexico.

December 5: The United States and Canada agree to speed up tariff cuts covering $6 billion in trade. Low-level talks continue to accelerate schedule for removing tariffs by 1998.

1990

May 22: President Carlos Salinas de Gortari calls for a free trade agreement with the United States and will also consider a similar accord with Canada but opposes a North American common market.

June 11: Presidents Bush and Salinas meet in Washington to initiate consultations. Commerce and trade officials are responsible for the process. They agree in principle on a free trade agreement but acknowledge major economic and political obstacles.

August 8: Both Mexico and the U.S. Trade and Commerce officials recommend initiating formal negotiations.

September 7: President Salinas formally asks the United States to open talks on a bilateral free trade agreement.

September 24: Mexican Secretary of Commerce Jaime Serra Puche announces the initiation of consultations in Mexico regarding creation of a free trade zone between the two countries.

September 25: President Bush requests authorization to speed up the free trade agreement.

November 27: President Bush completes a 28-hour visit to northern Mexico for talks with President Salinas.

1991

January 29: The United States, Mexico, and Canada agree to include Canada in the negotiations.

February 6: U.S. Congress Senate Finance Committee hearings begin on President Bush's plan to break down trade barriers between the United States and Mexico.

February 27: Congress authorizes fast-track procedure for NAFTA negotiations.

March 1: President Bush requests an extension of two years for the fast-track procedure.

April 24: U.S. Congress House Agriculture Committee holds hearing on President Bush's request for fast-track authority to negotiate the free trade agreement.

April 30: The Bush administration makes environmental and job security commitments to accompany the trade pact with Mexico in order to win fast-track authority from Congress.

May 14: Congressional committees in both houses vote overwhelmingly to endorse negotiations for the free trade agreement with Mexico.

May 23: The U.S. House of Representatives votes 231-192 to authorize President Bush to negotiate a free trade agreement with Mexico.

May 24: The U.S. Senate votes 59-36 to renew President Bush's authority to negotiate trade agreements and submit pacts to Congress with no amendments and limited debate allowed.

June 12: The first ministerial meeting that includes the three Secretaries of Commerce and Trade takes place in Toronto, Canada.

July 8: The first meeting of the chief negotiators is held in Washington, D.C.

1992

January 2: The first consolidated draft of the agreement is issued.

February 10: Trade negotiators from the United States, Canada, and Mexico meet to review their progress.

February 21: The sixth major round of talks ends in Dallas with no major breakthroughs.

May 20: President Bush and Prime Minister Brian Mulroney meet in Washington, D.C., to resolve trade disputes.

June 25: The International Trade Commission votes that imported Canadian lumber has hurt U.S. producers, causing controversy over the free trade draft.

July 13: Mexico agrees to open its banking, insurance, and securities industries to U.S. and Canadian companies, to further the trade talks.

July 14: President Bush and President Salinas meet in San Diego, where Mexico agrees to pay bonuses to U.S. and Canadian oil drillers for good performance.

July 24: The United States and Canada hamper free trade talks by imposing taxes on each other's beer shipments.

July 25: Trade ministers from the United States, Mexico, and Canada meet in Mexico City to resolve the remaining free trade issues.

August 3: Talks break down due to the success of a legal challenge by Peerless Clothing, Inc., a Canadian apparel maker, which ships a large number of suits to the United States.

August 12: Negotiations are concluded in Washington, D.C., and the United States, Canada, and Mexico formally announce the comprehensive North American Free Trade Agreement.

October 4: Governor Bill Clinton endorses NAFTA, but not in its current form. He states that it must include provisions to toughen environmental and worker-safety standards.

December 17: President Bush, President Salinas, and Prime Minister Mulroney each sign copies of NAFTA in their respective capitals.

1993

January 8: President-elect Clinton meets with President Salinas in Austin, Texas, assuring him that NAFTA will take effect as soon as Mexico agrees to side concessions.

February 17: The Mexican government's main development bank withdraws from the private investment fund set up to buy U.S. companies after U.S. Trade Representative Mickey Kantor states that negotiations cannot begin again until the side agreement issue is resolved.

May 27: Canada's House of Commons approves NAFTA, 140-124.

July 1: Judge Charles R. Richey orders the Clinton administration to prepare a lengthy study of the environmental effects of free trade, and the administration's appeal eventually delays the agreement.

July 28: The Clinton administration plans to set up binational authority with Mexico to issue up to $8 billion in bonds to pay for the cleanup of the Rio Grande and other rivers.

August 13: The United States reaches agreement with Canada and Mexico on many issues, including Mexican agreement to trade sanctions for violations of labor and environmental laws.

September 14: President Clinton holds an elaborate White House ceremony with former Presidents Bush, Carter, and Ford to garner support and influence opponents. President de Gortari signs the side agreements to NAFTA.

September 24: A U.S. Appeals Court rules that the Clinton administration can submit NAFTA to Congress without an environmental impact statement.

October 3: President Salinas announces plans to raise Mexican wages to address U.S. concerns over job loss.

November 9: Vice President Al Gore and Ross Perot discuss NAFTA in a nationally televised debate on the Cable News Network.

November 17: The U.S. House of Representatives approves NAFTA, 234-200; three-fifths of Democrats vote against the measure, while most Republicans approve it.

November 19: The U.S. Senate approves NAFTA, 61-38.

November 23: The Mexican Senate votes overwhelmingly in favor of the Tratado de Libre Comercio (TLC), or NAFTA, 56-2.

December 2: Canada drops its opposition to NAFTA after receiving concessions from the United States, removing the last uncertainty about treaty implementation.

December 8: In Mexico, President de Gortari signs the official enactment of TLC-NAFTA. In the United States, President Clinton signs the
official decree for NAFTA.

1994

January 1: NAFTA takes effect in the three member countries.

Appendix 3

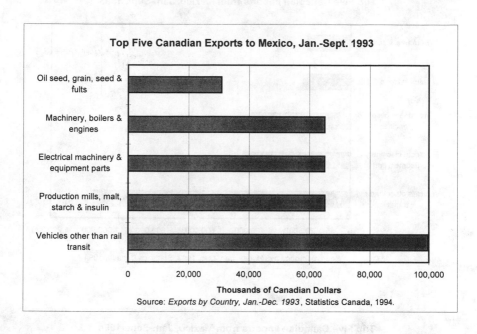

Top Five Canadian Exports to Mexico, Jan.-Sept. 1993

Oil seed, grain, seed & fults	
Machinery, boilers & engines	
Electrical machinery & equipment parts	
Production mills, malt, starch & insulin	
Vehicles other than rail transit	

Thousands of Canadian Dollars

Source: *Exports by Country, Jan.-Dec. 1993*, Statistics Canada, 1994.

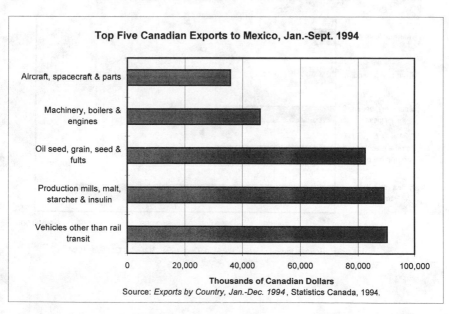

Top Five Canadian Exports to Mexico, Jan.-Sept. 1994

Aircraft, spacecraft & parts	
Machinery, boilers & engines	
Oil seed, grain, seed & fults	
Production mills, malt, starcher & insulin	
Vehicles other than rail transit	

Thousands of Canadian Dollars

Source: *Exports by Country, Jan.-Dec. 1994*, Statistics Canada, 1994.

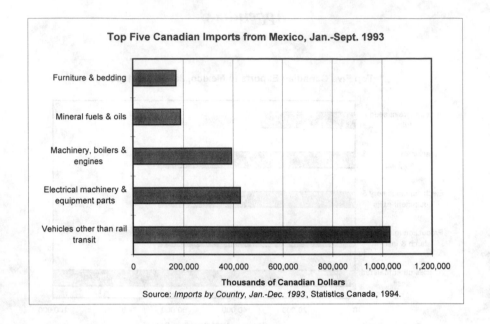

Top Five Canadian Imports from Mexico, Jan.-Sept. 1993

Source: *Imports by Country, Jan.-Dec. 1993*, Statistics Canada, 1994.

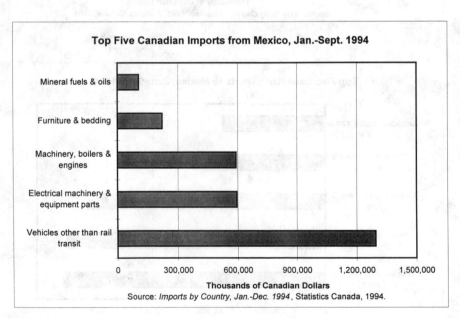

Top Five Canadian Imports from Mexico, Jan.-Sept. 1994

Source: *Imports by Country, Jan.-Dec. 1994*, Statistics Canada, 1994.

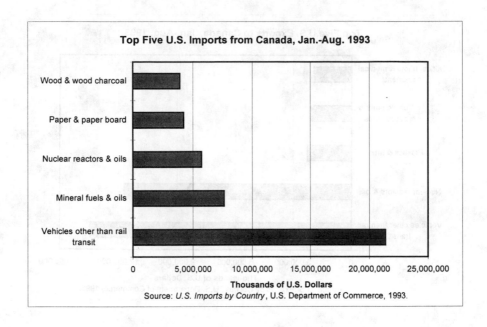

Top Five U.S. Imports from Canada, Jan.-Aug. 1993

Source: *U.S. Imports by Country*, U.S. Department of Commerce, 1993.

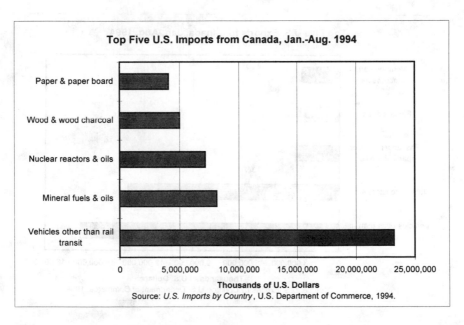

Top Five U.S. Imports from Canada, Jan.-Aug. 1994

Source: *U.S. Imports by Country*, U.S. Department of Commerce, 1994.

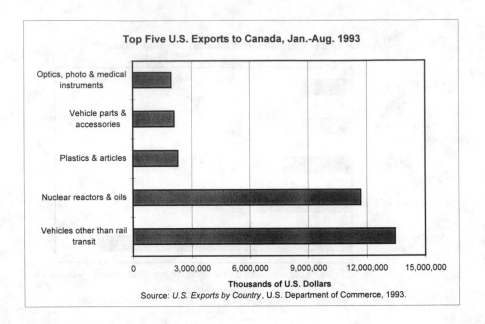

Top Five U.S. Exports to Canada, Jan.-Aug. 1993

Thousands of U.S. Dollars
Source: *U.S. Exports by Country*, U.S. Department of Commerce, 1993.

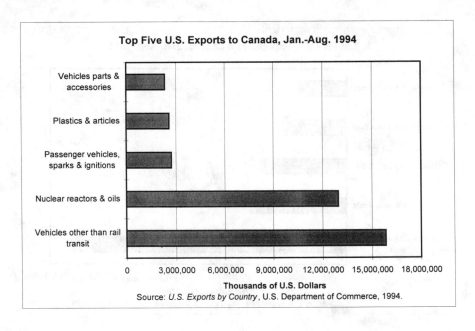

Top Five U.S. Exports to Canada, Jan.-Aug. 1994

Thousands of U.S. Dollars
Source: *U.S. Exports by Country*, U.S. Department of Commerce, 1994.

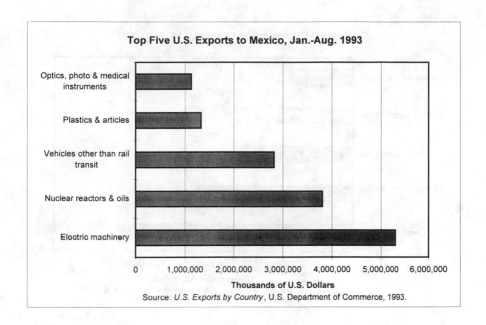

Top Five U.S. Exports to Mexico, Jan.-Aug. 1993

Thousands of U.S. Dollars

Source: *U.S. Exports by Country*, U.S. Department of Commerce, 1993.

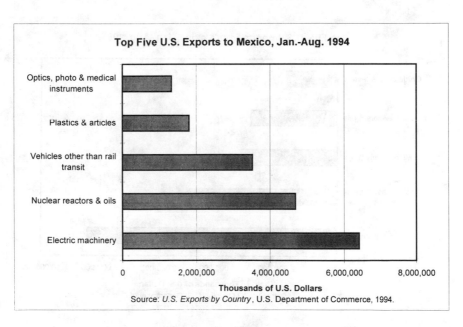

Top Five U.S. Exports to Mexico, Jan.-Aug. 1994

Thousands of U.S. Dollars

Source: *U.S. Exports by Country*, U.S. Department of Commerce, 1994.

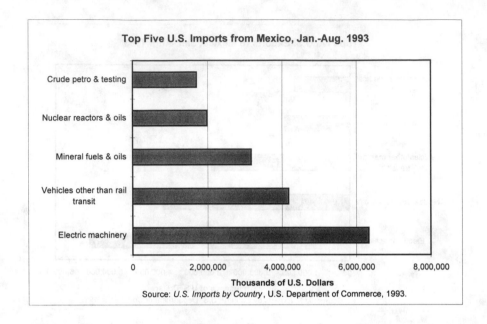

Top Five U.S. Imports from Mexico, Jan.-Aug. 1993

Thousands of U.S. Dollars
Source: *U.S. Imports by Country*, U.S. Department of Commerce, 1993.

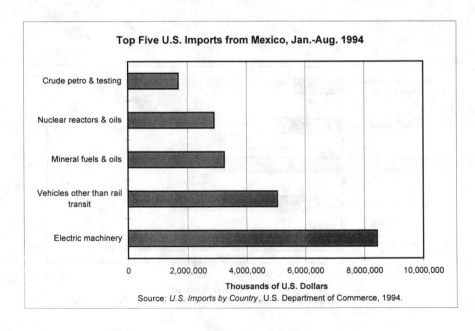

Top Five U.S. Imports from Mexico, Jan.-Aug. 1994

Thousands of U.S. Dollars
Source: *U.S. Imports by Country*, U.S. Department of Commerce, 1994.

About the Contributors

ROBERT APONTE

Robert Aponte received his Ph.D. in sociology from the University of Chicago and has taught at Indiana University and Michigan State University, where he is currently a faculty associate at the Julian Samora Research Institute (JSRI). There, he has led the Program on Social and Economic Demography. Previously, he directed a major research project at the University of Chicago for William Julius Wilson, with whom he has co-authored a number of papers. Aponte's research interests include poverty, Latinos in the United States, race and ethnicity, immigration, and contemporary Cuba. Among his most recent works are "The Informal Economy in the U.S." (forthcoming in *International Journal of Sociology and Social Policy*) and "Urban Employment and the Mismatch Dilemma: Accounting for the Immigrant Exception" (forthcoming in *Social Problems*). He also co-authored "Latinos in the Heartland: The Browning of the Midwest" (1994), a widely publicized JSRI research report on Midwestern Hispanics.

DAVID ARSEN

David Arsen is Associate Professor of Political Economy, James Madison College, Michigan State University. His published research focuses on economic growth, urban and regional development, public finance, and policy analysis. His current rearch focuses on education policy and the economic development consequences of public infrastructure. Arsen received his Ph.D. in economics from the University of California at Berkeley

RICHARD BLOCK

Richard N. Block is Professor, School of Labor and Industrial Relations, and faculty affiliate at the Institute for Public Policy and Social Research, Michigan State University. His work has appeared in all of the major journals in the industrial relations field. Topics include issues in union administration, the relationship between law and practice in industrial relations, industrial relations and structural economic change, labor arbitration, employee privacy, and government-sponsored employee training. Block is an experienced arbitrator. He was director of MSU's School of Labor and Industrial Relations from 1985 to 1993 and served on the Executive Board of the Industrial Relations Research Association from 1990 to 1993. Block received his Ph.D. in industrial and labor relations from Cornell University in 1977.

MANUEL CHAVEZ

Manuel Chavez is Assistant Director, Center for Latin American and Caribbean Studies, Michigan State University, and a visiting Assistant Professor in the Department of Resource Development. Chavez held a postdoctoral fellowship with the Julian Samora Research Institute at MSU and is currently an adjunct faculty member there. He received his Ph.D. in urban studies/sociology from the University of Wisconsin-Milwaukee. He is currently coediting a volume on NAFTA entitled "The Environmental Side Agreements, and the Role of Non-Governmental Organizations." His research focuses on interdependency and regionalism, particularly between Mexico and the United States; urban public policy; Latinos in the United States; and border studies. He has participated in different forums on the creation and effects of NAFTA. In addition, he has authored or coauthored a number of papers on ethnicity, social problems, and labor markets.

RICHARD CHAYKOWSKI

Richard Chaykowski is Associate Professor, School of Industrial Relations, Queen's University, where he has been a Queen's National Scholar. He has also been visiting professor at the Centre for Industrial Relations at the University of Toronto, visiting Associate Professor in the Faculty of Management at McGill University, and visiting scholar at the Sloan School of Management at the Massachusetts Institute of Technology. His teaching and research interests have a North American focus and include public policy in labor markets, pay equity, compensation systems, the effects of technological change on the organization of work and employee skills, labor unions and collective bargaining, and workplace governance systems. Chaykowski has been invited to speak about his research in a wide range of forums, including executive groups of major corporations, the Conference Board of Canada, and the Government of Canada. His *Industrial Relations in Canadian Industry* was published in 1992, and *Research in Canadian Workers' Compensation* is forthcoming. He received his Ph.D. in industrial and labor relations from Cornell University.

PETER DORMAN

Peter Dorman is Assistant Professor, James Madison College, Michigan State University. He teaches in political economy and has taught at Hamilton College, Smith College, and the University of California, Riverside. Dorman is an economist whose research interests include safety and environmental regulation, the role of labor standards in international trade, and the interaction between markets and institutions in the process of economic change. He earned his Ph.D. in economics from the University of Massachusetts and has published articles on NAFTA, international trade, workers' rights, and environmental standards. He is the author of *Markets and Mortality: Economics, Dangerous Work, and the Value of Human Life* (Cambridge University Press, March 1996).

LYNN DUGGAN

Lynn Duggan is Assistant Professor, Political Economy and Social Relations program, James Madison College, Michigan State University. She received her Ph.D. in economics from the University of Massachusetts, Amherst. Her research compares and analyzes family and social policy, focusing on Germany and the United States, and has appeared in *Feminist Economics* and other journals and books.

VINCENT FRILLICI

Vincent Frillici is a graduate of James Madison College at Michigan State University, having majored in political economy. In addition to serving as a research assistant at the Institute for Public Policy and Social Research, he has been a White House intern and represented the United States as a host/scholar at Expo'93 in Taejon, Korea. Currently he is on the staff of the Clinton/Gore '96 campaign in Washington, D.C.

KUNIKO FUJITA

Kuniko Fujita is Visiting Associate Professor, Department of Japanese Studies, National University of Singapore. She is coeditor of *Japanese Cities in the World Economy* (1993) and has published many articles on urban, industrial, and women's issues in Japan. She is currently researching the effect of Japanese transnational corporations on local development in Japan and Southeast Asia.

RICHARD CHILD HILL

Richard Child Hill is Professor of Sociology, Michigan State University. He is coauthor of *Restructuring the City: The Political Economy of Urban Redevelopment* (1983) and of *Detroit: Race & Uneven Development* (1987), and he is coeditor of *Japanese Cities in the World Economy* (1993). Hill has an enduring interest in the effect of transnational corporations on local development and is now researching this issue in Japan and Southeast Asia. He received his Ph.D. in sociology from the University of Wisconsin.

DOUG HYATT

Doug Hyatt is Assistant Professor of Economics and Industrial Relations, University of Wisconsin at Milwaukee, as well as a visiting professor at the Centre for Industrial Relations and research associate of the Institute for Policy Analysis at the University of Toronto. His research has appeared in a number of scholarly journals, including *Industrial and Labor Relations Review, Industrial Relations,* and *Relations Industrielles/Industrial Relations.* His academic interests include public sector collective bargaining, labor supply and the effect of child-care costs, public and private pension plans, occupational health and safety, and workers' compensation. Hyatt received his Ph.D. from the University of Toronto.

CORINNE KRUPP

Corinne Krupp is Assistant Professor of Economics, Michigan State University, and earned her Ph.D. in economics from the University of Pennsylvania. She teaches international trade and finance. Her research interests include strategic firm behavior in response to trade policies, empirical evidence of the market effect of antidumping laws, exchange rate uncertainty and trade, and the mechanics of trade and exchange-rate liberalization. She has served as economic consultant with Wilmer, Cutler, and Pickering (Washington, D.C.) and DuPont de Nemours and Company (Wilmington, Del.) on several antidumping cases. Krupp has published several articles and papers, one of the more recent being "Antidumping Cases in the U.S. Chemical Industry: A Panel Data Approach," *Journal of Industrial Economics,* 1994.

JAMES MCDONALD

James H. McDonald is Assistant Professor of Anthropology, University of Texas at San Antonio, and an affiliate of the Center for Latin

American and Caribbean Studies at Michigan State University. McDonald's main research examines the development of small-scale commercial agriculture in central Mexico. He has examined the transformation of Mexican agriculture under NAFTA and how this and related policy changes will affect domestic food production. Most recently he has done comparative research on the responses to NAFTA by dairy farmers in the United States and Mexico. The emphasis on commercial farming and a cross-border approach situates McDonald's work uniquely within anthropological research on NAFTA and agrarian change. Recent publications include "NAFTA and Basic Food Production: Dependency and Marginalization on Both Sides of the U.S./Mexico Border," *Research in Economic Anthropology* (1994), and "NAFTA and the Milking of Dairy Farmers in Central Mexico," *Culture & Agriculture* (1995).

GREGOR MURRAY

Gregor Murray is Associate Professor of Industrial Relations, Université Laval. His research interests concern trade unions, labor law, and industrial relations theory. He is the author, coauthor, or editor of a variety of publications on these themes, including *Flexibility and Labour Markets in Canada and the United States* (1989), *La négociation collective: adaptation ou disparition?* (1993), *Transformations du syndicalisme et des relations professionnelles* (1994), and *L'état des relations professionnelles* (1996).

JOSEPH OFORI-DANKWA

Joseph Ofori-Dankwa is Associate Professor of Management, Saginaw Valley State University and currently a visiting professor at the David Walker Research Insistute, Michigan State University. From January to May 1991 and again in 1994 he was a visiting professor at the School of Labor and Industrial Relations, Michigan State University. He has consulted with and conducted several diversimilarity workshops and strategic planning sessions for business and governmental units. An active member of the Mid Michigan Dispute Resolution

Center, Ofori-Dankwa holds a law degree from the University of Ghana, an M.A. in management from the University of Wales, and masters and doctoral degrees from the School of Labor and Industrial Relations at Michigan State University.

KAREN ROBERTS

Karen Roberts is Associate Professor, School of Labor and Industrial Relations, and a faculty affiliate in the Institute for Public Policy and Social Research, Michigan State University. She has worked as an economist at the Workers' Compensation Research Institute in Cambridge, Massachusetts and at DRI/McGraw Hill. Roberts is a labor economist who teaches about labor markets and has published on comparative labor markets, with particular emphasis on the United States and Canada. She has written on a variety of issues related to disability, including workers' compensation, the Americans with Disabilities Act, and related health care. Roberts received her Ph.D. from the Department of Urban Studies at MIT.

DAVID SCHWEIKHARDT

David Schweikhardt is Assistant Professor of Agricultural Economics, Michigan State University, specializing in agriculture and trade policy. He previously taught at Mississippi State University, where he conducted research on the effect of NAFTA on the U.S. cotton industry. Schweikhardt's recent research includes an examination of NAFTA's effects on Michigan and U.S. agriculture and an examination of the trade promotion policies of state governments. He received his Ph.D. in agricultural economics from MSU in 1989.

MARC TOMLINSON

Marc Tomlinson received his undergraduate degree in political economy from James Madison College at Michigan State University and a graduate degree in public administration from the Maxwell School at Syracuse University. He is currently in the doctoral program in economics at Michigan State University and serves as a graduate research assistant at the Institute for Public Policy and Social Research.

SCOTT WHITEFORD

Scott Whiteford is Professor of Anthropology and Director, Center for Latin American and Caribbean Studies, Michigan State University. His academic interests include political economy and social change, agrarian systems, and human modification of the physical environment. He has been actively engaged in research on these issues in six Latin American countries. His work has been published in multiple articles and in the six books he has written or edited. Most recently Whiteford's research focus is the interplay between Mexican neoliberal policies and NAFTA and their effects on rural communities and the environment.

MARK WILSON

Mark I. Wilson is Associate Professor, James Madison College, and a faculty affiliate at the Institute for Public Policy and Social Research, Michigan State University. He specializes in urban and regional economic analysis, labor markets, public policy, and the economic behavior of nonprofit organizations. At IPPSR, he focuses on Michigan's nonprofit sector and the globalization of service production. Wilson has published a number of articles and has held several research fellowships while leading the Michigan project. He earned his Ph.D. in regional science from the University of Pennsylvania.

DONALD WISMER

Donald T. Wismer was appointed Consul General of Canada in Detroit with accreditation to the states of Michigan, Indiana, Ohio, and Kentucky on 1 August 1994. He attended the Massachusetts Institute of Technology and holds a B.A. in economics from the University of Alberta. He joined the Canadian Federal Department of Industry, Trade and Commerce in 1966 as a foreign service officer.

Wismer has served Canada abroad in Rome, Milan, New York, Prague, Belgrade, Athens, and Madrid. From 1992 to 1993 he was Consul General in Cleveland. In Ottawa he has held the positions of director of the Western Europe Trade, Investment and Technology Division (1989-92) and, most recently, departmental ombudsman. From 1983 to 1985 he was Director of Trade and Tourism, Vancouver Department of Regional Industrial Expansion.

KANDEH YUMKELLA

Kandeh K. Yumkella is Assistant Professor of Agricultural Economics, Michigan State University. He is currently on leave from MSU to head the Ministry of Trade, Industry, and State Enterprises in Sierra Leone, where he is responsible for implementing market liberalization and export development and investment initiatives. His scholarship has focused on international trade in agricultural products and the effect of public policy on marketing and trade in that sector. He has done research on NAFTA and the economic integration of the United States, Mexico, and Canada. Yumkella is a graduate of Njala University.

JONAS ZONINSEIN

Jonas Zoninsein is Associate Professor, James Madison College, Michigan State University. He has been a visiting professor at Brown University's Center for Portuguese and Brazilian Studies and Center for the Comparative Study of Development. He has also taught at the Federal University of Rio de Janeiro. He specializes in economic development, international economics, and international political economy. He has published *Monopoly Capital Theory* and articles on economics in Brazil, Mexico, and the United States. Zoninsein received his Ph.D. in economics from the New School for Social Research in New York City.

Index